Bookkeeping

FOR

DUMMIES®

2ND EDITION

**by Jane Kelly, ACMA, Paul Barrow, MBA
and Lita Epstein, MBA**

 **WILEY**

A John Wiley and Sons, Ltd, Publication

Bookkeeping For Dummies,® 2nd Edition

Published by
John Wiley & Sons, Ltd
The Atrium
Southern Gate
Chichester
West Sussex
PO19 8SQ
England

E-mail (for orders and customer service enquires): cs-books@wiley.co.uk

Visit our Home Page on www.wiley.com

Copyright © 2011 John Wiley & Sons, Ltd, Chichester, West Sussex, England

Published by John Wiley & Sons, Ltd, Chichester, West Sussex

For general information on our other products and services, please contact our Customer Care Department within the U.S. at 877-762-2974, outside the U.S. at 317-572-3993, or fax 317-572-4002.

For technical support, please visit www.wiley.com/techsupport.

Wiley also publishes its books in a variety of electronic formats. Some content that appears in print may not be available in electronic books.

British Library Cataloguing in Publication Data: A catalogue record for this book is available from the British Library

ISBN: 978-0-470-97626-5 (paperback), ISBN: 978-0-470-97921-1 (ebk),

ISBN: 978-0-470-97731-6 (ebk), ISBN: 978-0-470-97732-3 (ebk)

Printed and bound in Great Britain by TJ International, Padstow, Cornwall

10 9 8 7 6 5 4 3 2

About the Authors

Jane Kelly is a qualified Chartered Management Accountant currently living and working in the Peak District. She has used Sage software for a number of years and has taught Bookkeeping to further education students, as well as edit and co-author this latest *Bookkeeping For Dummies* publication. Her first book *Sage 50 Accounts For Dummies* is currently selling well and is now into its second edition. Jane can be contacted via her blog which offers hints and tips for Sage 50 users. Please go to www.sagemadesimple.co.uk.

Paul Barrow trained and qualified as a Chartered Accountant with Deloitte & Touche before obtaining his MBA at Bradford University. As a senior consultant with Ernst & Young he was responsible for managing and delivering quality consulting assignments. During the mid-1980s, he was Investment Review Director for a UK venture capital business.

In 1998, as Group Finance Director of Adval Group plc, he was part of the team which took their software company on to the Alternative Investment Market. Adval specialises in providing multimedia training – both bespoke and generic. Paul has also been a director of several owner-managed businesses, and has started up and sold other businesses. He currently works with businesses as diverse as software, turkey farming, and food retailing.

Paul is a Visiting Fellow at Cranfield University where he teaches on the Business Growth Programme. This programme is designed specifically for owner managers who want to grow and improve their businesses. He also teaches at Warwick University and Oxford Brookes on similar programmes.

Whilst this is his first *For Dummies* book, Paul has written several other business books: *The Business Plan Workbook* and *Raising Finance* (both Kogan Page/Sunday Times); *The Best Laid Business Plans* and *The Bottom Line* (both Virgin Books). All these books are aimed at owner managers trying to grow and improve their businesses.

Lita Epstein, who earned her MBA from Emory University's Goizueta Business School, enjoys helping people develop good financial, investing, and tax planning skills.

While getting her MBA, Lita worked as a teaching assistant for the financial accounting department and ran the accounting lab. After completing her MBA, she managed finances for a small nonprofit organization and for the facilities management section of a large medical clinic.

She designs and teaches online courses on topics such as investing for retirement, getting ready for tax time, and finance and investing for women. She's written more than ten books, including *Streetwise Retirement Planning* and *Trading For Dummies*.

Lita was the content director for a financial services Web site, `MostChoice.com`, and managed the Web site Investing for Women. As a Congressional press secretary, Lita gained firsthand knowledge about how to work within and around the Federal bureaucracy, which gives her great insight into how government programmes work. In the past, Lita has been a daily newspaper reporter, magazine editor, and fundraiser for the international activities of former US President Jimmy Carter through The Carter Center.

Dedication

I would like to dedicate this book to my daughter Megan. At eight years old, she is already a great creative writer, and I'd like to think that my writing inspires her.

– Jane Kelly

To my late father, Colin Barrow who, out of kind desperation many years ago (when I could not decide how to make a living), introduced me to a partner in a Leeds firm of chartered accountants. I took up articles, which was akin to being a lowly paid slave, and suffered some years of financial hardship before surprising everyone (including myself) by qualifying as a chartered accountant.

The supreme irony has been that I left the profession the day I qualified, but that over the subsequent 30 years I have drifted in and out of the world of accountancy and bookkeeping. Having these skills and the immensely valuable chartered accountant's qualification after my name has enabled me to earn very well over the years. Thank you Dad.

– Paul Barrow

To my father, Jerome Kirschbrown, who taught me the importance of accounting, bookkeeping, and watching every detail.

– Lita Epstein

Authors' Acknowledgements

I hope that this book will help the many small businesses who may be struggling with their accounting systems, whether they be computerised or manual. I cannot emphasise enough, the need for proper accounting systems to be put in place. A well organised system will ensure the smooth running of any business, and should produce accurate and timely reports for the business managers.

I would like to thank everyone at Wiley for all their support throughout the process of updating this book, in particular to Jo Jones who helped me pull together all the chapters. I would also like to extend my thanks to Samantha Spickernell, who has worked with me right from the very start of my involvement with Wiley.

Thanks must also be given to Sage UK Ltd, who have kindly allowed us to use their software for illustration purposes throughout the book.

Finally, I would like to say thank you to my husband Malcolm, and my daughter Megan, for their never ending understanding and support when book deadlines loom!

– Jane Kelly

It has never ceased to amaze me how badly so many small businesses run the bookkeeping area of their business, relying on often inaccurate and mostly very late financial information. There is an often-used expression 'Garbage in, garbage out' which was initially applied to computerised systems, and which could equally be applied to computerised accounting systems – in the hands of the unskilled bookkeeper. Hopefully, this book will give its readers the confidence to prepare meaningful and timely accounts – both manual and computerised.

I am grateful to Sage UK Limited who provided me with the software that is featured in this book.

Also, I would like to thank my wife, Rachel, and my step daughter, Zoe, who had the business idea (Rachel and Zoe's Sewing Shop) that is featured throughout this book.

Finally, I would like to thank the team at Wiley who first of all let me write this book, and then edited it to be the finished product you now see. Thank you everyone.

– Paul Barrow

I want to take this opportunity to thank all the people who have helped make this book a reality. In particular, I want to thank the wonderful folks at Wiley who shepherded this book to completion – Stacy Kennedy, Kelly Ewing, and Elizabeth Rea. I also want to thank my technical advisor, Shellie Moore, who is a CPA and made sure that all the bookkeeping and accounting details were accurate. Finally, I want to thank my agent Jessica Faust at BookEnds, who helps find all my book projects.

– Lita Epstein

Publisher's Acknowledgements

We're proud of this book; please send us your comments through our Dummies online registration form located at `www.dummies.com/register/`.

Some of the people who helped bring this book to market include the following:

Acquisitions, Editorial, and Media Development

Project Editor: Jo Jones
   (Previous Edition: Steve Edwards)

Commissioning Editor: Samantha Spickernell

Assistant Editor: Ben Kemble

Proofreader: Charlie Wilson

Publisher: David Palmer

Production Manager: Daniel Mersey

Cover Photos: Paul Taylor

Cartoons: Ed McLachlan

Composition Services

Project Coordinator: Kristie Rees

Layout and Graphics: Claudia Bell, Carl Byers, Samantha K. Cherolis, Nikki Gately, Melanee Habig

Proofreader: Lindsay Amones

Indexer: Claudia Bourbeau

Special Help

Brand Reviewer: Jennifer Bingham

Contents at a Glance

Table of Contents

Introduction

. . . .

*B*ookkeepers manage all the financial data for small businesses. If you subscribe to the idea that information is power (and I do), you can see that the bookkeeper has a tremendous amount of power within a business. Information recorded in the books helps business owners make key decisions involving sales planning and product offerings, as well as manage many other financial aspects of their businesses.

Without the hard work of bookkeepers, businesses wouldn't have a clue about what's happening with their financial transactions. Without accurate financial bookkeeping, a business owner can't know how many sales are being made, how much cash is being collected or how much cash was paid for the products sold to customers during the year. The owner also can't know how much cash was paid to employees or spent on other business needs throughout the year.

Accurate and complete financial bookkeeping is crucial to any business owner, and also important to those who work with the business, such as investors, financial institutions and employees. People inside (managers, owners and employees) and outside the business (investors, lenders and HM Revenue & Customs) depend on the bookkeeper's accurate recording of financial transactions.

Yes, the bookkeeper's job is crucial and requires certain skills and talents. Bookkeepers must be detail-oriented, enjoy working with numbers and be meticulous about accurately entering those numbers in the books. They must be vigilant about keeping a paper trail and filing all needed backup information about the financial transactions entered into the books.

Whether you're a business owner keeping the books yourself or an employee keeping the books for a small-business owner, your job is critical to the smooth financial operation of the business.

About This Book

In this book, I introduce you to the key aspects of bookkeeping and how to set up and use your financial books. I walk you through the basics of book-keeping, starting with the process of setting up your business's books and developing:

✔ A list of your business's accounts, called the Chart of Accounts

✔ Your business's Nominal Ledger, which summarises all the activity in a business's accounts

✔ Your business's journals, which give details about all your financial transactions

Then I take you through the process of recording all your transactions – sales, purchases and other financial activity. I also talk about how to manage payroll, HM Revenue & Customs reporting and external financial reporting.

Finally, I show you how to start the yearly cycle all over again by closing the necessary accounts for the current year and opening up any new ones for the next year.

Bookkeeping is a continuous cycle, starting with financial transactions, recording those transactions in journals, posting those transactions to the Nominal Ledger, testing your books to be sure that they're in balance, making any necessary adjustments or corrections to the books to keep them in balance, preparing financial reports to understand how well the business did during the year, and finally getting ready to start the process all over again for the next year.

Conventions Used in This Book

I use Sage 50 Accounts computerised accounting system throughout this book and show you some of its advanced features where appropriate. As in every *For Dummies* book, *italics* indicate a defined term or a point of emphasis, and **bold face** text shows off the key phrase in a bulleted or numbered list.

Foolish Assumptions

While writing this book, I made some key assumptions about who you are and why you've picked up this book to get a better understanding of bookkeeping. I assume that you are one of the following:

✔ A business owner who wants to know how to do your own books. You have a good understanding of business and its terminology but have little or no knowledge of bookkeeping and accounting.

✔ A person who does, or plans to do, bookkeeping for a small business and needs to know more about how to set up and keep the books. You have some basic knowledge of business terminology but don't know much about bookkeeping or accounting.

✔ A staff person in a small business who's been asked to take over the bookkeeping duties. You need to know more about how transactions are entered into the books, how to check transactions to be sure that you're making entries correctly and accurately and how to prepare financial reports using the data you collect.

What You're Not to Read

Throughout *Bookkeeping For Dummies*, I include a number of examples on how to apply the basics of bookkeeping to real-life situations. If you're primarily reading this book to gain a general knowledge of the subject and don't need to delve into all the nitty-gritty day-to-day aspects of bookkeeping, you may want to skip over the paragraphs marked with the Example icon (see the section 'Icons Used in This Book' later in this Introduction). Skipping the examples doesn't interfere with your grasp of the key aspects of how to keep the books.

How This Book Is Organised

Bookkeeping For Dummies is divided into six parts, which I outline in the following sections. I also include a handy glossary at the end of the book where you can look up any of those terms you're not familiar with or have forgotten.

Part 1: Basic Bookkeeping: Why You Need It

In Part I, I discuss the importance of bookkeeping, explain how it works and help you get started with setting up your business's books. I also touch on the terms that are unique to bookkeeping and tell you how to set up the road-map for your books, the Chart of Accounts.

Part II: Keeping a Paper Trail

In Part II, I explain how you enter your financial transactions in the books, how you post transactions to your Nominal Ledger (the pinnacle of your bookkeeping system) and how you record all the transaction details in your journals. I also give tips for developing a good internal control system for managing your books and your business's cash, and I talk about your options if you decide to computerise your bookkeeping. I've also included a chapter that's all about planning your workload, with lots of useful hints and tips for running a well-organised bookkeeping system.

Part III: Recording Day-to-Day Business Operations

In Part III, I show you how to record your day-to-day business operations, including recording sales and purchases and any adjustments to those sales and purchases, such as discounts and returns. In addition, I talk about the basics of setting up and managing employee payroll, as well as all the HM Revenue & Customs paperwork you need to complete as soon as you decide to hire employees.

Part IV: Preparing the Books for Year- (Or Month-) End

In Part IV, I introduce you to the process of preparing your books for closing the accounting period, whether you're closing the books at the end of a month or the end of a year. The closing down process involves making key adjustments to record depreciation of your assets and calculating and recording your interest payments and receipts in your books. This part also covers various aspects of checking the accuracy of your books, from checking your cash and testing the balance of your books to making any needed adjustments or corrections.

Part V: Reporting Results and Starting Over

In Part V, I tell you how to use the information in your books to prepare reports that show how well your business – or your not-for-profit organisation – did during the month, quarter or year. I also lay out all the paperwork you have to deal with, including year-end HM Revenue & Customs forms. Finally, you find out how to close the books at year-end and get ready for the next year.

Part VI: The Part of Tens

The Part of Tens is the hallmark of the *For Dummies* series. In this part, I highlight the top ten accounts that you need to know how to manage and ten ways that you can use your books to manage your business's cash efficiently.

Icons Used in This Book

For Dummies books use little pictures, called _icons,_ to flag certain chunks of text. The icons in _Bookkeeping For Dummies_ are:

Look to this icon for ideas on how to improve your bookkeeping processes and manage your business accounts.

This icon marks anything I really, really want you to recall about bookkeeping after you've finished reading this book.

This icon points out any aspect of bookkeeping that comes with pitfalls or hidden dangers. I also use this icon to mark anything that can get you into trouble with HM Revenue & Customs, your bank, your suppliers, your employees or your investors.

The Example icon gives real-life specifics on how to do a particular bookkeeping function.

This icon highlights paragraphs that are a bit more technical than the rest of the book. This information can be handy, but you can skip over it without missing anything essential.

Where to Go from Here

Can you feel the excitement? You're now ready to enter the world of bookkeeping! Because of the way _Bookkeeping For Dummies_ is set up, you can start anywhere you like.

If you need the basics or you're a little rusty and want to refresh your knowledge of bookkeeping, start with Part I. However, if you already know bookkeeping basics, are familiar with the key terminology and know how to set up a Chart of Accounts, consider diving in at Part II.

If you've set up your books already and feel comfortable with the basics of bookkeeping, you may want to start with Part III and how to enter various transactions. On the other hand, if your priority is using the financial information you've already collected, check out the financial reporting options in Part V.

Part I
Basic Bookkeeping: Why You Need It

'So for all you eager investors, our latest financial report will be read to you by our new accountant, Mr Mesmero.'

In this part . . .

*N*ot sure why bookkeeping is important? In this part, I explain the basics of how bookkeeping works and help you get started with the task of setting up your books.

This part also exposes you to terms that have a unique meaning in the world of bookkeeping, such as ledger, journal, posting, debit, and credit. Finally, I start you on your bookkeeping journey by showing you how to set up the roadmap for your books, the Chart of Accounts.

Chapter 1

So You Want to Do the Books

*F*ew small-business owners actually employ accountants to work full time for them because the expense is probably too great. Instead, the owner employs a *bookkeeper* who does the day-to-day work, ready for the accountant to provide the finishing touches. In return, the *accountant* helps the bookkeeper develop good bookkeeping practices and reviews his or her work periodically (usually monthly).

In this chapter, I provide an overview of a bookkeeper's work. If you're just starting a business, you may be your own bookkeeper for a while until you can afford to employ one, so think of this chapter as your to-do list.

Delving into Bookkeeping Basics

Like most businesspeople, you probably have great ideas for running your own business and just want to get started. You don't want to be distracted by the small stuff, like keeping detailed records of every penny you spend; you just want to build a business in which you can make lots of money.

Well slow down there – you're not in a race! If you don't carefully plan your bookkeeping system and figure out exactly how and what financial details you want to track, you have absolutely no way to measure the success (or failure, unfortunately) of your business efforts.

Bookkeeping, when done properly, gives you an excellent measure of how well you're doing and also provides lots of information throughout the year. This information allows you to test the financial success of your business strategies and make any necessary course corrections early in the year to ensure that you reach your year-end profit goals.

Looking at basic accounting methods

You can't keep books unless you know how to go about doing so. The two basic accounting methods are *cash-based accounting* and *accrual accounting*. The key difference between the two methods is the point at which you record sales and purchases in your books. If you choose cash-based accounting, you only record transactions when cash changes hands. If you use accrual accounting, you record a transaction on its completion, even if cash doesn't change hands.

For example, suppose your business buys products to sell from a supplier but doesn't actually pay for those products for 30 days. If you're using cash-based accounting, you don't record the purchase until you actually lay out the cash to the supplier. If you're using accrual accounting, you record the purchase when you receive the products, and you also record the future debt in an account called Trade Creditors.

HM Revenue & Customs, who have an interest in every business in the UK, accept only the accrual accounting method. So, in reality you can't use cash-based accounting. However, a special concession for smaller businesses allows them to use a form of cash-based accounting for VAT purposes (which is covered in Chapter 23). In essence, you can complete your VAT return on a cash-based accounting method, which HM Revenue & Customs refer to as cash accounting.

I talk about the pros and cons of each type of accounting method in Chapter 2.

Understanding assets, capital and liabilities

Every business has three key financial parts that must be kept in balance: assets, capital and liabilities. Of course, for some of you these may be alien concepts, so maybe a quick accounting primer is in order. I use buying a house with a mortgage as an example. The house you're buying is an asset, that is, something of value that you own. In the first year of the mortgage you don't own all of it, but by the end of the mortgage period (typically 25 years), you will. The mortgage is a liability, or a debt you owe. As the years roll on and you reduce the mortgage (liability), your capital or ownership of the asset increases. That's it in a nutshell.

✔ **Assets** include everything the business owns, such as cash, stock, build-ings, equipment and vehicles.

✔ **Capital** includes the claims owners have on the assets based on their portion of ownership in the business.

✔ **Liabilities** include everything the business owes to others, such as sup-plier bills, credit card balances and bank loans.

The formula for keeping your books in balance involves these three elements:

Assets = Capital + Liabilities

Because this equation is so important, I talk a lot about how to keep your books in balance throughout this book. You can find an initial introduction to this concept in Chapter 2.

Introducing debits and credits

To keep the books, you need to revise your thinking about two common financial terms: debits and credits. Most non-bookkeepers and non-accountants think of debits as subtractions from their bank accounts. The opposite is true with credits – people usually see credits as additions to their accounts, in most cases in the form of refunds or corrections in favour of the account holders.

Well, forget all you think you know about debits and credits. Debits and cred-its are totally different animals in the world of bookkeeping. Because keep-ing the books involves a method called *double-entry bookkeeping,* you have to make at least two entries – a debit and a credit – into your bookkeeping system for every transaction. Whether that debit or credit adds or subtracts from an account depends solely upon the type of account.

I know all this debit, credit and double-entry stuff sounds confusing, but I promise this system is going to become much clearer as you work through this book. I start explaining this critical yet somewhat confusing concept in Chapter 2.

Charting your bookkeeping course

You can't just enter transactions in the books willy-nilly. You need to know exactly where those transactions fit into the larger bookkeeping system. To do this, you use your *Chart of Accounts,* which is essentially a list of all the accounts your business has and the types of transactions that go into each one. (I talk more about the Chart of Accounts in Chapter 3.)

Recognising the Importance of an Accurate Paper Trail

Keeping the books is all about creating an accurate paper trail. You want to keep track of all your business's financial transactions so that if a question comes up at a later date, you can turn to the books to figure out what went wrong.

An accurate paper trail is the only way to track your financial successes and review your financial failures, and so is vitally important for your business growth. You need to know what works successfully so that you can repeat it in the future and build on your success. On the other hand, you need to know what failed so that you can make corrections and avoid the same mistake again.

All your business's financial transactions are summarised in the Nominal Ledger, and journals keep track of the tiniest details of each transaction. You can make your information-gathering more effective by using a computerised accounting system, which gives you access to your financial information in many different formats. Controlling who enters this financial information into your books and who can access it afterwards is smart business practice, and involves critical planning on your part. I address all these concepts in the following sections.

You may get confused by the apparently indiscriminate use of the terms 'ledger', 'journal', 'book' and 'accounts'. The situation is not made any easier by the fact that in many cases the words appear to be interchangeable. So let's make some sense of it all:

✔ To start with, you have books of original (or prime) entry, that is, books in which you enter detailed transaction entries first of all. Examples of these books are:

- Sales journal for credit sales

- Purchases journal for credit purchases

- Returns Inwards journal for returns inwards from customers

- Returns Outwards journal for returns outwards to suppliers

- Cash book for receipts and payments of cash and cheques

- General journal for other items

I cover each of these in more detail later, but this is a quick introduction to the key books and journals you may need. So, you may well ask, what is the difference between a book and a journal? There is no real difference; it's just part of the foreign language that accountants use.

Some books are books and some books are journals. If you were to call the Sales journal the Sales book, accountants may turn up their noses at you, but they would know what you meant. All these books and journals are single-entry books, meaning they contain only debits or credits – not both.

✔ A **ledger** completes the double entry of the transactions contained in the books and journals. Instead of keeping all the double-entry accounts in one ledger, you keep several ledgers. The different types of ledger are:

- Sales Ledger for keeping customers' personal accounts

- Purchases Ledger for keeping suppliers' personal accounts

- Nominal Ledger for keeping the remaining double-entry accounts such as expenses, fixed assets, capital and so on. It is a summary of all business activity.

✔ So, for example, you may enter all the individual sales transactions initially in the Sales journal as credit entries and enter the debit entry (or double entry) in a personal account in the Sales Ledger. The original entry helps to give you daily/weekly/monthly sales figures, and the Sales Ledger shows who owes you what.

✔ **Accounts** is a collective term for all books, journals and ledgers.

I cover all these in more detail throughout this book.

Maintaining a ledger

The pinnacle of your bookkeeping system is the *Nominal Ledger*. In this ledger, you keep a summary of all your accounts and the financial activities that took place involving those accounts throughout the year.

You draw upon the Nominal Ledger's account summaries to develop your financial reports on a monthly, quarterly or annual basis. You can also use these account summaries to develop internal reports that help you make key business decisions. I talk more about developing and maintaining the Nominal Ledger in Chapter 4.

Keeping the books

Small businesses conduct hundreds, if not thousands, of transactions each year. If you keep every transaction in the Nominal Ledger, that record is sure to soon become unwieldy and difficult to use. Instead, most businesses keep a series of journals that detail activity in their most active accounts.

For example, almost every business has a *Cash book* to keep the details of all incoming cash receipts and outgoing cash. Other journals can detail sales, purchases, customer accounts, supplier accounts and any other key accounts that see significant activity.

You decide which accounts you want to create journals for based on your business operation and your need for information about key financial transactions.

I talk more about the importance of journals, the accounts commonly journalised and the process of maintaining journals in Chapter 5.

Considering computerising

Many businesses today use computerised accounting systems to keep their books. Consider using one of these systems rather than trying to keep your books on paper. A computerised system makes your bookkeeping quicker and probably more accurate. Having said that, the information input into a computer is only as good as the person entering it. It pays to have a basic understanding of how double-entry bookkeeping works, so that you can check the information that the computer is providing and know how to correct it if you make a mistake. I guide you through the rules of double-entry bookkeeping in Chapter 2.

In addition to increasing accuracy and speeding up your bookkeeping, computerised accounting also makes designing reports easier. These reports can then be used to help you make business decisions. Your computerised accounting system stores detailed information about every transaction, so you can group the detail in any way that assists your decision-making. I talk more about computerised accounting systems in Chapter 6.

Instituting internal controls

Every business owner needs to be concerned with keeping tight controls on business cash and how that cash is used. One way to institute this control is by placing internal restrictions on who can enter information into your books and who has the necessary access to use that information.

You also need to control carefully who has the ability to accept cash receipts and spend your business's cash. Separating duties appropriately helps you protect your business's assets from error, theft and fraud. I talk more about controlling your cash and protecting your financial records in Chapter 7.

Using Bookkeeping Tools to Manage Daily Finances

After you set up your business's books and put in place your internal controls, you're ready to use the systems you've established to manage the day-to-day operations of your business. A well-designed bookkeeping system quickly makes the job of managing your business's finances much easier.

Keeping stock

If your business keeps stock on hand or in warehouses, tracking the costs of the products you plan to sell is critical for managing your profit potential. When you see stock costs escalating, you may need to adjust your own prices in order to maintain your profit margin. You certainly don't want to wait until the end of the year to find out how much your stock cost you.

You also must keep careful watch on how much stock you have on hand and how much was sold. Stock can get damaged, discarded or stolen, meaning that your physical stock counts may differ from the counts you have in your books. Do a physical count periodically – at least monthly for most businesses and possibly daily for active retail stores.

In addition to watching for signs of theft or poor handling of stock, make sure that you have enough stock on hand to satisfy your customers' needs. I talk more about how to use your bookkeeping system to manage stock in Chapter 9.

If you have a service-based business, you can count yourself very lucky as stock is not as significant a cost in your business. You are predominantly selling time and using stocks of materials as a part of your service. However, you can't ignore your material costs, so the same lessons on stock control apply to you.

Tracking sales

Everyone wants to know how well sales are doing. If you keep your books up to date and accurate, you can easily get those numbers on a daily basis. You can also watch sales trends as often as you think necessary: daily, weekly or monthly.

Use the information collected by your bookkeeping system to monitor sales, review discounts offered to customers and track the return of products. All three elements are critical to monitoring the success of the sales of your products.

If you find you need to offer discounts more frequently in order to increase sales, you may need to review your pricing, and you definitely need to do market research to determine the cause of this sales weakness. The cause may be new activities by an aggressive competitor or simply a slowdown in your particular market. Either way, you need to understand the problem and work out how to maintain your profit objectives in spite of any obstacles.

When sales tracking reveals an increase in the number of your products being returned, you need to find the reason for the increase. Perhaps the quality of the product you're selling is declining, and you need to find a new supplier. Whatever the reason, an increased number of product returns is usually a sign of a problem that needs to be researched and corrected.

I talk more about how to use the bookkeeping system for tracking sales, discounts and returns in Chapter 10.

Handling payroll

Payroll can be a huge nightmare for many businesses. Payroll requires you to comply with loads of government and tax regulations and complete a lot of paperwork. You also have to worry about collecting and paying over such things as PAYE and National Insurance. And if you pay employee benefits, you have yet another layer of record-keeping to deal with.

I talk more about managing payroll and government requirements in Chapter 11. I also talk about year-end payroll obligations in Chapter 21.

Running Tests for Accuracy

Tracking your transactions is a waste of time if you don't periodically test to be sure that you've entered those transactions accurately. The old adage, 'Garbage in, garbage out' is particularly true for bookkeeping: if the numbers you put into your bookkeeping system are garbage, the reports you develop from those numbers are also garbage.

Checking the cash and bank

The first step in testing your books includes proving that your cash transactions are accurately recorded. This process involves checking a number of different transactions and elements, including the cash taken in on a daily basis by your staff and the accuracy of your bank account(s). I talk about all the necessary steps you can take to prove your cash is correct in Chapter 14.

Testing your balance

After you prove your cash is right (see Chapter 14), you can check that you've recorded everything else in your books just as precisely. Review the accounts for any glaring errors and then test whether or not they're in balance by doing a trial balance. You can find out more about trial balances in Chapter 16.

Doing bookkeeping corrections

You may not find your books in balance the first time you do a trial balance, but don't worry. Finding your books are in balance on the first try is rare. In Chapter 17, I explain common adjustments that may be needed as you close your books at the end of an accounting period, and I also explain how to make the necessary corrections.

Finally Showing Off Your Financial Success

You draw a metaphorical line at the end of each accounting period (month, quarter, year) and close off entries for that period. Effectively you say, 'That's it for now' and draw a line under it. In fact, in good old-fashioned bookkeeping, you do draw a line and total up entries for the period. This is called *closing your books*.

Closing your books and ensuring they balance means you finally get to show what your business has accomplished financially by developing reports to show to others. Think of this process as like putting your business on a stage and taking a bow – at least you hope you've done well enough to take a bow.

If you take advantage of your bookkeeping information, and review and consult that information throughout the year, the result gives a good idea of how well your business is doing. Also, as long as you've taken any necessary course corrections, your end-of-year reports are sure to look great.

Preparing financial reports

Most businesses prepare at least two key financial reports: the balance sheet and the profit and loss statement. These reports can be shown to business outsiders, including the financial institutions from which the business borrows money and the business's investors.

The *balance sheet* is a snapshot of your business's financial health as of a particular date, and ideally it shows that your business's assets are equal to the value of your liabilities and your capital. The balance sheet is so-called because of its balanced formula:

Assets = Capital + Liabilities

The *profit and loss statement* summarises your business's financial transactions for a particular time period, such as a month, quarter or year. This financial statement starts with your sales, subtracts the costs of goods sold and then subtracts any expenses incurred in operating the business. The bottom line of the profit and loss statement shows how much profit your business made during the accounting period. If you haven't done well, the profit and loss statement shows how much you've lost.

I explain how to prepare a balance sheet in Chapter 19, and I talk more about developing a profit and loss statement in Chapter 18.

Paying tax

Most small businesses don't have to pay taxes. Instead, their profits are reported on the annual tax returns of the business owners, whether one person (a *sole proprietorship*) or two or more people (a *partnership*). Only businesses that have incorporated must file and pay taxes. An incorporated business is one that has become a limited company – that is, a separate legal entity in which investors buy shares. (In Chapter 22, I explain shares in more detail and talk about business structures and how they're taxed.)

Chapter 2

Getting Down to Bookkeeping Basics

*A*ll businesses need to keep track of their financial transactions, which is why bookkeeping and bookkeepers are so important. Without accurate records, how can you tell if your business is making a profit or taking a loss?

In this chapter, I cover the key aspects of bookkeeping: I introduce you to the language of bookkeeping, familiarise you with how bookkeepers manage the accounting cycle and show you how to understand the more complex type of bookkeeping – double-entry bookkeeping.

Bookkeeping: The Record-Keeping of the Business World

Bookkeeping, the methodical way in which businesses track their financial transactions, is rooted in accounting. *Accounting* is the total structure of records and procedures used to record, classify and report information about a business's financial transactions. Bookkeeping involves the recording of that financial information into the accounting system while maintaining adherence to solid accounting principles.

The bookkeeper's job is to work day in and day out to ensure that transactions are accurately recorded. Bookkeepers need to be very detail-oriented and love working with numbers, because numbers and the accounts the numbers go into are what these people deal with all day long.

Bookkeepers aren't required to belong to any recognised professional body, such as the Institute of Chartered Accountants of England and Wales. You can recognise a chartered accountant by the letters *ACA* after the name, which indicates that he or she is an Associate of the Institute of Chartered Accountants. If they've been qualified much longer, they may use the letters *FCA*, which indicate that the accountant is a Fellow of the Institute of Chartered Accountants.

Of course, both Scotland and Ireland have their own chartered accountant bodies with their own designations. Other accounting qualifications exist, offered by the Institute of Chartered Management Accountants (ACMA and FCMA), the Institute of Chartered Certified Accountants (ACCA and FCMA) and the Chartered Institute of Public Finance Accountants (CIPFA).

The Association of Accounting Technicians offers a bookkeeping certificate (ABC) programme, which provides a good grounding in this subject. In reality, most bookkeepers tend to be qualified by experience.

If you're after an accountant to help your business, use the appropriate chartered accountants or a chartered certified accountant as they have the most relevant experience.

On starting up their businesses, many small-business people serve as their own bookkeepers until the business is large enough to hire a dedicated person to keep the books. Few small businesses have accountants on the payroll to check the books and prepare official financial reports; instead, they have bookkeepers (either on the payroll or hired on a self-employed basis) who serve as the outside accountants' eyes and ears. Most businesses do seek out an accountant, usually a chartered accountant (ACA or FCA), but this is typically to submit annual accounts to the Inland Revenue, which is now part of HM Revenue & Customs.

In many small businesses today, a bookkeeper enters the business transactions on a daily basis while working inside the business. At the end of each month or quarter, the bookkeeper sends summary reports to the accountant who then checks the transactions for accuracy and prepares financial statements such as the profit and loss (see Chapter 18), and balance sheet (see Chapter 19) statements.

In most cases, the accounting system is initially set up with the help of an accountant. The aim is to ensure that the system uses solid accounting principles and that the analysis it provides is in line with that required by the business, the accountant and HM Revenue & Customs. That accountant periodically reviews the system's use to make sure that transactions are being handled properly.

Accurate financial reports are the only way to ensure that you know how your business is doing. These reports are developed using the information you, as the bookkeeper, enter into your accounting system. If that information isn't accurate, your financial reports are meaningless: remember, 'Garbage in, garbage out'.

Wading through Basic Bookkeeping Lingo

Before you can take on bookkeeping and start keeping the books, you first need to get a handle on the key accounting terms. This section describes the main terms that all bookkeepers use on a daily basis.

Note: This list isn't exhaustive and doesn't contain all the unique terms you have to know as a bookkeeper. For full coverage of bookkeeping terminology, turn to the Glossary at the back of the book.

Accounts for the balance sheet

Here are a few terms you need to know:

- **Balance sheet:** The financial statement that presents a snapshot of the business's financial position (assets, liabilities and capital) as of a particular date in time. The balance sheet is so-called because the things owned by the business (assets) must equal the claims against those assets (liabilities and capital).

  On an ideal balance sheet, the total assets need to equal the total liabilities plus the total capital. If your numbers fit this formula, the business's books are in balance. (I discuss the balance sheet in greater detail in Chapter 19.)

- **Assets:** All the items a business owns in order to run successfully, such as cash, stock, buildings, land, tools, equipment, vehicles and furniture.

- **Liabilities:** All the debts the business owes, such as mortgages, loans and unpaid bills.

- **Capital:** All the money the business owners invest in the business. When one person (sole trader) or a group of people (partnership) own a small business, the owners' capital is shown in a Capital account. In an incorporated business (limited company), the owners' capital is shown as shares.

Another key Capital account is *Retained Earnings,* which shows all business profits that have been reinvested in the business rather than paid out to the owners by way of dividends. Unincorporated businesses show money paid out to the owners in a Drawings account (or individual drawings accounts in the case of a partnership), whereas incorporated businesses distribute money to the owners by paying *dividends* (a portion of the business's profits paid out to the ordinary shareholders, typically for the year).

Accounts for the profit and loss statement

Following are a few terms related to the profit and loss statement that you need to know:

- **Profit and loss statement:** The financial statement that presents a summary of the business's financial activity over a certain period of time, such as a month, quarter or year. The statement starts with Sales made, subtracts out the Costs of Goods Sold and the Expenses, and ends with the bottom line – Net Profit or Loss. (I show you how to develop a profit and loss statement in Chapter 18.)

- **Income:** All sales made in the process of selling the business's goods and services. Some businesses also generate income through other means, such as selling assets the business no longer needs or earning interest from investments. (I discuss how to track income in Chapter 10.)

- **Cost of Goods Sold:** All costs incurred in purchasing or making the products or services a business plans to sell to its customers. (I talk about purchasing goods for sale to customers in Chapter 9.)

- **Expenses:** All costs incurred to operate the business that aren't directly related to the sale of individual goods or services. (I review common types of expenses in Chapter 3.)

Other common terms

Some other common terms include the following:

- **Accounting period:** The time for which financial information is being prepared. Most businesses monitor their financial results on a monthly basis, so each accounting period equals one month. Some businesses choose to do financial reports on a quarterly basis, so the accounting period is three months. Other businesses only look at their results on a yearly basis, so their accounting period is 12 months. Businesses that track their financial activities monthly usually also create quarterly and *annual reports* (a year-end summary of the business's activities and financial results) based on the information they gather.

✔ **Accounting year-end:** In most cases a business accounting year is 12 months long and ends 12 months on from when the business started or at some traditional point in the trading cycle for that business. Many businesses have year-ends of 31 March (to tie in with the tax year) and 31 December (to tie in with the calendar year). You're allowed to change your business year-end to suit your business.

For example, if you started your business on July 1, your year-end will be 30 June (12 months later). If, however, it is traditional for your industry to have 31 December as the year-end, it is quite in order to change to this date. For example, most retailers have 31 December as their year-end. You of course have to let HM Revenue & Customs know and get their formal acceptance.

✔ **Trade Debtors (also known as Accounts Receivable):** The account used to track all customer sales made on credit. *Credit* refers not to credit-card sales, but to sales in which the business gives a customer credit directly, and which the business needs to collect from the customer at a later date. (I discuss how to monitor Trade Debtors in Chapter 10.)

✔ **Trade Creditors (also known as Accounts Payable):** The account used to track all outstanding bills from suppliers, contractors, consultants and any other businesses or individuals from whom the business buys goods or services. (I talk about managing Trade Creditors in Chapter 9.)

✔ **Depreciation:** An accounting method used to account for the ageing and use of assets. For example, if you own a car, you know that the value of the car decreases each year (unless you own one of those classic cars that goes up in value). Every major asset a business owns ages and eventually needs replacement, including buildings, factories, equipment and other key assets. (I discuss how you monitor depreciation in Chapter 12.)

✔ **Nominal (or General) Ledger:** Where all the business's accounts are summarised. The Nominal Ledger is the master summary of the bookkeeping system. (I discuss posting to the Nominal Ledger in Chapter 4.)

✔ **Interest:** The money a business needs to pay when it borrows money from anybody. For example, when you buy a car using a car loan, you must pay not only the amount you borrowed (capital or principal), but also additional money, or interest, based on a percentage of the amount you borrowed. (I discuss how to deal with interest expenses in a business's books in Chapter 13.)

✔ **Stock (or Inventory):** The account that tracks all products sold to customers. (I review stock valuation and control in Chapter 9.)

✔ **Journals:** Where bookkeepers keep records (in chronological order) of daily business transactions. Each of the most active accounts, including cash, Trade Creditors and Trade Debtors, has its own journal. (I discuss entering information into journals in Chapter 5.)

✔ **Payroll:** The way a business pays its employees. Managing payroll is a key function of the bookkeeper and involves reporting many aspects of payroll to HM Revenue & Customs, including Pay As You Earn (PAYE) taxes to be paid on behalf of the employee and employer, and National Insurance Contributions (NICs). In addition, a range of other payments such as Statutory Sick Pay (SSP) and maternity/paternity pay may be part of the payroll function. (I discuss employee payroll in Chapter 11 and the government side of payroll reporting in Chapter 21.)

✔ **Trial balance:** How you test to ensure that the books are in balance before pulling together information for the financial reports and closing the books for the accounting period. (I discuss how to do a trial balance in Chapter 16.)

Pedalling through the Accounting Cycle

As a bookkeeper, you complete your work by completing the tasks of the accounting cycle, so-called because the workflow is circular: entering transactions, manipulating the transactions through the accounting cycle, closing the books at the end of the accounting period and then starting the entire cycle again for the next accounting period.

The accounting cycle has eight basic steps, shown in Figure 2-1.

1. **Transactions:** Financial transactions start the process. Transactions can include the sale or return of a product, the purchase of supplies for business activities or any other financial activity that involves the exchange of the business's assets, the establishment or payoff of a debt or the deposit from or payout of money to the business's owners. All sales and expenses are transactions that must be recorded. I cover transactions in greater detail throughout the book as I discuss how to record the basics of business activities – recording sales, purchases, asset acquisition or disposal, taking on new debt or paying off debt.

2. **Journal entries:** The transaction is listed in the appropriate journal, maintaining the journal's chronological order of transactions. (The journal is also known as the *book of original entry* and is the first place a transaction is listed.) I talk more about journal entries in Chapter 5.

3. **Posting:** The transactions are posted to the relevant account. These accounts are part of the Nominal Ledger, where you can find a summary of all the business's accounts. I discuss posting in Chapters 4 and 5.

4. **Trial balance:** At the end of the accounting period (which may be a month, quarter or year depending on your business's practices), you prepare a trial balance.

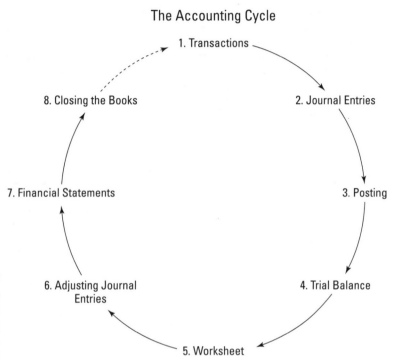

The Accounting Cycle

1. Transactions

8. Closing the Books

2. Journal Entries

7. Financial Statements

3. Posting

6. Adjusting Journal Entries

4. Trial Balance

5. Worksheet

Figure 2-1:
The
Accounting
Cycle.

5. **Worksheet:** Unfortunately, often your first trial balance shows that the books aren't in balance. In this case, you look for errors and make corrections called *adjustments,* which are tracked on a worksheet. Adjustments are also made to account for the depreciation of assets and to adjust for one-time payments (such as insurance) that need to be allocated on a monthly basis to match monthly expenses with monthly revenues more accurately. After you make and record adjustments, you take another trial balance to be sure that the accounts are now in balance.

6. **Adjusting journal entries:** You post any necessary corrections to the relevant accounts after your trial balance shows that the accounts balance (after the necessary adjustments are made to the accounts). You don't need to make adjusting entries until the trial balance process is completed and all needed corrections and adjustments have been identified.

7. **Financial statements:** You prepare the balance sheet and profit and loss statement using the corrected account balances.

8. **Closing the books:** You close the books for the Revenue and Expense accounts and begin the entire cycle again.

At the end of the accounting year (year-end) all the accounting ledgers are closed off. This situation means that Revenue and Expense accounts must start with a zero balance at the beginning of each new accounting year. In contrast, you carry over Asset, Liability and Capital account balances from year to year, because the business doesn't start each cycle by getting rid of old assets and buying new assets, paying off and then taking on new debt or paying out all claims to owners and then collecting the money again.

Understanding Accounting Methods

Many not-for-profit organisations, such as sports clubs, have very simple accounting needs. These organisations aren't responsible to shareholders to account for their financial performance, though they are responsible to their members for the safe custody of their subscriptions and other funds. Consequently, the accounting focus isn't on measuring profit but more on accounting for receipts and payments. In these cases, a simple cash-based accounting system may well suffice, which allows for only cash transactions – no provisions are made for giving or receiving credit. (I cover not-for-profit organisations in more detail in Chapter 20.)

However, complications may arise when members don't pay their subscriptions during the current accounting year, and the organisation needs to reflect this situation in its accounts. In this case, the accrual accounting method is best.

A few businesses operate on a cash basis, and their owners can put forward a good case for using this method. However most accountants and HM Customs & Revenue don't accept this method as it doesn't give a very accurate measure of profit (or loss) for accounting periods.

In the next sections, I briefly explain how cash-based accounting works before dismissing it in favour of the more accepted and acceptable accrual method.

Realising the limitations of cash-based accounting

With *cash-based accounting*, you record all transactions in the books when cash actually changes hands, which means when the business receives cash payment from customers or pays out cash for purchases or other services. Cash receipt or payment can be in the form of cash, cheque, credit card, electronic transfer or other means used to pay for an item.

Cash-based accounting can't be used when a business sells products on credit and collects the money from the customer at a later date. No provision exists in the cash-based accounting method to record and track money due from customers at some point in the future.

This situation also applies for purchases. With the cash-based accounting method, the business only records the purchase of supplies or goods that are to be sold later when it actually pays cash. When the business buys goods on credit to be paid later, it doesn't record the transaction until the cash is actually paid out.

Depending on the size of your business, you may want to start out with cash-based accounting. Many small businesses run by a sole proprietor or a small group of partners use the easier cash-based accounting system. When your business model is simple – you carry no stock, start and finish each job within a single accounting period, and pay and get paid within this period – the cash-based accounting method can work for you. But as your business grows, you may find it necessary to switch to accrual accounting in order to track revenues and expenses more accurately and to satisfy the requirements of the external accountant and HM Revenue & Customs. The same basic argument also applies to not-for-profit organisations.

Cash-based accounting does a good job of tracking cash flow, but the system does a poor job of matching revenues earned with money laid out for expenses. This deficiency is a problem particularly when, as often happens, a business buys products in one month and sells those products in the next month. For example, you buy products in June paying £1,000 cash, with the intent to sell them that same month. You don't sell the products until July, which is when you receive cash for the sales. When you close the books at the end of June, you have to show the £1,000 expense with no revenue to offset it, meaning you have a loss that month. When you sell the products for £1,500 in July, you have a £1,500 profit. So, your monthly report for June shows a £1,000 loss, and your monthly report for July shows a £1,500 profit, when in reality you had revenues of £500 over the two months. Using cash-based accounting, you can never be sure that you have an accurate measure of profit or loss – but as cash-based accounting is for not-for-profit organisations, this is not surprising.

Because accrual accounting is the only accounting method acceptable to accountants and HM Revenue & Customs, I concentrate on this method throughout the book. If you choose to use cash-based accounting because you have a cash-only business and a simple trading model, don't panic: most of the bookkeeping information here is still useful, but you don't need to maintain some of the accounts, such as Trade Debtors and Trade Creditors, because you aren't recording transactions until cash actually changes hands. When you're using a cash-based accounting system and you start to sell things on credit, though, you better have a way to track what people owe you.

Our advice is to use the accrual accounting method right from the beginning. When your business grows and your business model changes, you need the more sophisticated and legally required accrual accounting.

Recording right away with accrual accounting

With *accrual accounting,* you record all transactions in the books when they occur, even when no cash changes hands. For example, when you sell on credit, you record the transaction immediately and enter it into a Trade Debtors account until you receive payment. When you buy goods on credit, you immediately enter the transaction into a Trade Creditors account until you pay out cash.

Like cash-based accounting, accrual accounting has drawbacks; it does a good job of matching revenues and expenses, but a poor job of tracking cash. Because you record income when the transaction occurs and not when you collect the cash, your profit and loss statement can look great even when you don't have cash in the bank. For example, suppose you're running a contracting business and completing jobs on a daily basis. You can record the revenue upon completion of the job even when you haven't yet collected the cash. When your customers are slow to pay, you may end up with lots of income but little cash. Remember – *never* confuse profit and cash. In the short term, cash flow is often more important than profit, but in the long term profit becomes more important. But don't worry just yet; in Chapter 9, I tell you how to manage your Trade Debtors so that you don't run out of cash because of slow-paying customers.

Many businesses that use the accrual accounting method monitor cash flow on a weekly basis to be sure that they have enough cash on hand to operate the business. If your business is seasonal, such as a landscaping business with little to do during the winter months, you can establish short-term lines of credit through your bank to maintain cash flow through the lean times.

Seeing Double with Double-Entry Bookkeeping

All businesses use *double-entry bookkeeping* to keep their books, whether they use the cash-based accounting method or the accrual accounting method. Double-entry bookkeeping – so-called because you enter all transactions twice – helps minimise errors and increase the chance that your books balance.

When it comes to double-entry bookkeeping, the key formula for the balance sheet (Assets = Liabilities + Capital) plays a major role.

In the bookkeeping world, you use a combination of debits and credits to adjust the balance of accounts. You may think of a debit as a subtraction, because debits usually mean a decrease in your bank balance. On the other hand, you probably like finding unexpected credits in your bank account or on your credit card, because they mean more money has been added to the account in your favour. Now forget everything you know about debits or credits. In the world of bookkeeping, their meanings aren't so simple.

The only definite thing when it comes to debits and credits in the bookkeeping world is that a debit is on the left side of a transaction and a credit is on the right side of a transaction. Everything beyond that can get very muddled. I show you the basics of debits and credits in this chapter, but don't worry if you find these concepts difficult to grasp. You get plenty of practice using these concepts throughout this book.

Before I get into all the technical mumbo-jumbo of double-entry bookkeeping, here's an example of the practice in action. Suppose you purchase a new desk for your office that costs £1,500. This transaction actually has two parts: you spend an asset – cash – to buy another asset, furniture. So, you must adjust two accounts in your business's books: the Cash account and the Furniture account. The transaction in a bookkeeping entry is as follows (I talk more about how to do initial bookkeeping entries in Chapter 4):

Account	*Debit*	*Credit*
Furniture	£1,500	
Cash		£1,500

To purchase a new desk for the office.

In this transaction, you record the accounts impacted by the transaction. The debit increases the value of the Furniture account, and the credit decreases the value of the Cash account. For this transaction, both accounts impacted are Asset accounts so, looking at how the balance sheet is affected, you can see that the only changes are to the asset side of the balance sheet equation:

Assets = Liabilities + Capital

Furniture increase = No change to this side of the equation

Cash decrease

Double-entry bookkeeping goes way back

No one's really sure who invented double-entry bookkeeping. The first person to put the practice on paper was Benedetto Cotrugli in 1458, but mathematician and Franciscan monk Luca Pacioli is most often credited with developing double-entry bookkeeping. Although Pacioli is called the Father of Accounting, accounting actually occupies only one of five sections of his book, *Everything About Arithmetic, Geometry and Proportions,* which was published in 1494.

Pacioli didn't actually *invent* double-entry bookkeeping; he just described the method used by merchants in Venice during the Italian Renaissance period. He's most famous for his warning to bookkeepers: 'A person should not go to sleep at night until the debits equal the credits!'

In this case, the books stay in balance because the exact pounds sterling amount that increases the value of your Furniture account decreases the value of your Cash account. At the bottom of any journal entry, include a brief explanation that explains the purpose of the entry. In the first example, I indicate this entry was 'To purchase a new desk for the office'.

To show you how you record a transaction that impacts both sides of the balance sheet equation, here's an example that records the purchase of stock. Suppose that you purchase £5,000 worth of widgets on credit. (Have you always wondered what widgets were? Can't help you. They're just commonly used in accounting examples to represent something purchased where what is purchased is of no real significance.) These new widgets add value to your Stock Asset account and also add value to your Trade Creditors account. (Remember, the Trade Creditors account is a Liability account where you track bills that need to be paid at some point in the future.) The bookkeeping transaction for your widget purchase looks as follows:

Account	Debit	Credit
Stock	£5,000	
Trade Creditors		£5,000

To purchase widgets for sale to customers.

This transaction affects the balance sheet equation as follows:

Assets = Liabilities + Capital

Stock increases = Creditor increases + No change

In this case, the books stay in balance because both sides of the equation increase by $5,000.

You can see from the two example transactions how double-entry bookkeeping helps to keep your books in balance – as long as you make sure that each entry into the books is balanced. Balancing your entries may look simple here, but sometimes bookkeeping entries can get very complex when the transaction impacts more than two accounts.

Don't worry, you don't have to understand double-entry bookkeeping totally now. Throughout the book, I show you how to enter transactions, depending upon the type of transaction being recorded. I'm just giving you a quick overview to introduce the subject right now.

Differentiating Debits and Credits

Because bookkeeping's debits and credits are different from the ones you're used to encountering, you're probably wondering how you're supposed to know whether a debit or credit increases or decreases an account.

Believe it or not, identifying the difference becomes second nature as you start making regular entries in your bookkeeping system. But to make things easier for you, Table 2-1 is a chart that bookkeepers and accountants commonly use. Yep, everyone needs help sometimes.

Table 2-1	How Credits and Debits Impact Your Accounts	
Account Type	*Debits*	*Credits*
Assets	Increase	Decrease
Liabilities	Decrease	Increase
Income	Decrease	Increase
Expenses	Increase	Decrease

Copy Table 2-1 and post it at your desk when you start keeping your own books (a bit like the chief accountant in the nearby 'Sharing a secret' sidebar). I guarantee that the table helps to keep your debits and credits straight.

Sharing a secret

Don't feel embarrassed if you forget which side the debits go on and which side the credits go on. One often-told story is of a young clerk in an accounts office plucking up courage to ask the chief accountant, who was retiring that day, why for 30 years he had at the start of each day opened up his drawer and read the contents of a piece of paper before starting work. The chief accountant at first was reluctant to spill the beans, but ultimately decided he had to pass on his secret – and who better than an up-and-coming clerk? Swearing the young clerk to secrecy, he took out the piece of paper and showed it to him. The paper read: 'Debit on the left and Credit on the right.'

Chapter 3

Outlining Your Financial Roadmap with a Chart of Accounts

Can you imagine what a mess your cheque book would be if you didn't record each cheque you write? Like me, you've probably forgotten to record a cheque or two on occasion, but you certainly found out quickly enough when an important payment bounced as a result. Yikes!

Keeping the books of a business can be a lot more difficult than maintaining a personal cheque book. Each business transaction must be carefully recorded to make sure that it goes into the right account. This careful bookkeeping gives you an effective tool for working out how well the business is doing financially.

As a bookkeeper, you need a roadmap to help you determine where to record all those transactions. This roadmap is called the Chart of Accounts. In this chapter, I tell you how to set up the Chart of Accounts, which includes many different accounts. I also review the types of transactions you enter into each type of account in order to track the key parts of any business – assets, liabilities, capital, income and expenses.

Getting to Know the Chart of Accounts

The *Chart of Accounts* is the roadmap that a business creates to organise its financial transactions. After all, you can't record a transaction until you know where to put it! Essentially, this chart is a list of all the accounts a business has, organised in a specific order; each account has a description that includes the type of account and the types of transactions to be entered into that account. Every business creates its own Chart of Accounts based on how the business is operated, so you're unlikely to find two businesses with the exact same Charts of Accounts.

However, some basic organisational and structural characteristics are common to all Charts of Accounts. The organisation and structure are designed around two key financial reports: the *balance sheet,* which shows what your business owns and what it owes, and the *profit and loss statement,* which shows how much money your business took in from sales and how much money it spent to generate those sales. (You can find out more about profit and loss statements in Chapter 18 and balance sheets statements in Chapter 19.)

The Chart of Accounts starts with the balance sheet accounts, which include the following:

- **Fixed Assets:** Includes all accounts that show things the business owns that have a lifespan of more than 12 months, such as buildings, furniture, plant and equipment, motor vehicles and office equipment

- **Current Assets:** Includes all accounts that show things the business owns and expects to use in the next 12 months, such as cash, Trade Debtors (also known as Accounts Receivable, which is money due from customers), prepayments and stock

- **Current Liabilities:** Includes all accounts that show debts the business must repay over the next 12 months, such as Trade Creditors (also known as Accounts Payable, which is bills from suppliers, contractors and consultants), hire purchase and other loans, VAT and income/corporation tax, accruals and credit cards payable

- **Long-Term Liabilities:** Includes all accounts that show debts the business must pay over a period of time longer than the next 12 months, such as mortgages repayable and longer-term loans that are repayable

- **Capital:** Includes all accounts that show the owners of the business and their claims against the business's assets, including any money invested in the business, any money taken out of the business and any earnings that have been reinvested in the business

The rest of the chart is filled with profit and loss statement accounts, which include the following:

- ✔ **Income:** Includes all accounts that track sales of goods and services as well as revenue generated for the business by other means

- ✔ **Cost of Goods Sold:** Includes all accounts that track the direct costs involved in selling the business's goods or services

- ✔ **Expenses:** Includes all accounts that track expenses related to running the businesses that aren't directly tied to the sale of individual products or services

When developing the Chart of Accounts, start by listing all the Asset accounts, the Liability accounts, the Capital accounts, the Revenue accounts and finally, the Expense accounts. All these accounts feed into two statements: the balance sheet and the profit and loss statement.

In this chapter, I review the key account types found in most businesses, but this list isn't cast in stone. You need to develop an account list that makes the most sense for how you're operating your business and the financial information you want to track. As I explore the various accounts that make up the Chart of Accounts, I point out how the structure may differ for different types of businesses.

The Chart of Accounts is a money-management tool that helps you follow your business transactions, so set it up in a way that provides you with the financial information you need to make smart business decisions. You're probably going to tweak the accounts in your chart annually and, if necessary, you may add accounts during the year if you find something for which you want more detailed tracking. You can add accounts during the year, but don't delete accounts until the end of a 12-month reporting period. I discuss adding and deleting accounts from your books in Chapter 17.

Starting with the Balance Sheet Accounts

The first part of the Chart of Accounts is made up of balance sheet accounts, which break down into the following three categories:

- ✔ **Assets:** These accounts are used to show what the business owns. Assets include cash on hand, furniture, buildings, vehicles and so on.

- ✔ **Liabilities:** These accounts show what the business owes, or more specifically, claims that lenders have against the business's assets. For example, mortgages on buildings and long-term loans are two common types of liabilities. Also, a mortgage (a legal charge) is a good example of a claim that the lender (bank or building society) has over a business asset (in this case, the premises being bought through the mortgage).

✔ **Capital:** These accounts show what the owners put into the business and the claims the owners have against the business's assets. For example, shareholders are business owners that have claims against the business's assets.

The balance sheet accounts, and the financial report they make up, are so-called because they have to *balance* out. The value of the assets must be equal to the claims made against those assets. (Remember, these claims are liabilities made by lenders and capital made by owners.)

I discuss the balance sheet in greater detail in Chapter 19, including how to prepare and use it. This section, however, examines the basic components of the balance sheet, as reflected in the Chart of Accounts.

Tackling assets

The accounts that track what the business owns – its assets – are always the first category on the chart. The two types of Asset accounts are fixed assets and current assets.

Fixed assets

Fixed assets are assets that you anticipate your business is going to use for more than 12 months. This section lists some of the most common fixed assets, starting with the key accounts related to buildings and business premises that the business owns:

✔ **Land and Buildings:** This account shows the value of the land and buildings the business owns. The initial value is based on the cost at the time of purchase, but this asset can be (and often is) revalued as property prices increase over time. Because of the virtually indestructible nature of this asset, it doesn't depreciate at a fast rate. *Depreciation* is an accounting method that shows an asset is being used up. I talk more about depreciation in Chapter 12.

✔ **Accumulated Depreciation – Land and Buildings:** This account shows the cumulative amount this asset has depreciated over its useful lifespan.

✔ **Leasehold Improvements:** This account shows the value of improvements to buildings or other facilities that a business leases rather than purchases. Frequently when a business leases a property, it must pay for any improvements necessary in order to use that property as the business requires. For example, when a business leases a shop, the space leased is likely to be an empty shell or filled with shelving and other items that don't match the particular needs of the business. As with land and buildings, leasehold improvements depreciate as the value of the asset ages – usually over the remaining life of the lease.

✔ **Accumulated Depreciation – Leasehold Improvements:** This account tracks the cumulative amount depreciated for leasehold improvements.

The following are the types of accounts for smaller long-term assets, such as vehicles and furniture:

✔ **Vehicles:** This account shows any cars, lorries or other vehicles owned by the business. The initial value of any vehicle is listed in this account based on the total cost paid to put the vehicle into service. Sometimes this value is more than the purchase price if additions were needed to make the vehicle usable for the particular type of business. For example, when a business provides transportation for the handicapped and must add additional equipment to a vehicle in order to serve the needs of its customers, that additional equipment is added to the value of the vehicle. Vehicles also depreciate through their useful lifespan.

✔ **Accumulated Depreciation – Vehicles:** This account shows the depreciation of all vehicles owned by the business.

✔ **Furniture and Fixtures:** This account shows any furniture or fixtures purchased for use in the business. The account includes the value of all chairs, desks, store fixtures and shelving needed to operate the business. The value of the furniture and fixtures in this account is based on the cost of purchasing these items. These items are depreciated during their useful lifespan.

✔ **Accumulated Depreciation – Furniture and Fixtures:** This account shows the accumulated depreciation of all furniture and fixtures.

✔ **Plant and Equipment:** This account shows equipment that was purchased for use for more than 12 months, such as process-related machinery, computers, copiers, tools and cash registers. The value of the equipment is based on the cost to purchase these items. Equipment is also depreciated to show that over time it gets used up and must be replaced.

✔ **Accumulated Depreciation – Plant and Equipment:** This account tracks the accumulated depreciation of all the equipment.

The following accounts show the fixed assets that you can't touch (accountants refer to these as *intangible assets*), but that still represent things of value owned by the business, such as start-up costs, patents and copyrights. The accounts that track them include:

- ✔ **Start-up Costs:** This account shows the initial start-up expenses to get the business off the ground. Many such expenses can't be set off against business profits in the first year. For example, special licences and legal fees must be written off over a number of years using a method similar to depreciation, called *amortisation,* which is also tracked. I discuss amortisation in greater detail in Chapter 13.

- ✔ **Amortisation – Start-up Costs:** This account shows the accumulated amortisation of these costs during the period in which they're being written-off.

- ✔ **Patents:** This account shows the costs associated with *patents,* grants made by governments that guarantee to the inventor of a product or service the exclusive right to make, use and sell that product or service over a set period of time. Like start-up costs, patent costs are amortised. The value of this asset is based on the expenses the business incurs to get the right to patent its product.

- ✔ **Amortisation – Patents:** This account shows the accumulated amortisation of a business's patents.

- ✔ **Copyrights:** This account shows the costs incurred to establish copyrights, the legal rights given to an author, playwright, publisher or any other distributor of a publication or production for a unique work of literature, music, drama or art. This legal right expires after a set number of years, so its value is amortised as the copyright gets used up.

- ✔ **Goodwill:** This account is needed only if a business buys another business for more than the actual value of its tangible assets. Goodwill reflects the intangible value of this purchase for things like business reputation, store locations, customer base and other items that increase the value of the business bought. The value of goodwill is not everlasting, and so like other intangible assets, must be amortised.

- ✔ **Research and Development:** This account shows the investment the business has made in future products and services, which may not see the light of day for several years. These costs are written off (amortised) over the life of the products and services as and when they reach the marketplace.

If you hold a lot of assets that aren't of great value, you can also set up an Other Assets account to show those assets that don't have significant business value. Any asset you show in the Other Assets account that you later want to show individually can be shifted to its own account. I discuss adjusting the Chart of Accounts in Chapter 17.

Current assets

Current assets are the key assets that your business uses up within a 12-month period and are likely not to be there the next year. The accounts that reflect current assets on the Chart of Accounts are:

- ✔ **Current account:** This account is the business's primary bank account for operating activities, such as depositing receipts and paying expenses. Some businesses have more than one account in this category; for example, a business with many divisions may have an account for each division.

- ✔ **Deposit account:** This account is used for surplus cash. Any cash not earmarked for an immediate plan is deposited in an interest-earning savings account. In this way, the cash earns interest while the business decides what to do with it.

- ✔ **Cash on Hand:** This account is used to record any cash kept at retail stores or in the office. In retail stores, cash must be kept in registers in order to provide change to customers. In the office, petty cash is often kept for immediate cash needs that pop up from time to time. This account helps you keep track of the cash held outside the various bank and deposit accounts.

- ✔ **Trade Debtors:** This account shows the customers who still owe you money when you offer your products or services to customers on credit (by which I mean *your* own credit system).

  Trade Debtors isn't used to show purchases made on other types of credit cards, because your business gets paid directly by banks, not customers, when credit cards are used. Check out Chapter 10 to read more about this scenario and the corresponding type of account.

- ✔ **Stock:** This account shows the value of the products you have on hand to sell to your customers. The value of the assets in this account varies depending upon the way you decide to track the flow of stock into and out of the business. I discuss stock valuation and recording in greater detail in Chapter 9.

- ✔ **Prepayments:** This account shows goods or services you pay for in advance: the payment is credited as it gets used up each month. For example, say you prepay your property insurance on a building you own one year in advance. Each month you reduce the amount that you prepaid by one-twelfth as the prepayment is used up.

Depending upon the type of business you're setting up, you may have other current Asset accounts to set up. For example, say you're starting a service business in consulting. You're likely to have an account called Consulting Fees for tracking cash collected for those services.

Laying out your liabilities

After you deal with assets, the next stop on the bookkeeping journey is the accounts that show what your business owes to others. These others can include suppliers from whom you buy products or supplies, financial institutions from which you borrow money and anyone else who lends money to your business. Like assets, liabilities are lumped into current liabilities and long-term liabilities.

Current liabilities

Current liabilities are debts due in the next 12 months. Some of the most common types of current liabilities accounts that appear on the Chart of Accounts are as follows:

- ✔ **Trade Creditors:** This account shows money the business owes to suppliers, contractors and consultants that must be paid in less than 12 months. Most of these liabilities must be paid in 30 to 90 days from initial invoicing.

- ✔ **Value Added Tax (VAT):** This account shows your VAT liability. You may not think of VAT as a liability, but because the business collects the tax from the customer and doesn't pay it immediately to HM Customs & Revenue, the taxes collected become a liability. Of course you're entitled to offset the VAT that the business has been charged on its purchases before making a net payment. A business usually collects VAT throughout the month and then pays the net amount due on a quarterly basis. I discuss paying VAT in greater detail in Chapter 23.

- ✔ **Accrued Payroll Taxes:** This account shows payroll taxes, such as PAYE and National Insurance, collected from employees and the business itself, which have to be paid over to HM Customs & Revenue. Businesses don't have to pay these taxes over immediately and may pay payroll taxes on a monthly basis. I discuss how to handle payroll taxes in Chapter 11.

- ✔ **Credit Cards Payable:** This account shows all credit card accounts for which the business is liable. Most businesses use credit cards as short-term debt and pay them off completely at the end of each month, but some smaller businesses carry credit card balances over a longer period of time. In Chart of Accounts, you can set up one Credit Card Payable account, but you may want to set up a separate account for each card your business holds to improve your ability to track credit card usage.

The way you set up your current liabilities – and how many individual accounts you establish – depends upon the level of detail that you want to use to track each type of liability.

Long-term liabilities

Long-term liabilities are debts due in more than 12 months. The number of long-term Liability accounts you maintain on your Chart of Accounts depends on your debt structure. For example, if you have several different loans, then set up an account for each one. The most common type of long-term Liability accounts is Loans Payable. This account tracks any long-term loans, such as a mortgage on your business building. Most businesses have separate Loans Payable accounts for each of their long-term loans. For example, you can have *Loans Payable – Mortgage Bank* for your building and *Loans Payable – Vehicles* for your vehicle loan.

In addition to any separate long-term debt that you may want to track in its own account, you may also want to set up an account called *Other Liabilities*. You can use this account to track types of debt that are so insignificant to the business that you don't think they need their own accounts.

Controlling the capital

Every business is owned by somebody. *Capital accounts* track owners' contributions to the business as well as their share of ownership. For a limited company, ownership is tracked by the sale of individual shares because each stockholder owns a portion of the business. In smaller businesses owned by one person or a group of people, capital is tracked using Capital and Drawing accounts. Here are the basic Capital accounts that appear in the Chart of Accounts:

- ✔ **Ordinary Share Capital:** This account reflects the value of outstanding ordinary shares sold to investors. A business calculates this value by multiplying the number of shares issued by the value of each share of stock. Only limited companies need to establish this account.

- ✔ **Retained Earnings:** This account tracks the profits or losses accumulated since a business opened. At the end of each year, the profit or loss calculated on the profit and loss statement is used to adjust the value of this account. For example, if a business made a £100,000 profit after tax in the past year, the Retained Earnings account is increased by that amount; if the business lost £100,000, that amount is subtracted from this account. Any dividends paid to shareholders reduce the profit figure transferred to Retained Earnings each year.

- ✔ **Capital:** This account is only necessary for small, unincorporated businesses, such as sole traders or partnerships. The Capital account reflects the amount of initial money the business owner contributed to the business as well as any additional contributions made after initial start-up. The value of this account is based on cash contributions and other assets contributed by the business owner, such as equipment, vehicles or buildings. When a small company has several different partners, each partner gets his or her own Capital account to track his or her contributions.

✔ **Drawing:** This account is only necessary for businesses that aren't incorporated. The Drawing account tracks any money that a business owner takes out of the business. If the business has several partners, each partner gets his or her own Drawing account to track what he or she takes out of the business.

Keeping an Eye on the Profit and Loss Statement Accounts

The profit and loss statement is made up of two types of accounts:

✔ **Revenue:** These accounts track all income coming into the business, including sales, interest earned on savings and any other methods used to generate income.

✔ **Expenses:** These accounts track all costs that a business incurs in order to keep itself afloat.

The bottom line of the profit and loss statement shows if your business made a profit or a loss for a specified period of time. I discuss how to prepare and use a profit and loss statement in greater detail in Chapter 18.

This section examines the various accounts that make up the profit and loss statement portion of the Chart of Accounts.

Recording the profit you make

Accounts that show revenue coming into the business are first up in the profit and loss statement section of the Chart of Accounts. If you choose to offer discounts or accept returns, that activity also falls within the revenue grouping. The most common income accounts are:

✔ **Sales of Goods or Services:** This account, which appears at the top of every profit and loss statement, shows all the money that the business earns selling its products, services or both.

> ✔ **Sales Discounts:** This account shows any reductions to the full price of merchandise (necessary because most businesses offer discounts to encourage sales).
>
> ✔ **Sales Returns:** This account shows transactions related to returns, when a customer returns a product.

When you examine a profit and loss statement from a business other than the one you own or are working for, you usually see the following accounts summarised as one line item called *Revenue* or *Net Revenue*. Because not all income is generated by sales of products or services, other income accounts that may appear on a Chart of Accounts include the following:

> ✔ **Other Income:** This account shows income a business generates from a source other than its primary business activity. For example, a business that encourages recycling and earns income from the items recycled records that income in this account.
>
> ✔ **Interest Income:** This account shows any income earned by collecting interest on a business's savings accounts. If the business lends money to employees or to another business and earns interest on that money, that interest is recorded in this account as well.

Recording the cost of goods sold

Of course, before you can sell a product, you must spend money to buy or make that product. The type of account used to track the money spent is called a Cost of Goods Sold account. The most common Cost of Goods Sold accounts are:

> ✔ **Purchases:** This account shows the purchases of all items you plan to sell.
>
> ✔ **Purchase Discount:** This account shows the discounts you may receive from suppliers when you pay for your purchase quickly. For example, a business may give you a 2 per cent discount on your purchase when you pay the bill in ten days rather than wait until the end of the 30-day payment period.
>
> ✔ **Purchase Returns:** This account shows the value of any returns when you're unhappy with a product you bought.
>
> ✔ **Freight Charges:** This account shows any charges related to shipping items you purchase for later sale. You may or may not want to keep this detail.
>
> ✔ **Other Sales Costs:** This account is a catchall account for anything that doesn't fit into one of the other Cost of Goods Sold accounts.

Acknowledging the other costs

Expense accounts take the cake for the longest list of individual accounts. Anything you spend on the business that can't be tied directly to the sale of an individual product falls under the Expense account category. For example, advertising a sale isn't directly tied to the sale of any one product, so the costs associated with advertising fall under the Expense account category.

The Chart of Accounts mirrors your business operations, so you decide how much detail you want to keep in your Expense accounts. Most businesses have expenses that are unique to their operations, so your list is likely to be longer than the one I present here. However, you also may find that you don't need some of these accounts. Small businesses typically have expense headings that mirror those required by HM Revenue & Customs on their self-assessment returns.

On your Chart of Accounts, the Expense accounts don't have to appear in any specific order, so I list them alphabetically. The most common Expense accounts are:

- ✔ **Advertising:** This account shows all expenses involved in promoting a business or its products. Expenditure on newspaper, television, magazine and radio advertising is recorded here, as well as any costs incurred to print flyers and mailings to customers. Also, when a business participates in community events such as cancer walks or craft fairs, associated costs are shown in this account.

- ✔ **Amortisation:** This account is very similar to the depreciation account (later in this list) and shows the ongoing monthly charge for the current financial year for all your intangible assets.

- ✔ **Bank Service Charges:** This account shows any charges made by a bank to service a business's bank accounts.

- ✔ **Depreciation:** This account shows the ongoing monthly depreciation charge for the current financial year for all your fixed assets – buildings, cars, vans, furniture and so on. Of course, when the individual depreciation values are large for each fixed asset category, you may open up individual depreciation accounts.

- ✔ **Dues and Subscriptions:** This account shows expenses related to business-club membership or subscriptions to magazines for the business.

- ✔ **Equipment Rental:** This account records expenses related to renting equipment for a short-term project. For example, a business that needs to rent a van to pick up some new fixtures for its shop records that van rental in this account.

- ✔ **Insurance:** This account shows insurance costs. Many businesses break this account down into several accounts such as Building Insurance, Public Liability Insurance and Car Insurance.

✔ **Legal and Accounting:** This account shows the cost of legal or accounting advice.

✔ **Miscellaneous Expenses:** This account is a catch-all account for expenses that don't fit into one of a business's established accounts. If certain miscellaneous expenses occur frequently, a business may choose to add an account to the Chart of Accounts and move related expenses into that new account by subtracting all related transactions from the Miscellaneous Expenses account and adding them to the new account. With this shuffle, you need to carefully balance out the adjusting transaction to avoid any errors or double counting.

✔ **Office Expenses:** This account shows any items purchased in order to run an office. For example, office supplies such as paper and pens or business cards fit in this account. As with miscellaneous expenses, a business may choose to track some office expense items in their own accounts. For example, when you find your office is using a lot of copy paper and you want to track that separately, set up a Copy Paper Expense account. Just be sure that you really need the detail because a large number of accounts can get unwieldy and hard to manage.

✔ **Payroll Taxes:** This account records any taxes paid related to employee payroll, such as Pay As You Earn (PAYE), Statutory Sick Pay (SSP) and maternity/paternity pay.

✔ **Postage:** This account shows any expenditure on stamps, express package shipping and other shipping. If your business does a large amount of shipping through suppliers such as UPS or Federal Express, you may want to track that spending in separate accounts for each supplier. This option is particularly helpful for small businesses that sell over the Internet or through mail-order sales.

✔ **Profit (or Loss) on Disposal of Fixed Assets:** This account records any profit when a business sells a fixed asset, such as a car or furniture. Make sure that you only record revenue remaining after subtracting the accumulated depreciation from the original cost of the asset.

✔ **Rent:** This account records rental costs for a business's office or retail space.

✔ **Salaries and Wages:** This account shows any money paid to employees as salary or wages.

✔ **Travel and Entertainment:** This account records any expenditure on travel or entertainment for business purposes. Some businesses separate these expenses into several accounts, such as Travel and Entertainment – Meals; Travel and Entertainment – Travel; and Travel and Entertainment – Entertainment, to keep a close watch.

✔ **Telephone:** This account shows all business expenses related to the telephone and telephone calls.

✔ **Utilities:** This account shows utility costs, such as electricity, gas and water.

✔ **Vehicles:** This account shows expenses related to the operation of business vehicles.

Setting Up Your Chart of Accounts

You can use all the lists of accounts provided in this chapter to set up your business's own Chart of Accounts. No secret method exists for creating your own chart – just make a list of the accounts that apply to your business.

When first setting up your Chart of Accounts, don't panic if you can't think of every type of account you may need for your business. You can easily add to the Chart of Accounts at any time. Just add the account to the list and distribute the revised list to any employees who use the Chart of Accounts for recording transactions into the bookkeeping system. (Employees who code invoices or other transactions and indicate the account to which those transactions are to be recorded need a copy of your Chart of Accounts as well, even if they aren't involved in actual bookkeeping.)

The Chart of Accounts usually includes at least three columns:

✔ **Account:** Lists the account names

✔ **Type:** Lists the type of account – Asset, Liability, Capital, Income, Cost of Goods Sold or Expense

✔ **Description:** Contains a description of the type of transaction that is to be recorded in the account

Many businesses also assign numbers to the accounts, to be used for coding charges. If your company uses a computerised system, the computer automatically assigns the account number. For example, Sage 50 Accounts provides you with a standard Chart of Accounts that you can adapt to suit your business. Sage also allows you to completely customise your Chart of Accounts to codes that suit your business; however, most businesses find that the standard Chart of Accounts is sufficient. A typical numbering system is as follows:

✔ Asset accounts: 0010 to 1999

✔ Liability accounts: 2000 to 2999

✔ Capital accounts: 3000 to 3999

✔ Sales and Cost of Goods Sold accounts: 4000 to 6999

✔ Expense accounts: 7000 to 9999

This numbering system matches the one used by some computerised accounting systems, so you can easily make the transition if you decide to automate your books using a computerised accounting system in the future.

One major advantage of a computerised accounting system is the number of different Charts of Accounts that have been developed based on the type of business you plan to run. When you get your computerised system, whichever accounting software you decide to use, you can review the list of chart options included with that software for the type of business you run, delete any accounts you don't want and add any new accounts that fit your business plan.

If you're setting up your Chart of Accounts manually, be sure to leave a lot of room between accounts to add new accounts. For example, number your Trade Debtors account 1100 and then start your bank accounts from 1200. If you have a number of bank accounts, you can number them 1210, 1220, 1230 and so on. That leaves you plenty of room to add new bank accounts as well as petty cash. The same applies to your revenue accounts: you need to allow plenty of room in your codes for your business to grow. For example, 4000 may be Retail Sales from your shop, but you may start to develop an online presence and need a code to track Online Sales, so you could use 4050. Further codes could be added for Foreign Online Sales as opposed to UK online sales. Don't be too rigid in your choice of codes – leave as large a gap as possible between codes to give you maximum flexibility.

Figure 3-1 is a sample Chart of Accounts developed using Sage 50 Accounts, the accounts package I use throughout this book. This sample chart highlights the standard overhead accounts that Sage has already set up for you.

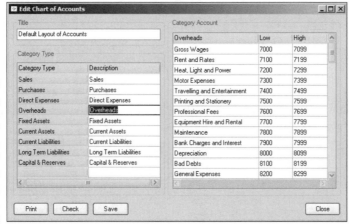

Figure 3-1:
The top portion of a sample Chart of Accounts showing overheads.

Chapter 4

Looking at Ledgers

As a bookkeeper, you may dream of having a single source that you can turn to when you need to review all entries that impact your business's accounts. (Okay, so maybe you're not exactly dreaming that, but just work with me here!) The Nominal Ledger is your dream come true, because here you find a summary of transactions and a record of the accounts that those transactions impact.

In this chapter, you discover the purpose of the Nominal Ledger. I tell you how to develop entries for the ledger and also how to enter (or post) them. In addition, I explain how you can change already posted information or correct entries in the Nominal Ledger and how this entire process is streamlined when you use a computerised accounting system.

Keeping Watch: The Eyes and Ears of a Business

The Nominal Ledger serves as the figurative eyes and ears of bookkeepers and accountants who want to know what financial transactions have taken place historically in a business. By reading the Nominal Ledger – not exactly interesting reading unless you love numbers – you can see, account by account, every transaction that has taken place in the business. (And to uncover more details about those transactions, you can turn to your business's journals, where transactions are kept on a daily basis. See Chapter 5 for the low-down on journals.)

The Nominal Ledger is the master summary of your business. You can find all the transactions that ever occurred in the history of the business in the Nominal Ledger account. In just one place you can find transactions that impact Cash, Stock, Trade Debtors (Accounts Receivable), Trade Creditors (Accounts Payable) and any other account included in your business's Chart of Accounts. (See Chapter 3 for more information about setting up the Chart of Accounts and the kind of transactions you can find in each account.)

Developing Entries for the Ledger

Because your business's transactions are first entered into journals, you develop many of the entries for the Nominal Ledger based on information pulled from the appropriate journal. For example, cash receipts and the accounts that those receipts impact are listed in the Cash Receipts book. Cash payments and the accounts those payments impact are listed in the Cash Payments book. The same is true for transactions found in the Sales journal, Purchases journal, General journal and any other special journals you may be using in your business.

At the end of each month, you summarise each journal by adding up the columns and then use that summary to develop an entry for the Nominal Ledger. Believe me, this process takes a lot less time than entering every transaction in the Nominal Ledger.

I introduce you to the process of entering transactions and summarising journals in Chapter 5. Near the end of that chapter, I even summarise one journal and develop this entry for the Nominal Ledger:

Account	Debit	Credit
Cash	£2,900	
Trade Debtors		£500
Sales		£900
Capital		£1,500

Note that the Debits and Credits are in balance – £2,900 each. Remember the cardinal rule of double-entry bookkeeping: all entries to the Nominal Ledger must be balanced entries. For more detail about double-entry bookkeeping, read Chapter 2.

In this entry, the Cash account is increased by £2,900 to show that cash was received. The Trade Debtors account is decreased by £500 to show customers paid their bills and the money is no longer due. The Sales account is increased by £900, because additional revenue was collected. The Capital account is increased by £1,500 because the owner put more cash into the business.

You need a selection of accountancy pads to write up your journals. I get my pads from high street stationers, so you shouldn't have a problem doing the same. A good all-purpose pad is the A4 six-column cash pad. Vestry produces a range of pads to suit all purposes, but any similar brand is fine too.

Figures 4-1 to 4-4 summarise the remaining journal pages prepared in Chapter 5. Reviewing those summaries, I developed the following entries for the Nominal Ledger:

Figure 4-1 – Summarised Cash Payments book

Figure 4-2 – Summarised Sales journal

Figure 4-3 – Summarised Purchases journal

Figure 4-4 – Summarised General journal

The following Nominal Ledger entry is based on the transactions that appear in Figure 4-1, a summary of the Cash Payments book:

Account	*Debit*	*Credit*
Rent	£800	
Trade Creditors	£750	
Salaries	£350	
Credit Card Payable	£150	
Cash		£2,050

This Nominal Ledger summary balances out at £2,050 each for the debits and credits. The Cash account is decreased to show the cash outlay, the Rent and Salaries Expense accounts are increased to show the additional expenses and the Trade Creditors and Credit Card Payable accounts are decreased to show that bills were paid and are no longer due.

In a small business, you use the Cash book to record both payments and receipts made by cheque or cash. In Figure 4-1, a column records the cheque number, which is useful if any queries crop up later.

Figure 4-2 shows the Sales journal for a sample business.

Rachel & Zoe's Sewing Shop
Cash Book (Payments)
June 2010

Date	Account Debited	Folio	Cheque No.	Nominal Debit	Trade Creditor Debit	Salaries Debit		Cash Credit
1/6	Rent		1065	800 —				800 —
3/6	Trade Creditor - Henry's		1066		500 —			500 —
3/6	Trade Creditor - Helen's		1067		250 —			250 —
4/6	Salaries		1068			350 —		350 —
10/3	Credit Card - Barclays		1069	150 —				150 —
				950 —	750 —	350 —		2,050 —

Rachel & Zoe's Sewing Shop
Sales Journal
June 2010

Date	Customer Acct. Debited		Invoice No.	Trade Debtors Debit	Sales Credit			
1/6	S. Smith		243	200 —	200 —			
1/6	Charlie's Garage		244	300 —	300 —			
3/6	P. Perry		245	100 —	100 —			
5/6	J. Jones		246	200 —	200 —			
				800 —	800 —			

The following Nominal Ledger entry is based on the transactions that appear in Figure 4-2:

Account	Debit	Credit
Trade Debtors	£800	
Sales		£800

Note that this entry is balanced. The Trade Debtors account is increased to show that customers owe the business money because they bought items on credit. The Sales account is increased to show that even though no cash changed hands, the business in Figure 4-2 took in revenue. Cash is going to be collected when the customers pay their bills.

Figure 4-3 shows the business's Purchases journal for one month. The following Nominal Ledger entry is based on the transactions that appear in Figure 4-3:

Account	Debit	Credit
Purchases	£925	
Trade Creditors		£925

Like the entry for the Sales account, this entry is balanced. The Trade Creditors account is increased to show that money is due to suppliers, and the Purchases Expense account is also increased to show that more supplies were purchased.

Figure 4-4 shows the General journal for a sample business. The following Nominal Ledger entry is based on the transactions that appear in Figure 4-4:

Account	Debit	Credit
Sales Returns	£60	
Trade Creditors	£200	
Vehicles	£10,000	
Trade Debtors		£60
Purchase Returns		£200
Capital		£10,000

Checking for balance – Debits and Credits both total to £10,260.

In this entry, the Sales Returns and Purchase Returns accounts are increased to show additional returns. The Trade Creditors and Trade Debtors accounts are both decreased to show that money is no longer owed. The Vehicles account is increased to show new business assets, and the Capital account, which is where the owner's deposits into the business are recorded, is increased accordingly.

Figure 4-3:
A Purchases journal keeps track of all purchases of goods to be sold. This figure shows how to summarise those transactions so that they can be posted to the Nominal Ledger.

Rachel & Zoe's Sewing Shop
Purchases Journal
June 2010

Date	Supplier Credited	Invoice No.	Purchases Debit	Trade Creditors Credit			
1/6	Supplier from Henry's	1575	750 —	750 —			
5/6	Barry's – packaging	1285	100 —	100 —			
8/6	Helen's – paper	1745	75 —	75 —			
			925 —	925 —			

Figure 4-4:
A General journal keeps track of all miscellaneous transactions not tracked in a specific journal, such as a Sales journal or a Purchases journal. This figure shows how to summarise those transactions so that they can be posted to the Nominal Ledger.

Rachel & Zoe's Sewing Shop
General Journal
June 2010

Date	Account	Nominal Debit	Nominal Credit	Trade Creditors Debit	Trade Debtors Credit		
3/6	Sales Return	60 —					
	S. Smith				60 —		
	Credit Memo 124						
5/6	Henry's Bakery			200 —			
	Purchase Return		200 —				
	Debit Memo 346						
8/6	Vehicles	10,000 —					
	Rachel's Capital		10,000 —				
				200 —	60 —		

Posting Entries to the Ledger

After you summarise your journals and develop all the entries you need for the Nominal Ledger (see the previous section), you post your entries into the Nominal Ledger accounts whenever you sit down to do the bookkeeping.

When posting to the Nominal Ledger, include transaction pound amounts as well as references to where material was originally entered into the books so that you can track a transaction back if a question arises later. For example, you may wonder what a number means, your boss or the owner may wonder why certain money was spent, or an auditor (an outside accountant who checks your work for accuracy) may raise a question.

Whatever the reason for questioning an entry in the Nominal Ledger, you definitely want to be able to find the point of original entry for every transaction in every account. Use the reference information that guides you to where the original detail about the transaction is located in the journals to answer any question that arises.

For this particular business, three of the accounts – Cash, Trade Debtors and Trade Creditors – are carried over month to month, so each has an opening balance. Just to keep things simple, in this example I start each account with a £2,000 balance. One of the accounts, Sales, is closed at the end of each accounting period, and so starts with a zero balance.

Most businesses close their books at the end of each month and produce financial reports. Others close them at the end of a quarter or end of a year. (I talk more about which accounts are closed at the end of each accounting period and which accounts remain open, as well as why, in Chapter 24.) For the purposes of this example, I assume that this business closes its books monthly. And in the figures that follow, I only give examples for the first five days of the month to keep things simple.

As you review the figures for the various accounts in this example, notice that the balance of some accounts increase when a debit is recorded and decrease when a credit is recorded. Other accounts increase when a credit is recorded and decrease when a debit is recorded. This feature is the mystery of debits, credits and double-entry accounting. For more, flip to Chapter 2.

The Cash account (see Figure 4-5) increases with debits and decreases with credits. Ideally, the Cash account always ends with a debit balance, which means money is still in the account. A credit balance in the Cash account indicates that the business is overdrawn, and you know what that means – cheques are returned for non-payment.

	Rachel & Zoe's Sewing Shop								
	Cash Account								
	June 2010								
Date	Description	Ref. No.	Debit	Credit			Balance		
1/6	Opening Balance						2,000 —		
30/6	From Cash Receipts book	Jnl Page 1	2,900 —						
30/6	From Cash Payments Journal	Jnl Page 2		2,050 —					
	Closing Balance						2,850 —		

Figure 4-5: Cash account in the Nominal Ledger.

The Trade Debtors account (see Figure 4-6) increases with debits and decreases with credits. Ideally, this account also has a debit balance that indicates the amount still due from customer purchases. If no money is due from customers, the account balance is zero. A zero balance isn't necessarily a bad thing if all customers have paid their bills. However, a zero balance may be a sign that your sales have slumped, which can be bad news.

	Rachel & Zoe's Sewing Shop								
	Debtors account								
	June 2010								
Date	Description	Ref. No.	Debit	Credit			Balance		
1/6	Opening Balance						2,000 —		
30/6	From Cash Receipts book	Jnl Page 1		500 —					
30/6	From Sales Jnl	Jnl Page 3	800 —						
3/6	Credit Memo 124 Gen. Jnl	Jnl Page 5		60 —					
	Closing Balance						2,240 —		

Figure 4-6: Trade Debtors account in the Nominal Ledger.

The Trade Creditors account (see Figure 4-7) increases with credits and decreases with debits. Ideally, this account has a credit balance because money is still due to suppliers, contractors and others. A zero balance here means no outstanding bills.

			Rachel & Zoe's Sewing Shop						
			Creditors account						
			June 2010						
Date	Description		Ref. No.	Debit	Credit				Balance
1/6	Opening Balance								2,000 —
30/6	From Cash Book		Jnl Page 2	750 —					
30/6	From Purchase Jnl.		Jnl Page 4		925 —				
5/6	Debit Memo 346		Jnl Page 5	200 —					
	Closing Balance								1,975 —

Figure 4-7: Trade Creditors account in the Nominal Ledger.

These three accounts – Cash, Trade Debtors and Trade Creditors – are part of the balance sheet, which I explain fully in Chapter 19. Asset accounts on the balance sheet usually carry debit balances because they reflect assets (in this case, cash) that the business owns. Cash and Trade Debtors are Asset accounts. Liability and Capital accounts usually carry credit balances because Liability accounts show claims made by creditors (in other words, money the business owes to financial institutions, suppliers or others), and Capital accounts show claims made by owners (in other words, how much money the owners have put into the business). Trade Creditors is a Liability account.

Here's how these accounts impact the balance of the business:

Assets	=	Liabilities	+	Capital
Cash		Trade Creditors		Trade Debtors
(Usually debit balance)		(Usually credit balance)		(Usually debit balance)

Here's how these accounts affect the balances of the business.

The Sales account (see Figure 4-8) isn't a balance sheet account. Instead, the Sales account is used to develop the profit and loss statement, which shows whether or not a business made profit in the period being examined. (For the low-down on profit and loss statements, see Chapter 18.) Credits and debits are pretty straightforward in the Sales account: credits increase the account and debits decrease it. Fortunately, the Sales account usually carries a credit balance, which means the business had income.

What's that, you say? The Sales account should carry a credit balance? That may sound strange, but the key is the relationship between the Sales account and the balance sheet. The Sales account is one of the accounts that feed the bottom line of the profit and loss statement, which shows whether your business made a profit or suffered a loss. A profit means that you earned more through sales than you paid out in costs or expenses. Expense and cost accounts usually carry a debit balance.

The profit and loss statement's bottom line figure shows whether or not the business made a profit. When the business makes a profit, the Sales account credits exceed expense and cost account debits. The profit is in the form of a credit, which gets added to the Capital account called Retained Earnings, which tracks how much of your business's profits are reinvested to grow the business. When the business loses money and the bottom line of the profit and loss statement shows that costs and expenses exceeded sales, the number is a debit. That debit is subtracted from the balance in Retained Earnings, to show the reduction to profits reinvested in the business.

		Rachel & Zoe's Sewing Shop							
		Sales Account							
		June 2010							
Date	Description	Ref. No.	Debit	Credit			Balance
1/6	Opening Balance						— —
30/6	From Cash Receipts Jnl.	Jnl Page 1		900 —			
30/6	From Sales Jnl.	Jnl Page 3		800 —			
	Closing Balance						1,700 —

Figure 4-8: Sales account in the Nominal Ledger.

When your business earns a profit at the end of the accounting period, the Retained Earnings account increases thanks to a credit from the Sales account. When you lose money, your Retained Earnings account decreases.

Because the Retained Earnings account is a Capital account and Capital accounts usually carry credit balances, Retained Earnings usually carries a credit balance as well.

After you post all the Nominal Ledger entries, you need to record details about where you posted the transactions on the journal pages. I show you how to carry out that process in Chapter 5.

Adjusting for Nominal Ledger Errors

Your entries in the Nominal Ledger aren't cast in stone. If necessary, you can always change or correct an entry with an *adjusting entry.* Four of the most common reasons for Nominal Ledger adjustments are:

- ✔ **Depreciation:** A business shows the ageing of its assets through depreciation. Each year, a portion of the original cost of an asset is written off as an expense, and that change is noted as an adjusting entry. Determining how much is to be written off is a complicated process that I explain in greater detail in Chapter 12.

- ✔ **Prepaid expenses:** Expenses that are paid up front, such as a year's worth of insurance, are allocated by the month using an adjusting entry. This type of adjusting entry is usually done as part of the closing process at the end of an accounting period. I show you how to develop entries related to prepaid expenses in Chapter 17.

- ✔ **Adding an account:** Accounts can be added by way of adjusting entries at any time during the year. If the new account is being created to track transactions separately that once appeared in another account, you must move all transactions already in the books to the new account. You do this transfer with an adjusting entry to reflect the change.

- ✔ **Deleting an account:** Only delete an account at the end of an accounting period.

I talk more about adjusting entries and how you can use them in Chapter 17.

Using Computerised Transactions to Post and Adjust in the Nominal Ledger

If you keep your books using a computerised accounting system, your accounting software does the posting to the Nominal Ledger behind the scenes. You can view your transactions right on the screen. I show you how to do this using the following simple steps in Sage 50 Accounts, so you don't have to make a Nominal Ledger entry. Other computerised accounting programs allow you to view transactions right on the screen too. Sage 50 Accounts is the most popular of the computerised accounting systems, which is why I use it to produce examples throughout the book.

1. **Click on the Company button, which opens up the Nominal Ledger screen.**

2. **Click the Record icon.**

   The Nominal Ledger Record screen appears.

3. **Select Nominal Code (NC) 2100 to view a summary of the Trade Creditors account.**

   This summary shows how much in total you owe (see Figure 4-9).

4. **Click on the Activity tab for more detail.**

   Figure 4-10 shows the sales transactions entered for July.

Be sure that you can trust whoever has access to your computerised system and that you set up secure password access. People can manipulate the system and process incorrect or fraudulent information very easily. Also, establish a series of checks and balances for managing your business's cash and accounts. Chapter 7 covers safety and security measures in greater detail.

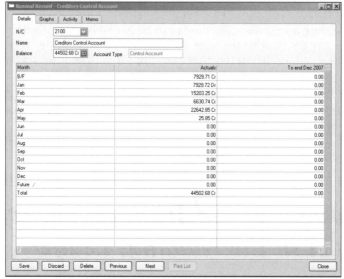

Figure 4-9: A summary of a Trade Creditors account in Sage 50 Accounts.

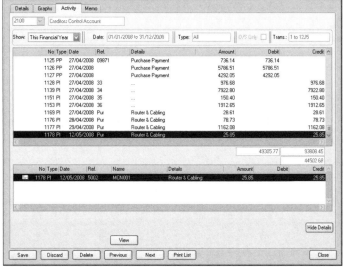

Figure 4-10:
Look inside
the Trade
Creditors
account
in Sage 50
Accounts.

Part II
Keeping a Paper Trail

'This is <u>real</u> hell – The books
down here <u>never</u> balance!'

In this part . . .

This part introduces you to the basics of entering financial transactions, posting transactions to your Nominal Ledger (the pinnacle of your bookkeeping system), and recording all the transaction details in your journals.

Good internal controls are a must-have for any bookkeeping system, and so I tell you how to put them in place to be sure that all your financial transactions are not only entered into the books but also entered correctly. In addition, you want to be sure that cash coming in and going out of the business is properly handled, and so I provide recommendations of how to separate various money-related duties.

Finally, I introduce you to your options when it comes to computerised accounting systems and share the benefits of using these types of systems to keep your business's books.

Chapter 5

Keeping Journals

. . . .

In This Chapter

▶ Starting things off with point of original entry

▶ Recording cash, sales and purchases

▶ Posting to the appropriate accounts

▶ Simplifying the journals process with computers

. . . .

*W*hen doing your books, you have to start somewhere. You can take a shortcut and just list every transaction in the affected accounts, but after recording hundreds – maybe thousands – of transactions in one month, imagine the nightmare if your books don't balance and you need to find the error. Talk about looking for a needle in a haystack – a haystack of numbers!

Because in a double-entry bookkeeping system you enter every transaction in two places – as a debit in one account and a credit in another account – you need to have a place where you can easily match those debits and credits. (For more on the double-entry system, flip to Chapter 2.)

Long ago, bookkeepers developed a system of *journals* to give businesses a starting point for each transaction. In this chapter, I introduce you to the process of journalising your transactions; I tell you how to set up and use journals, how to post the transactions to the accounts impacted and how to use a computerised bookkeeping program to simplify this entire process.

Establishing a Transaction's Point of Entry

In most businesses that don't use computerised bookkeeping programs, a transaction's original point of entry into the bookkeeping system is through a system of journals.

Each transaction goes in the appropriate journal in chronological order. The entry includes information about the date of the transaction, the accounts to which the transaction was posted and the source material used for developing the transaction.

If, at some point in the future, you need to follow how a credit or debit ended up in a particular account, you can find the necessary detail in the journal where you first posted the transaction. (Before being posted to various accounts in the bookkeeping system, each transaction gets a reference number to help you backtrack to the original entry point.) For example, suppose a customer calls you and wants to know why his account has a $500 charge. To find the answer, you go to the posting in the customer's account, follow the charge back to its original point of entry in the Sales journal, use that information to locate the source for the charge, make a copy of the source (most likely a sales invoice or receipt) and post the evidence to the customer.

If you filed everything properly, you can easily find the original source material and settle any issue that arises regarding any transaction. For more on what papers you need to keep and how to file them, see Chapter 7.

Although you can keep a single general journal for all your transactions, one big journal can be very hard to manage because you're likely to have thousands of entries in that journal by the end of the year. Instead, most businesses employ a system of journals that includes a Cash book (or books), which are really journals but are traditionally called books, for both incoming cash and outgoing cash. In the one-book system, cash receipts are entered on one page (usually the left-hand page) and cash payments are entered on the opposite page (the right-hand page). This system works well if you have roughly equal numbers of cash receipts and payments. However, if your business makes more payments than it has receipts (which is usual), you may want to have a Cash Payments book and a separate Cash Receipts book.

Not all transactions involve cash, however, so the two most common non-cash journals are the Sales journal and the Purchases journal. I show you how to set up and use each of these journals in the following sections.

Watching Cash Change Hands

Businesses deal with cash transactions every day, and as a business owner, you definitely want to know where every penny is going. The best way to get a quick daily summary of cash transactions is by reviewing the entries in your Cash book. In this section, I assume that you're keeping a separate Cash Payments book and a Cash Receipts book because you have a very busy business.

Keeping track of incoming cash

The Cash Receipts book is the first place you record cash received by your business. The majority of cash received each day comes from daily sales; other possible sources of cash include deposits of capital from the business's owner, customer invoice payments, new loan proceeds and interest from savings accounts.

Each entry in the Cash Receipts book must not only indicate how the cash was received, but also designate the account into which the cash is to be recorded.

Every Cash Receipts book has at least two columns in common:

- ✔ **Date:** The date of the transaction, whether a sale, a receipt, a credit transaction or whatever.

- ✔ **Folio:** This column shows where the transaction is to be posted at the end of the month. This information is filled in at the end of the month when you do the posting to the Nominal Ledger accounts. If the entry to be posted to the accounts is summarised and totalled at the bottom of the page, you can just put a tick mark next to the entry in the Folio column. For transactions listed in the General Credit or General Debit columns, indicate an account number for the account in which the transaction is posted.

Remember, in double-entry bookkeeping, every transaction is entered twice – once as a debit and once as a credit. For example, cash taken in for sales is credited to the Sales account and debited to the Cash account. In this case, both accounts increase in value. (For more about debits and credits, flip to Chapter 2.)

In the Cash Receipts book, the Cash account is always the debit because you initially deposit your money there. The credits vary depending upon the source of the funds. Figure 5-1 shows you what a series of transactions look like when they're entered into a Cash Receipts book.

					Rachel & Zoe's Sewing Shop						
					Cash Book (Receipts)						
					June 2010						
					Trade						
Date	Account	Folio	General	Debtors	Sales			Cash			
	Credited		Credit	Credit	Credit			Debit			
1/6	Sales				300 —			300 —			
2/6	Sales				250 —			250 —			
3/6	Cheque 121 - S. Smith			200 —				200 —			
3/6	Sales				150 —			150 —			
4/6	H.G. Capital	1,500 —						1,500 —			
5/6	Cheque 325 - J. Jones			100 —				100 —			
5/6	Cheque 567 - P. Perry			200 —				200 —			
5/6	Sales				200 —			200 —			

Figure 5-1: The Cash Receipts book is the first point of entry for incoming cash.

Most of your incoming cash (received by the cashier) is recorded each day, and is called *cash register sales* or simply *sales* in the journal. When you record cheques received from customers, you list the customer's cheque number and name as well as the amount. In Figure 5-1, the only other cash received is a cash deposit from H.G. to cover a cash shortfall.

The Cash Receipts book in Figure 5-1 has seven columns of information, including the Date and Folio columns explained earlier in this section:

✔ **Account Credited:** The name of the account credited.

✔ **General Credit:** For transactions that don't have their own columns; these transactions are entered individually into the accounts impacted.

For example, according to Figure 5-1, H.G. deposited £1,500 of his own money into the Capital account on 4 June in order to pay invoices. The credit shown is to be posted to the Capital account at the end of the month, because the Capital account tracks all information about assets H.G. pays into the business.

> ✔ **Trade Debtors (Accounts Receivable) Credit:** Any transactions that are posted to the Trade Debtors account (which tracks information about customers who buy products on credit).
>
> ✔ **Sales Credit:** Credits for the Sales account.
>
> ✔ **Cash Debit:** Anything that is going to be added to the Cash account.

You can set up your Cash Receipts book with more columns when you have accounts with frequent cash receipts. The big advantage to having individual columns for active accounts is that, when you total the columns at the end of the month, the total for the active accounts is the only thing you have to add to the Nominal Ledger accounts, which is a lot less work than entering every Sales transaction individually in the Nominal Ledger account. This approach saves a lot of time posting to accounts that involve multiple transactions every month. Individual transactions listed in the General Credits column each need to be entered into the affected accounts separately, which takes a lot more time that just entering a column total.

The top right-hand corner of the Cash Receipts book provides space for the person who prepared the journal, and for someone who approves the entries, to sign and date. If your business deals with cash, incorporate a system of checks and balances to ensure that cash is properly handled and recorded. For more safety measures, see Chapter 7.

Following outgoing cash

Cash going out of the business to pay invoices, salaries, rents and other necessities has its own journal, the Cash Payments book. This journal is the point of original entry for all business cash paid out to others.

No businessperson likes to see money go out the door, but imagine what creditors, suppliers and others think if they don't get the money they're due. Put yourself in their shoes: would you be able to buy needed supplies if other businesses didn't pay what they owed you? Not a chance.

You need to monitor your outgoing cash just as carefully as you monitor incoming cash (see the preceding section). Each entry in the Cash Payments book must not only indicate how much cash was paid out, but also designate which account is to be decreased in value because of the cash disbursal. For example, cash disbursed to pay invoices is credited to the Cash account (which goes down in value) and is debited to the account from which the invoice or loan is paid, such as Trade Creditors (Accounts Payable). The debit decreases the amount still owed in the Trade Creditors account.

In the Cash Payments book, the Cash account is always the credit, and the debits vary depending upon the outstanding debts to be paid. Figure 5-2 shows you what a series of transactions look like when they're entered in a Cash Payments book.

					Trade				
Date	Account	Folio	Cheque	Nominal	Creditors	Salaries			Cash
	Debited		No.	Debit	Debit	Debit			Credit
1/6	Rent		1065	800 —					800 —
3/6	Trade Creditors - Henry's		1066		500 —				500 —
3/6	Trade Creditors - Helen's		1067		250 —				250 —
4/6	Salaries		1068			350 —			350 —
10/3	Credit Card - Barclays		1069	150 —					150 —
				950 —	750 —	350 —			2,050 —

Rachel & Zoe's Sewing Shop
Cash Book (Payments)
June 2010

Figure 5-2:
The Cash Payments book is the first point of entry for outgoing cash.

The Cash Payments book in Figure 5-2 has eight columns of information. (For an explanation of the Date and Folio columns, see the preceding section 'Keeping track of incoming cash'.)

- ✔ **Account Debited:** The name of the account debited, as well as any detail about the reason for the debit.

- ✔ **Cheque No.:** The number of the cheque used to pay the debt.

- ✔ **General Debit:** Any transactions that don't have their own columns; these transactions are entered individually into the accounts they impact.

  For example, according to Figure 5-2, rent was paid on 1 June and is to be indicated by a debit in the Rent Expense account.

- ✔ **Trade Creditors Debit:** Any transactions that are posted to the Trade Creditors account (which tracks invoices due).

- ✔ **Salaries Debit:** Debits to the Salaries Expense account, which increase the amount of salaries expenses paid in a particular month.

- ✔ **Cash Credit:** Anything deducted from the Cash account.

You can set up your Cash Payments book with more columns if you have accounts with frequent cash disbursals. For example, in Figure 5-2, the bookkeeper for this fictional business added one column each for Trade Creditors and Salaries because cash for both accounts is disbursed on multiple occasions during the month. Rather than having to list each disbursement in the Trade Creditors and Salaries accounts, she can just total each journal column at the end of the month and add totals to the appropriate accounts. This approach saves a lot of time when you're working with your most active accounts.

Managing Sales Like a Pro

Not all sales involve the collection of cash; many businesses allow customers to buy products on credit using a credit account facility.

Credit comes into play when a customer is allowed to take a business's products without paying immediately because his account is invoiced monthly. This can be done by using a credit card issued by the shop (in the case of a retail business) or some other method the business uses to record customer credit purchases, such as having the customer sign a sales receipt indicating that the amount is to be charged to the customer's account.

Sales made on credit don't involve cash until the customer pays his invoice. (In contrast, with credit card sales, the store gets a cash payment from the card-issuing bank before the customer even pays the credit card invoice.) If your business sells on credit, the total value of the products bought on any particular day becomes an item for the Trade Debtors account, which records all money due from customers. I talk more about managing Trade Debtors in Chapter 10.

Before allowing customers to buy on credit, make sure that you require them to apply for credit in advance so that you can check their credit references.

When something's sold on credit, usually the cashier or accounts department drafts an invoice for the customer to sign when picking up the product. The invoice lists the items purchased and the total amount due. After getting the customer's signature, the invoice is recorded in both the Trade Debtors account and the customer's individual account.

Transactions for sales made on credit first enter your books in the Sales journal. Each entry in the Sales journal must indicate the customer's name, the invoice number and the amount charged.

In the Sales journal, the Trade Debtors account is debited, which increases in value. The bookkeeper must also remember to make an entry to the customer's account records because the customer has not yet paid for the item. The transaction also increases the value of the Sales account, which is credited.

Figure 5-3 shows a few days' worth of transactions related to credit sales.

					Trade					
Date	Customer Acct. Debited			Invoice No.	Debtors Debit	Sales Credit				
1/6	S. Smith			243	200 —	200 —				
1/6	Charlie's Garage			244	300 —	300 —				
3/6	P. Perry			245	100 —	100 —				
5/6	J. Jones			246	200 —	200 —				
					800 —	800 —				

Rachel & Zoe's Sewing Shop
Sales journal
June 2010

Figure 5-3: The Sales journal is first point of entry for sales made on credit.

The columns in the Sales journal in Figure 5-3 include the following:

- **Customer Account Debited:** The name of the customer whose account is debited
- **Invoice Number:** The invoice number for the purchase
- **Trade Debtors Debit:** Increases to the Trade Debtors account
- **Sales Credit:** Increases to the Sales account

(For an explanation of the Date and Folio columns, see the earlier 'Keeping track of incoming cash' section.)

At the end of the month, the bookkeeper can just total the Trade Debtors and Sales columns shown in Figure 5-3 and post the totals to those Nominal Ledger accounts. She doesn't need to post all the detail because she can always refer back to the Sales journal. However, each invoice noted in the Sales journal must be carefully recorded in each customer's account. Otherwise, the bookkeeper doesn't know who and how much to invoice.

Keeping Track of Purchases

Purchases of products to be sold to customers at a later date are a key type of non-cash transaction. All businesses must have something to sell, whether they manufacture it themselves or buy a finished product from some other business. Businesses usually make these purchases on credit from the business that makes the product. In this case, the business becomes the customer of another business.

Transactions for purchases bought on credit first enter your books in the Purchases journal. Each entry in the Purchases journal must indicate the supplier from whom the purchase was made, the supplier's invoice number and the amount charged.

In the Purchases journal, the Trade Creditors account is credited and the Purchases account is debited, meaning both accounts increase in value. The Trade Creditors account increases because the business now owes more money to creditors, and the Purchases account increases because the amount spent on goods to be sold goes up.

Figure 5-4 shows some store purchase transactions as they appear in the business's Purchases journal.

Rachel & Zoe's Sewing Shop											
Purchases journal											
June 2010											
Date	Supplier Credited	Folio	Invoice No.	Purchases Debit	Trade Creditors Credit						
1/6	Supplies from Henry's		1575	750 —	750 —						
5/6	Barry's – packaging		1285	100 —	100 —						
8/6	Helen's – paper		1745	75 —	75 —						
				925 —	925 —						

Figure 5-4: The Purchases journal is first point of entry for purchases bought on credit.

Including the standard Date and Folio columns, which are explained in the previous 'Keeping track of incoming cash' section, the Purchases journal in Figure 5-4 has six columns of information:

- **Supplier Account Credited:** The name of the supplier from whom the purchases were made
- **Invoice Number:** The invoice number for the purchase that the supplier assigned
- **Purchases Debit:** Additions to the Purchases account
- **Trade Creditors Credit:** Increases to the Trade Creditors account

At the end of the month, the bookkeeper can just total the Purchases and Trade Creditors columns and post the totals to the corresponding Nominal Ledger accounts. He can refer back to the Purchases journal for details if necessary. However, each invoice needs to be carefully recorded in each supplier's accounts so that a running total of outstanding invoices exists for each supplier. Otherwise, the bookkeeper doesn't know who, and how much, is owed.

Dealing with Transactions that Don't Fit

Not all your transactions fit in one of the four main journals (Cash Receipts, Cash Payments, Sales and Purchases). If you need to establish other special journals as the original points of entry for transactions, go ahead. The sky's the limit!

If you keep your books the old-fashioned way – on paper – be aware that paper is vulnerable to being mistakenly lost or destroyed. In this case, you may want to keep the number of journals you maintain to a minimum.

For transactions that don't fit in the 'big four' journals but don't necessarily warrant the creation of their own journals, consider keeping a General journal for miscellaneous transactions. Using columnar paper similar to that used for the other four journals, create Date and Folio columns (see the previous section, 'Keeping track of incoming cash') as well as the following columns:

- **Account:** The account that the transaction impacts. More detail is needed here because the General journal impacts so many different accounts with so many different types of transactions. For example, you find only sales transactions in the Sales journal and Purchase transactions in the Purchase journal, but you can find any type of transaction in the General journal affecting many less active accounts. (Place this column after the Date column and before the Folio column.)
- **General Debit:** Contains most debits.
- **General Credit:** Contains most credits.

If you have certain very active accounts, start a column for those accounts as well. In Figure 5-4, I added a column for Trade Creditors, and in Figure 5-5, I added columns for Trade Creditors and Trade Debtors. The big advantage of having a separate column for an account is that you're able to total that column at the end of the month and just put the total in the Nominal Ledger. You don't have to enter each transaction separately.

Many businesses also add columns for Trade Creditors and Trade Debtors because non-cash transactions commonly impact those accounts.

All the transactions in the General journal are non-cash transactions. Cash transactions go into one of the two cash journals: Cash Receipts (see the section 'Keeping track of incoming cash') and Cash Payments (see the section 'Following outgoing cash').

In a General journal, you enter transactions on multiple lines because each transaction impacts two accounts (and sometimes more than two). For example, in the General journal shown in Figure 5-5, the first transaction listed is the return of product by S. Smith. This return of products sold must be posted to the customer's account as a credit as well as to the Trade Debtors account. Also, the Sales Return account, where the business tracks all products returned by the customer, has to be debited. Here are some sample transactions from Figure 5-5:

- ✔ 5 June – Return a portion of purchase from Henry's Supplies, £200, Debit memo 346. When a business returns a product purchased, track it in the Purchase Return account, which is credited. A debit must also be made to the Trade Creditors account, as well as to the supplier's account, because less money is now owed. Cash doesn't change hands with this transaction.

- ✔ 8 June – Rachel transfers a car to the business, £10,000. This transaction is posted to the Vehicle Asset account and the Capital account in Owner's Capital. Rather than deposit cash into the business, Rachel made her personal vehicle a business asset.

In addition to the other columns, the General journal in Figure 5-5 has the following two columns:

- ✔ **Trade Creditors Debit:** Decreases to the Trade Creditors account

  The bookkeeper working with this journal anticipated that many of the business's transactions were going to impact Trade Creditors. She created this column so that she can subtotal it and make just one entry to the Trade Creditors account in the Nominal Ledger.

- ✔ **Trade Debtors Credit:** Decreases to the Trade Debtors account

			Trade	Trade		

Rachel & Zoe's Sewing Shop
General journal
June 2010

Date	Account	Folio	Nominal Debit	Nominal Credit	Trade Creditors Debit	Trade Debtors Credit			
3/6	Sales Return		60 —						
	S. Smith					60 —			
	Credit Memo 124								
5/6	Henry's Bakery				200 —				
	Purchase Return			200 —					
	Debit Memo 346								
8/6	Vehicles		10,000 —						
	Rachel's Capital			10,000 —					
					200 —	60 —			

Figure 5-5:
The General journal is the point of entry for miscellaneous transactions.

At the end of the month, the bookkeeper can just total this journal's Trade Creditors and Trade Debtors columns and post those totals to the corresponding Nominal Ledger accounts. All transaction details remain in the General journal. However, because the miscellaneous transactions impact Nominal Ledger accounts, the transactions need to be posted to each affected account separately (see the section 'Posting Journal Information to Accounts').

Posting Journal Information to Accounts

When you close your books at the end of the month, you summarise all the journals by totalling the columns and posting the information to update all the accounts involved.

Posting journal pages is a four-step process:

1. **Number each journal page at the top if not already numbered.**

2. **Total any column not titled General Debit or General Credit.**

   Any transactions recorded in the General Debit or General Credit columns need to be recorded individually in the Nominal Ledger.

3. **Post the entries to the Nominal Ledger account.**

   Each transaction in the General Credit or General Debit column must be posted separately. You just need to post totals to the Nominal Ledger for the other columns in which transactions for more active accounts were entered in the General journal. List the date and journal page number as well as the amount of the debit or credit, so that you can quickly find the entry for the original transaction if you need more details.

   The Nominal Ledger account shows only debit or credit (whichever is appropriate to the transaction). Only the journals have both sides of a transaction. (I show you how to work with Nominal Ledger accounts in Chapter 4.)

4. **Record information about where the entry is posted in the Folio column.**

   If the entry to be posted to the accounts is summarised and totalled at the bottom of the page, you can just put a tick mark next to the entry in the Folio column. For transactions listed in the General Credit or General Debit columns, indicate an account number for the account into which the transaction is posted. This process helps you confirm that you've posted all entries in the Nominal Ledger.

Posting to the Nominal Ledger is done at the end of an accounting period as part of the process of closing the accounts. I cover the closing process in greater detail in Chapter 15.

Figure 5-6 shows a summarised journal page, specifically the Cash Receipts book. You can see that entries listed in the Sales Credit and Cash Debit columns on the Cash Receipts book are just ticked. Only one entry was placed in the General Credit column, and that entry has an account number in the Folio column. Although I don't list here all the transactions for the month, which would of course be a much longer list, I do show how you summarise the journal at the end of the month.

					Trade						
Date	Account	Folio	General	Debtors	Sales				Cash		
	Credited		Credit	Credit	Credit				Debit		
1/6	Sales	✓			300 —				300 —		
2/6	Sales	✓			250 —				250 —		
3/6	Cheque 121 - S. Smith	✓		200 —					200 —		
3/6	Sales	✓			150 —				150 —		
4/6	H.G. Capital	3300	1,500 —						1,500 —		
5/6	Cheque 325 - J. Jones	✓		100 —					100 —		
5/6	Cheque 567 - P. Perry	✓		200 —					200 —		
5/6	Sales	✓			200 —				200 —		
			1,500 —	500 —	900 —				2,900 —		
		✓	(1100)	(4000)					(1000)		

Rachel & Zoe's Sewing Shop
Cash Book (Receipts)
June 2010

Nominal Codes

Figure 5-6: Summary of Cash Receipts book entries after the first five days.

As shown in Figure 5-6, after summarising the Cash Receipts book, you only need to post entries into four Nominal Ledger accounts (General Credit, Trade Debtors Credit, Sales Credit and Cash Debit) and three customer accounts (S. Smith, J. Jones and P. Perry). For the Nominal Ledger transactions, I show the Nominal Ledger account numbers (or codes) that each posting goes to – 3300, 1100, 4000 and 1000. You use codes like this if you choose to computerise your accounts. Even better, the entries balance: £2,900 in debits and £2,900 in credits! (The customer accounts total £500, which is good news because it matches the amount credited to Trade Debtors. The Trade Debtors account is decreased by £500 because payments were received, as is the amount due from the individual customer accounts.)

Simplifying Your Journaling with Computerised Accounting

The process of posting first to the journals and then to the Nominal Ledger and individual customer or supplier accounts can be very time-consuming.

Luckily, most businesses today use computerised accounting software, so the same information doesn't need to be entered as many times. The computer does the work for you.

If you're working with a computerised accounting software package (see Chapter 6), you only have to enter a transaction once. All the detail that normally needs to be entered into one of the journal pages, one of the Nominal Ledger accounts, and customer, supplier and other accounts is posted automatically. Voilà!

The method you use to enter your transaction initially varies depending on the type of transaction. To show you what's involved in making entries into a computerised accounting system, the following figures show one entry each from the Cash Receipts book (see Figure 5-7 for a customer payment), the Cash Payments book (see Figure 5-8 for a list of invoices to be paid) and the Sales journal (see Figure 5-9 for an invoice). (The screenshots are all from Sage 50 Accounts, a popular computerised bookkeeping system.)

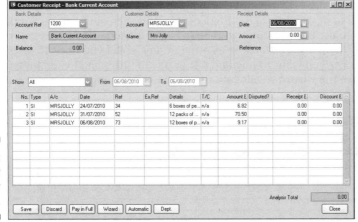

Figure 5-7:
Payment by
customer
Mrs Jolly.

As shown in Figure 5-7, to enter the payment by Mrs Jolly, all you need to do is click on the Bank button and then select the customer icon within the Bank Accounts screen. Ensure that you have selected the correct bank account and enter **MrsJolly** in the A/C box. All outstanding invoices for that account appear. You can then decide to accept payment for individual invoices by clicking on the Receipts column and then click the Pay In Full button or let the Wizard allocate the money to the invoices in chronological order. I favour the individual allocation of invoices, because that way you can be more accurate allocating the cash. The customer often sends a Remittance Advice slip with their cheque that identifies exactly which invoices they are paying. When you are done, click on Save and Close.

When you use a software package to track your cash receipts, the following accounts are automatically updated:

- ✔ The Cash account is debited the appropriate amount.
- ✔ The Trade Debtors account is credited the appropriate amount.
- ✔ The corresponding customer account is credited the appropriate amount.

You can see how much simpler this computerised system is than adding the transaction to the Cash Receipts book, closing the journal at the end of the month, adding the transactions to the accounts impacted by the cash receipts and then (finally!) closing the books.

Cash disbursements are just as easy when you have a computerised system on your side. For example, when paying invoices (see Figure 5-8), all you need to do is click on the Bank button and then click on the Supplier icon within the Bank Account screen in Sage 50 Accounts. In this example, all the June invoices are showing as outstanding, so all you need to do is select the invoices you want to pay and either pay in full against each individual invoice or use the wizard to allocate the payment automatically.

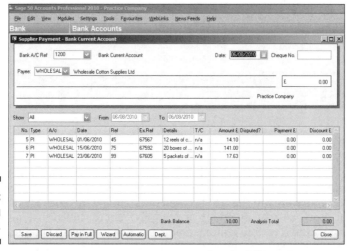

Figure 5-8:
Paying
invoices.

The invoice-paying perks of this system include:

- ✔ Cheques can be automatically printed by the software package.
- ✔ Each of the supplier accounts are updated to show that payment is made.
- ✔ The Trade Creditors account is debited the appropriate amount for your transaction, which decreases the amount due to suppliers.
- ✔ The Cash account is credited the appropriate amount for your transaction, which decreases the amount of cash available (because the cash is designated for use to pay corresponding invoices).

When you make the necessary entries into your computerised accounting system for the information normally to be found in a Sales journal (for example, when a customer pays for your product on credit), you can automatically create a sales invoice. Figure 5-9 shows what that invoice looks like when generated by a computerised accounting system. Adding the customer name in the Customer box automatically fills in all the necessary customer information. The date appears automatically, and the system assigns a customer invoice number. You add the quantity and select the type of product bought in the Item Code section, and the rest of the invoice is calculated automatically. When the invoice is final, you print it out and send it off to the customer.

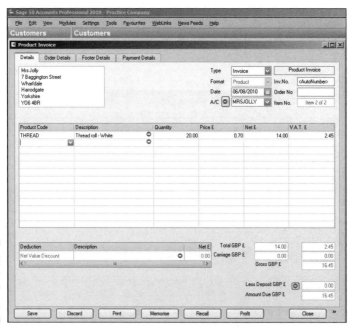

Figure 5-9: Customer invoice for Mrs Jolly.

Figure 5-9 shows Value Added Tax, which the system automatically calculates. I cover Value Added Tax in Chapter 23.

Filling out the invoice in the accounting system also updates the affected accounts:

- ✔ The Trade Debtors account is debited the appropriate amount, which increases the amount due from customers by that amount.

- ✔ The Sales account is credited the appropriate amount, which increases the revenue received by that amount.

- ✔ The invoice is added to the customer's outstanding invoices so that when the customer makes a payment, the outstanding invoice appears on the Payment screen.

Chapter 6

Surveying Computer Options

In This Chapter

▶ Finding the right accounting software for your business

▶ Getting your computerised books up and running

Some small-business owners who've been around a while still do things the old-fashioned way – keeping their books in paper journals and ledgers. However, in this age of technology and instant information, the majority of today's businesses computerise their books.

Not only is computerised bookkeeping easier, but it also minimises the chance of errors, because most of the work done to a computerised system's ledgers and journals (see Chapters 4 and 5, respectively) involves inputting data on forms that can be understood even by someone without training in accounting or bookkeeping. The person entering the information doesn't need to know whether something is a debit or credit (see Chapter 2 for an explanation of the difference) because the computerised system takes care of everything.

In this chapter, I explore three popular accounting software packages for small businesses, discuss the basics of setting up your own computerised books, talk about how you can customise a program for your business and give you some pointers on converting your manual bookkeeping system into a computerised one.

Most businesses start with a manual accounting system and progress to computerisation as the business grows. The real benefit of computerised accounting systems is that they enable you to do your bookkeeping much faster as your business grows. Also, most reports you may want are available at the click of a menu button. However, remember that in a significant number of business situations no accounting software package does exactly what you did before in the same way. Every accounting package is a compromise because it offers the features that someone else decided are important for the majority of businesses. You may have to choose whether to modify your business processes to fall into line with the new accounting software or have some bespoke modification to the accounting software package you decide to buy. The simplest and cheapest solution is to fall into line with your chosen accounting software.

Surveying Your Software Options

Many types of accounting software programs are on the market, and all are designed to computerise your bookkeeping. The more sophisticated ones target specific industry needs, such as food services or utilities, and can cost thousands of pounds.

Use an Internet search engine to find a list of accounting software in the UK.

As a further resource, ask your auditors or external accountants for their advice. Don't be surprised if they recommend Sage 50 Accounts, the number one accounting software package for small (and bigger) businesses in the UK. Most accountants are resellers of these accounting packages.

Luckily, as a small-business owner, you probably don't need all the bells and whistles that the top-of-the-line programs offer. Instead, the three software programs that I review in this chapter can meet the needs of most small businesses. You can buy one of the three systems I recommend from as little as £100. Such a program may not be fancy, but basic computerised accounting software can do a good job of helping you keep your books. And you can always upgrade to a more expensive program, if needed, as your business grows. The third accounting solution, Sage 50 Accounts, is a full-featured software package costing around £550. This amount may seem like a big investment, but the Sage 50 Accounts system can grow with your business.

The three programs I describe that meet any small business's basic bookkeeping needs are QuickBooks, Mamut and Sage 50 Accounts. The most affordable of the three is QuickBooks Simple Start, which I've seen for around £100 at various Internet sites. Mamut and Sage also offer simple systems, but if you can afford the cost, I recommend that you step up at least one notch to Sage 50 Accounts or QuickBooks Pro.

Accounting software packages are updated almost every year, because tax laws and laws involving many other aspects of operating a business change so often. In addition, computer software companies are always improving their products to make computerised accounting programs more user-friendly, so ensure that you always buy the most current version of an accounting software package.

QuickBooks

QuickBooks (www.intuit.co.uk) offers an easy user interface (for the novice) and extensive bookkeeping and accounting features (for the experienced bookkeeper or accountant). In 2010, QuickBooks (Pro and Premier versions) became even better by providing a real-time overview of your business via the Company Snapshot feature. It shows the Income and Expenditure trend for your business, as well as listing debtors and creditors and showing a list of account balances that can be customised to meet your needs. The Snapshot screens are updated throughout the day as transactions are posted. Various other improvements have also been made to the software; for example, you can download your data to your accountant directly from the software. This feature allows your accountant to work on the accounts and make adjustments at the year-end, while you continue entering transactions for the new financial period.

QuickBooks Simple Start, priced around £100, can meet most of your bookkeeping and accounting needs. If you want to track stock and handle multiple currencies, you need to get QuickBooks Pro 2010, which sells for around £250 for up to three users. A Premier version retails at £500 and allows you to highlight unbilled expenses before you invoice, has more advanced stock capabilities than Pro, allows you to forecast your cash flow and has accountant friendly features, such as a Client Data review tool.

From MYOB to Mamut

You may have heard about MYOB, which was an accounting system that was withdrawn from the UK market in 2008. A new piece of software has been created for MYOB users that allows them to migrate to a package called Mamut.

If you have MYOB software and want to know how you can move across to Mamut, contact Mamut Software Ltd on 0800 0325616 to discuss your requirements. You can test drive Mamut for free at www.mamut.com. Mamut offers many different accounting options, and the website helps you determine which package suits you best, depending on the type of business you operate.

For example, Mamut One gives you web-based access to your accounting information from £29 per month. For this, you get contact management software as well as accounting and payroll software with the ability to access the information online from anywhere. You can also upgrade to Mamut Platinum, which offers more functionality and dedicated implementation services.

Mac users can buy a dedicated accounts package called Mamut AccountEdge. Prices start from £149+ VAT for the basic package.

Sage

I'd be negligent if I didn't mention Sage accounting products (www.sage. co.uk). Sage offers a wide range of accounting software for businesses of every size. Sage probably has the biggest user-base in the UK among small and medium-sized businesses using accounting software. They offer something for businesses of every size and level of sophistication. Also, Sage products are easy and quick to obtain because virtually every high street software retailer stocks them.

Sage even has software packages designed for businesses that have yet to get started. Sage Start-Up offers business planning tools and online advice to help you run your business. Sage Instant Accounts is their budget accounting software package range and offers basic accounting, but you can add on Payroll, the ACT! contact manager feature and Forecasting at additional cost. Sage Instant Accounts covers most of the basic accounting features a small business needs. This software allows you to organise and record your sales and purchases, customer and supplier contacts, invoicing and VAT. The bank reconciliation process allows you to match money recorded in Instant Accounts with your bank statements. This software package even lets you create and customise quotations and then automate the invoicing process. The program also creates your VAT return. You can add a Pay Now button to your system to process credit card payments, although an additional Sage charge applies.

Sage Instant Accounts starts at £115, and you can also buy Sage Instant Accounts Plus, which gives you a two-user licence and allows you to control your stock and see business summaries at a glance, so you can spot business opportunities and grow your business.

One of the real beauties of Sage software is the attractive and familiar screens. For many years, when its competitors were hiding behind off-putting, text-based, non-Windows screens, Sage offered a welcoming approach. I know of many bookkeepers and accountants who still have fond memories of using Sage, long after they've moved to businesses that use other accounting software packages. By and large, Sage users are happy users.

Most reasonable-sized businesses are really going to start with the Sage 50 Accounts range, which starts at around £500 for Sage 50 Accounts and rises to £1,075+ VAT for the top of the range Sage 50 Accounts Professional. At the time of writing, you can get 10 per cent off the software if you take out SageCover, the support package offered by Sage. Sage 50 Accounts comes in three versions: Accounts, Accounts Plus and Accounts Professional. All versions have an impressive feature list, and if you aren't an importer/exporter with a need to run multi-currencies, Accounts or Accounts Plus meets most of your needs. Of course, all these software packages cover your basic accounting needs. Accounts Plus, however, adds some nice touches like project costing, individual customer pricing and custom price lists, multiple delivery addresses, cheque printing and improved stock allocation and bill of materials. Accounts Professional, the top of the range package, also offers Intrastat support, Foreign Trader, cash sales, sales order processing and purchase order processing.

In addition to these accounting software packages, Sage also offers payroll and HR software solutions, reporting and analysis software and customer contact software. However, the real strength of Sage is that you're buying into a family of products and services that can grow with your business. Sage run their own training courses, which are available regionally, and numerous books are available to show you how to use their various packages, including *Sage 50 Accounts For Dummies* by Jane Kelly.

Sage offer a full range of stationery that you can use with their software to improve the image of your business.

For all these reasons, I use Sage 50 Accounts to demonstrate various bookkeeping functions throughout this book.

Setting Up Your Computerised Books

After you pick your software, the hard work is done because setting up the package probably takes you less time than researching your options and picking your software. All three packages I discuss in this chapter (see the earlier section 'Surveying Your Software Options') have good start-up tutorials to help you set up the books. QuickBooks even has an interactive interview that asks questions about all aspects of how you want to run your business and then sets up what you need based on your answers.

All the featured accounting software packages produce a number of sample Charts of Accounts (see Chapter 3) that automatically appear after you choose the type of business you plan to run and within which industry your business falls. Start with one of the sample charts that the software offers, as shown in Figure 6-1, and then tweak the chart to your business's needs.

When your Chart of Accounts appears, all three programs ask you to enter a company name, address and tax identification numbers to get started. You then select an accounting period. If the calendar year is your accounting period, you don't have to change anything. But if you operate your business based on another 12-month period, you must enter that information. Most accounting packages assume you run on a 12-month financial year.

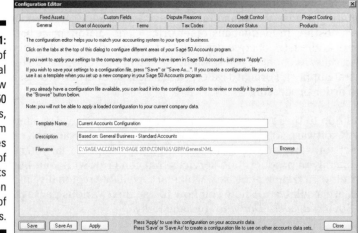

If you don't change your accounting period to match how you plan to develop your financial statements, you have to delete the business from the system and start over.

After you set up your business, you can customise the software so that it matches your business's needs.

Customising software to match your operations

With the basics set up (see the preceding section), you can customise the software to fit your business's operations. For example, you can pick the type of invoices and other business forms you want to use.

You're also now ready to input information about your bank accounts and other key financial data (see Figure 6-2). Use your main business bank account as the first account listed in your software program.

After entering your bank and other financial information, enter data unique to your business. If you want to use the program's budgeting features, enter your budget information before entering other data. Then add your supplier and customer accounts so that when you start entering transactions, the information is already in the system. If you don't have any outstanding bills or customer payments due, you can wait and enter supplier and customer information as the need arises.

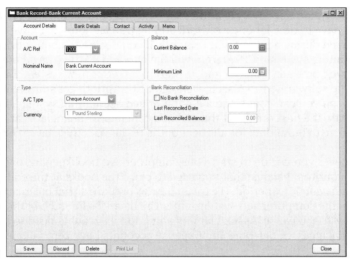

Figure 6-2:
Sage 50
Accounts
collects
informa-
tion about
your bank
accounts
via the Bank
Record
screen,
which is
accessed
from the
Bank tab.

You can import data about your customers, suppliers and Nominal Ledger from software packages you currently use to track that information, such as Microsoft Excel or Access. The accounting program you choose comes with full instructions for importing data, so you can save a lot of time if you have extensive customer and supplier records. Simply follow the instructions in the program and the system does all the hard work for you! You just need to make sure that you correctly format the data in a way that the accounting program understands.

You also need to enter information about whether you're VAT registered and if so, the appropriate VAT rates. Also, you can pick a format for your invoices, set up payroll data and make arrangements for how you want to pay bills.

Converting your manual bookkeeping to a computerised system

When you're converting a manual bookkeeping system to a computerised system, your conversion takes a bit more time than just starting fresh, because you need to be sure that your new system starts with information that matches your current books. The process for entering your initial data varies depending on the software you've chosen, so I don't go into detail about that process here. To ensure that you properly convert your book-keeping system, use the information that comes with your software; read through the manual, review the start-up suggestions made as you set up the system and pick the methods that best match your style of operating.

The best time to convert is at the end of an accounting period. That way, you don't have to do a lot of extra work adding transactions that have already occurred during a period. For example, if you decide to computerise your accounting system on 15 March, you have to add all the transactions that occurred between 1 March and 15 March into your new system. Even if you buy the software on 15 March, waiting until 1 April to get started is easier. Although you can convert to a computerised accounting system at the end of a month, the best time is at the end of a calendar or financial year. Otherwise, you have to input data for all the months of the year that have passed.

Whenever you decide to start your computerised bookkeeping, use the data from your trial balance that you used to close the books at the end of the most recent accounting period. (I explain how to prepare a trial balance in Chapter 16.) In the computerised system, enter the balances for each of the accounts in your trial balance. Asset, Liability and Capital accounts need to have carry-over balances, but Income and Expense accounts have zero balances.

Of course, when you're starting a new business, you don't have a previous trial balance. In this case, just enter any balances you may have in your cash accounts, any assets your business may own as it starts up and any liabilities that your business may already owe relating to start-up expenses. Also add any contributions from owners that were made to get the business started in the Capital accounts.

After you enter your opening balances, you can run a series of financial reports, such as a profit and loss statement and balance sheet, to be sure that the data is entered and formatted the way you prefer. You can edit your Chart of Accounts to ensure that your Profit and Loss account and your balance sheet are customised to suit your business needs. For example, you may not want Product Sales as the revenue title in your Profit and Loss account, you may prefer Consultancy Fees instead.

You need to be sure that you've entered the right numbers, so verify that the new accounting system's financial reports match what you created manually. If the numbers are different, now's the time to find out why. Otherwise the reports you do at the end of the accounting period are going to be wrong. If the numbers don't match, don't assume that the error is in the data entered. You may find that the error is in the reports you developed manually. Of course, check your entries first, but if the profit and loss statement and balance sheet still don't look right, double-check your trial balances as well.

Chapter 7

Controlling Your Books, Your Records and Your Money

*C*ash is an extremely important asset in any business, and it must be accurately recorded and monitored. Every business takes in cash in some form or another: notes and coins, cheques, and credit card and electronic payments are all eventually deposited as cash into the business's accounts. Before you take in that first penny, your initial concern must be controlling that cash and making sure that none of it walks out the door improperly.

Finding the right level of cash control, while at the same time allowing your employees the flexibility to sell your products or services and provide ongoing customer service, can be a monumental task. If you don't have enough controls, you risk theft or embezzlement. Yet if you have too many controls, employees may miss sales or anger customers.

In this chapter, I explain the basic protections you need to put in place to be sure that all cash coming into or going out of your business is clearly documented and controlled. I also review the type of paperwork you need to document the use of cash and other business assets. Finally, I tell you how to organise your staff to control the flow of your assets properly and insure yourself against possible misappropriation of those assets.

Putting Controls on Your Business's Cash

Think about how careful you are with your personal cash. You find various ways to protect the cash you carry around, you dole it out carefully to your family members and you may even hide cash in a safe place in the house just in case you need it for unexpected purposes.

You're very protective of your cash when you're the only one who handles it, but consider the vulnerability of your business cash. After all, you aren't the only one handling that cash. You have some employees encountering incoming cash at cash registers, others opening the mail and finding cheques for orders to purchase products or pay bills, as well as cheques from other sources. And don't forget that employees may need petty cash to pay for postage and other small items that the business requires.

If you watch over every transaction in which cash enters your business, you have no time to do the things you need to do to grow your business. When the business is small, you can sign all cheques and maintain control of cash going out, but as soon as the business grows, you just may not have the time.

The good news is that just putting in place the proper controls for your cash can help protect it. Cash flows through your business in four key ways:

- ✔ Deposits and payments into and out of your current accounts
- ✔ Deposits and payments into and out of your savings accounts
- ✔ Petty cash funds in critical locations where quick access to cash may be needed
- ✔ Transactions made in your cash registers

The following sections cover some key controls for each of these cash-flow points.

Current accounts

Almost every penny that comes into your business flows through your business's current account (at least that *should* happen). Whether the cash is collected at your cash registers, payments received in the mail, cash used to fill the cash registers or petty cash accounts, payments sent out to pay business obligations or any other cash need, this cash enters and exits your current account. Thus, your current account is your main tool for protecting your cash flow.

The high cost of employee versus customer theft

According to the Centre for Retail Research based in the UK, internal theft by employees cost UK retailers £1,479 million in 2009. You don't hear much about it, though, because many businesses choose to keep quiet. Four key situations in the workplace provide opportunities for theft and embezzlement: poor internal controls, too much control given to certain individuals, lax management and failure to pre-screen employees adequately. By comparison, customer theft cost retailers £1,767 million in the same year. It seems that retailers are getting a pretty raw deal!

Choosing the right bank

Finding the right bank to help you set up your current account and the controls that limit access to that account is crucial. When evaluating your banking options, ask yourself the following questions:

- ✔ Does this bank have a branch conveniently located for my business?
- ✔ Does this bank operate at times when I need it most?
- ✔ Does this bank offer secure ways to deposit cash even when the bank is closed?

   Most banks have secure deposit boxes for cash so that you can pay in cash receipts as quickly as possible at the end of the business day rather than secure the cash overnight yourself. You don't have to wait in a queue to deposit cash at the counter, simply fill out a paying-in slip, put it and the money into an envelope supplied by the bank and post the envelope into a special deposit box within the bank.

Visit local bank branches yourself and check out the type of business services each bank offers. Pay particular attention to:

- ✔ The type of personal attention you receive
- ✔ How questions are handled
- ✔ What type of charges may be tacked on for personalised attention

Some banks require business account holders to call a centralised line for assistance rather than depend on local branches. Most banks charge if you use a cashier rather than an ATM (automatic teller machine). Other banks charge for every transaction, whether a deposit, withdrawal or cheque. Many banks have charges that differ for business accounts. If you plan to accept credit cards, compare the services offered for that as well.

The general rule is that banks charge businesses for everything they do. However, they charge less for tasks that can be automated and thus involve less manual effort. So, you save money when you use electronic payment and receipt processes. In other words, pay your suppliers electronically and get your customers to pay you the same way to reduce your banking costs.

Deciding on types of cheques

After you choose your bank, you need to consider what type of cheques you want to use in your business. For example, you need different cheques depending upon whether you handwrite each cheque or print cheques from your computerised accounting system.

Writing cheques manually

If you plan to write your cheques, you're most likely to use a business cheque book, which in its simplest form is exactly the same as a personal cheque book, with a counter foil (or cheque stub) on the left and a cheque on the right. This arrangement provides the best control for manual cheques because each cheque and counter foil is numbered. When you write a cheque, you fill out the counter foil with details such as the date, the cheque's recipient and the purpose of the cheque. The counter foil also has a space to keep a running total of your balance in the account.

Printing computer-generated cheques

If you plan to print cheques from your computerised accounting system, you need to order cheques that match that system's programming. Each computer software program has a unique template for printing cheques, and some provide bespoke stationery for their accounting software. The key information is exactly what you expect to see on any cheque – payee details, date and amount in both words and numbers.

Unlike a manual cheque, you don't have a counter foil to fill in, which is not a problem because your computerised accounting system records this information for you: it keeps an internal record of all cheques issued. If you need to check that you issued a cheque correctly, you can always run a report or make an on-screen enquiry on your computerised accounting system.

Initially, when the business is small, you can sign each cheque and keep control of the outflow of money. But as the business grows, you may find that you need to delegate cheque-signing responsibilities to someone else, especially if you travel frequently. Many small business owners set up cheque-signing procedures that allow one or two of their staff to sign cheques up to a designated amount, such as £5,000. Any cheques above that designated amount require the owner's signature, or the signature of an employee and a second designated person, such as an officer of the business.

Making deposits in the current account

Of course, you aren't just withdrawing from your business's current account (that would be a big problem). You also need to deposit money into that account, and you want to be sure that your paying-in slips contain all the necessary detail as well as documentation to back up the deposit information. Most banks provide printed paying-in slips with all the necessary detail to be sure that the money is deposited into the appropriate account, together with who wrote each cheque, the value and the date received.

A good practice is to record cheques immediately as part of a daily morning routine. Enter the details onto the paying-in slip and update your computerised or manual accounting system at the same time. Make sure that you pay in any money received before 3.30 p.m. on the same day, to ensure that your bank account gets credit that day rather than the next. (I talk more about controls for incoming cash in the 'Dividing staff responsibilities' section, later in this chapter.) If you get both personal and business cheques sent to the same address, instruct the person opening the mail about how to differentiate the types of cheques and how each type of cheque needs to be handled to best protect your incoming cash, whether for business or personal purposes.

You may think that making bank deposits is as easy as 1-2-3, but when it comes to business deposits and multiple cheques, things get a bit more complicated. To make deposits to your business's current account properly, follow these steps:

1. **Record on the paying-in slip the full details of all cheques being deposited as well as the total cash being deposited. Also make a note of how many cheques you're paying into the bank on that paying-in slip.**

2. **Record the details regarding the source of the deposited cash before you make the deposit. If you're operating a manual system, you can write the entries in your Cash Receipts book, or if using a computerised system, you can enter the details from the paying-in slip directly into the computer.** (I talk more about filing in the section 'Keeping the Right Paperwork', later in this chapter.)

3. **Make sure that the cashier at the bank stamps the paying-in slip as confirmation that the bank has received all the cheques and cash.**

   If you're paying in cheques via the ATM, treat it exactly as if you were paying in via the cashier. Still prepare your own paying-in slip and make sure that you pick up the receipt that the ATM gives you. This doesn't ensure that things won't go wrong, but it means you have a paper trail if they do. Note on your paying-in slip counterfoil that you have paid via the deposit box or ATM.

Savings accounts

Some businesses find that they have more cash than they need to meet their immediate plans. Rather than keep that extra cash in a non-interest-bearing account, many businesses open a savings account to store the extra cash.

If you're a small business owner with few employees, you probably control the flow of money into and out of your savings account yourself. As you grow and find that you need to delegate the responsibility for the business's savings, ensure that you think carefully about who gets access and how you can document the flow of funds into and out of the savings account. Treat a savings account like a current account and use paying-in slips to record deposits and cheque-book stubs to record payments. Alternatively, you can arrange for the bank to automatically transfer surplus funds from your current account across to your savings account when the current account reaches a specified amount.

Petty cash accounts

Every business needs cash on almost a weekly basis. Businesses need to keep some cash on hand, called *petty cash,* for unexpected expenses such as money to pay for letters and packages delivered COD, money to buy a few emergency stamps to get the mail out or money for some office supplies needed before the next delivery.

You certainly don't want to have a lot of cash sitting around in the office, but try to keep £50 to £100 in a petty cash box. If you subsequently find that you're faced with more or less cash expenses than you expected, you can always adjust the amount kept in petty cash accordingly.

No matter how much you keep in petty cash, make sure that you set up a good control system that requires anyone who uses the cash to write a petty cash voucher specifying how much was used and why. Also ask that a cash receipt, for example from the shop or post office, is attached to the voucher in order to justify the cash withdrawal whenever possible. In most cases, a member of staff buys something for the business and then gets reimbursed for that expense. If the expense is small enough, you can reimburse through the petty cash fund. If the expense is more than a few pounds, ask the person to fill out an expense account form and get reimbursed by cheque. Petty cash is usually used for minor expenses of £10 or less.

The best way to control petty cash is to pick one person in the office to manage the use of all petty cash. Before giving that person more cash, he or she should be able to prove the absence of cash used and why it was used.

Poor control of the petty cash box can lead to small but significant losses of cash. Quite often you can find it difficult or impossible to identify or prove who took the cash. The best solution is to make it slightly more difficult for employees to obtain petty cash; a locked box in a cupboard works very well.

For the ultimate control of cash, use the imprest system in which a fixed amount is drawn from the bank and paid into petty cash (the float). After that, cash is issued only against a petty cash voucher. This system means that, at any point, cash, or cash plus vouchers, should be equal to the total of the petty cash float. At the end of the week (or month) the vouchers are removed and the cash made up to the original amount.

Cash registers

Have you ever gone into a business and tried to pay with a large note only to find out that the cashier has no change? This frustrating experience happens in many businesses, especially those that don't carefully monitor the money in their cash registers. Most businesses empty cash registers each night and put any cash not being deposited in the bank that night into a safe. However, many businesses instruct their cashiers to deposit their cash in a business safe periodically throughout the day and get a paper voucher to show the cash deposited. These daytime deposits minimise the cash held in case the store is the victim of a robbery.

All these types of controls are necessary parts of modern business operations, but they can have consequences that make customers angry. Most customers just walk out the door and don't come back when they can't buy what they want using the notes they have on hand.

At the beginning of the day, cashiers usually start out with a set amount of cash in the register. As they collect money and give out change, the register records the transactions. At the end of the day, the cashier must count out the amount of change left in the register, run a copy of all transactions that passed through that register and total the cash collected. Then the cashier must prove that the amount of cash remaining in that register totals the amount of cash the register started with plus the amount of cash collected during the day. After the cashier balances the register, the person in charge of cash deposits (usually the shop manager or someone on the accounting or bookkeeping staff) takes all the cash out, except the amount needed for the next day, and deposits it in the bank. (I talk more about separation of staff duties in the section 'Dividing staff responsibilities', later in this chapter.)

In addition to having the proper amount of cash in the register necessary to give customers the change they need, you also must make sure that your cashiers are giving the right amount of change and actually recording all sales on their cash registers. Keeping an eye on cashier activities is good business practice in any case, but you can also protect against cash theft by your employees in this way. Three ways exist in which cashiers can pocket some extra cash:

✔ **They don't record the sale in the cash register and instead pocket the cash.** The best deterrent to this type of theft is supervision. You can decrease the likelihood of theft through unrecorded sales by printing up sales tickets that the cashier must use to enter a sale in the cash register and open the cash drawer. If cash register transactions don't match sales receipts, the cashier must show a voided transaction for the missing ticket or explain why the cash drawer was opened without a ticket.

✔ **They don't provide a sales receipt and instead pocket the cash.** In this scenario the cashier neglects to give a sales receipt to one customer in the queue. The cashier gives the next customer the unused sales receipt but doesn't actually record the second transaction in the cash register. Instead, he or she just pockets the cash. In the business's books, the second sale never took place. The customer whose sale wasn't recorded has a valid receipt though it may not match exactly what was bought. Therefore, the customer is unlikely to notice any problem unless something needs to be returned later. Your best defence against this type of deception is to post a sign reminding all customers that they must get a receipt for all purchases and that the receipt is required to get a refund or exchange. Providing numbered sales receipts that include a duplicate copy can also help prevent this problem; cashiers need to produce the duplicates at the end of the day when proving the amount of cash flow that passed through their registers.

In addition to protection from theft by cashiers, the printed sales receipt system can be used to monitor shoplifters and prevent them from getting money for merchandise they never bought. For example, suppose a shoplifter takes a blouse out of a store, as well as some blank sales receipts. The next day the shoplifter comes back with the blouse and one of the stolen sales receipts filled out as though the blouse had actually been purchased the day before. You can spot the fraud because that sales receipt is part of a numbered batch of sales receipts that you've already identified as missing or stolen. You can quickly identify that the customer never paid for the merchandise and call the police.

✔ **They record a false credit voucher and keep the cash for themselves.** In this case the cashier writes up a credit voucher for a nonexistent customer and then pockets the cash refund. Most shops use a numbered credit voucher system to control this problem, so each credit can be carefully monitored with some detail that proves its connection to a previous customer purchase, such as a sales receipt. Customers are often asked to provide an address and telephone number before receiving a refund. Although this may not put off the determined fraudster, the opportunist thief is likely to be deterred. Also, shops usually require that a manager review the reason for the credit voucher, whether a return or exchange, and approve the transaction before cash or credit is given. When the bookkeeper records the sales return in the books, the number for the credit voucher is recorded with the transaction so that the detail about that credit voucher is easy to find if a question is raised later about the transaction.

Even if cashiers don't deliberately pocket cash, they can inadvertently give the wrong change. If you run a retail outlet, training and supervising your cashiers is a critical task that you must handle yourself or hand over to a trusted employee.

Keeping the Right Paperwork

When handling cash, you can see that a lot of paper changes hands, whether from the cash register, deposits into your current accounts or petty cash withdrawals. Therefore, careful documentation is paramount to control the movement of cash into and out of your business properly. And don't forget about organisation; you need to be able to find that documentation if questions about cash flow arise later.

Monitoring cash flow isn't the only reason why you need to keep loads of paperwork. In order to do your taxes and write off business expenses, you need receipts for those expenses. You also need details about the money you pay to employees, and tax and National Insurance contributions collected for your employees, in order to file the proper reports with HM Revenue & Customs. (I discuss taxes in Chapter 22 and dealing with HM Revenue & Customs in relation to employee matters in Chapter 11.) Setting up a good filing system and knowing what to keep and for how long is very important for any small-business person.

Creating a filing system

To get started setting up your filing system, you need the following supplies:

- ✔ **Filing cabinets:** Pretty self-explanatory – you can't have a filing system with nothing to keep the files in.

- ✔ **File folders:** Set up separate files for each of your suppliers, employees and customers who buy on credit, as well as files for backup information on each of your transactions. Many bookkeepers file transaction information using the date the transaction was added to their journal. If the transaction relates to a customer, supplier or employee, they add a duplicate copy of the transaction to the individual files as well.

Even if you have a computerised accounting system, you need to file paperwork related to the transactions you enter into your computer system. You still need to maintain employee, supplier and customer files in hard copy just in case something goes wrong – for example, if your computer system crashes, you need the originals to restore the data. Back up your computerised accounting system's data regularly to minimise the effects of such a crisis. Daily backups are best; one week is the longest you should ever go without a backup.

✔ **Ring binders:** These binders are great for things like your Chart of Accounts (see Chapter 3), your Nominal Ledger (see Chapter 4) and your system of journals (see Chapter 5) because you add to these documents regularly and the binders make adding additional pages easy. Make sure that you number the pages as you add them to the binder, so that you can quickly spot a missing page. How many binders you need depends on how many financial transactions you have each accounting period. You can keep everything in one binder, or you may want to set up a binder for the Chart of Accounts and Nominal Ledger and then a separate binder for each of your active journals. The decision is based on what makes your job easier.

✔ **Expandable files:** These files are the best way to keep track of current supplier activity and any bills that may be due. Make sure that you have:

- **An alphabetical file:** Use this file to track all your outstanding purchase orders by supplier. After you fill the order, you can file all details about that order in the supplier's individual file in case questions about the order arise later.

- **A 12-month file:** Use this file to keep track of bills that you need to pay. Simply place the bill in the slot for the month payment is due. Many businesses also use a 30-day expandable file. At the beginning of the month, the bills are placed in the 30-day expandable file based on the dates that they need to be paid. This approach provides a quick and organised visual reminder for bills that are due.

If you're using a computerised accounting system, you don't need the expandable files because your accounting system can remind you when bills are due. You can also print an Aged Debtor report, which shows you who owes you money, and an Aged Creditor report, which shows you how much money you owe your suppliers and how many days overdue your invoices are.

✔ **Rewritable CDs** can be used to backup your computerised system on a daily basis. Keep the backup discs in a fire safe or somewhere unaffected if a fire destroys the business. (A fire safe is the best way to keep critical financial data safe, and is therefore a must for any business.) If you don't have a fire safe, use two different CDs for backup on alternate days. Take the most recent backup off-site each night and leave the other CD at the office. In the event that disaster strikes, you are only ever one day behind with your backup data.

Working out what to keep and for how long

As you can probably imagine, the pile of paperwork you need to hold on to can get very large very quickly. As they see their files getting thicker and thicker, most businesspeople wonder what they can toss, what they really need to keep and how long they need to keep it.

Generally, keep most transaction-related paperwork for as long as HM Revenue & Customs can come and audit your books. For most types of audits, that means six years. But if you fail to file your tax return or file it fraudulently (and I hope this doesn't apply to you), HM Revenue & Customs may question you about it any time, because no time limitations exist in these cases.

HM Revenue & Customs isn't the only reason to keep records around for longer than one year. You may need proof-of-purchase information for your insurance company if an asset is lost, stolen or destroyed by fire or other accident. Also, you need to hang on to information regarding any business loan until paid off, just in case the bank questions how much you paid. After the loan's paid off, ensure that you keep proof of payment indefinitely in case a question about the loan ever arises. Information about property and other asset holdings needs to be kept around for as long as you hold the asset and for at least six years after the asset is sold. You're legally required to keep information about employees for at least three years after the employee leaves.

Keep the current year's files easily accessible in a designated filing area and keep the most recent past year's files in accessible filing cabinets if you have room. Box up records when they hit the two-year-old mark and put them in storage. Make sure that you date your boxed records with information about what they are, when they were put into storage and when you can destroy them. Many people forget that last detail, and boxes pile up until total desperation sets in and no more room is left. Then someone must take the time to sort through the boxes and figure out what needs to be kept and what can be destroyed – not a fun job.

It is a legal requirement to keep information about all transactions for six years. After that, make a list of things you want to hold on to longer for other reasons, such as asset holdings and loan information. Check with your lawyer and accountant to get their recommendations on what to keep and for how long.

Protecting Your Business Against Internal Fraud

Many businesspeople start their operations by carefully hiring people they can trust, thinking: 'We're a family – they'd never steal from me.'

Often a business owner finds out too late that even the most loyal employee may steal from the business if the opportunity arises and the temptation becomes too great – or if the employee gets caught up in a serious personal financial dilemma and needs fast cash. In this section, I talk about the steps you can take to prevent people stealing from your business.

Facing the reality of financial fraud

The four basic types of financial fraud are:

- **Embezzlement,** which is the illegal use of funds by a person who controls those funds. For example, a bookkeeper may use business money for his or her own personal needs. Many times, embezzlement stories don't appear in the newspapers because businesspeople are so embarrassed that they choose to keep the affair quiet. They usually settle privately with the embezzler rather than face public scrutiny.

- **Internal theft,** which is the stealing of business assets by employees, such as taking office supplies or products the business sells without paying for them. Internal theft is often the culprit behind stock shrinkage.

- **Payoffs and kickbacks,** which are situations in which employees accept cash or other benefits in exchange for access to the business, often creating a scenario where the business that the employee works for pays more for the goods or products than necessary. That extra money finds its way into the pocket of the employee who helped facilitate the access. For example, say Business A wants to sell its products to Business B. An employee in Business B helps Business A get in the door. Business A prices its product a bit higher and gives the employee of Business B the extra profit in the form of a kickback for helping it out. A payoff is paid before the sale is made, essentially saying 'please'. A kickback is paid after the sale is made, essentially saying 'thank you'. In reality, payoffs and kickbacks are a form of bribery, but few businesses report or litigate this problem (although employees are fired when deals are uncovered).

- **Skimming,** which occurs when employees take money from receipts and don't record the revenue on the books.

Caught with fingers in the till

Alice is a bookkeeper who's been with Business A for a long time. She was promoted to office manager after being with the business for 20 years. She's like a family member to the business owner, who trusts her implicitly. Because he's so busy with other aspects of running the business, he gives her control of the daily grind of cash flow. The beloved office manager handles or supervises all incoming and outgoing cash, reconciles the bank statements, handles payroll, signs all the cheques and files the business's tax returns.

All that control gives her the opportunity, credibility and access to embezzle a lot of money. At first, the trust is well founded, and Alice handles her new responsibilities very well. But after about three years in the role as office manager,

she develops a gambling habit and the debts mount up.

Alice decides to pay herself more money. She adds her husband to the payroll and documents the cheques for him as consulting expenses. She draws large cash cheques to buy non-existent office supplies and equipment, and then, worst of all, she files the business's tax returns and pockets the money that should go to paying the tax due. The business owner doesn't find out about the problem until HM Revenue & Customs comes calling, and by then, the office manager has retired and moved away.

This story may sound far-fetched, but you can read about similar embezzlement schemes in the national newspapers.

Although any of these financial crimes can happen in a small business, the one that hits small businesses the hardest is embezzlement. This crime happens most frequently when one person has access or control over most of the business's financial activities. For example, a single bookkeeper may write cheques, make deposits and balance the monthly bank statement – talk about having your fingers in a very big till.

Dividing staff responsibilities

Your primary protection against financial crime is properly separating staff responsibilities when the flow of business cash is involved. Basically, never have one person handling more than one of the following tasks:

✔ **Bookkeeping:** Involves reviewing and entering all transactions into the business's books. The bookkeeper makes sure that transactions are accurate, valid, appropriate and have the proper authorisation. For example, if a transaction requires paying a supplier, the bookkeeper makes sure that the charges are accurate and someone with proper authority has approved the payment. The bookkeeper can review documentation of cash receipts and the overnight deposits taken to the bank, but shouldn't actually make the deposit. Also, if the bookkeeper is responsible for handling payments from external parties, such as customers or suppliers, he or she shouldn't enter those transactions in the books.

✔ **Authorisation:** Involves being the manager or managers delegated to authorise expenditures for their departments. You may decide that transactions over a certain amount must have two or more authorisations before cheques can be sent to pay a bill. Spell out authorisation levels clearly and make sure that everyone follows them, even the owner or managing director of the business. (Remember, as owner, you set the tone for how the rest of the office operates; when you take shortcuts, you set a bad example and undermine the system you put in place.)

✔ **Money-handling:** Involves direct contact with incoming cash or revenue, whether cheque, credit card or credit transactions, as well as outgoing cash flow. People who handle money directly, such as cashiers, shouldn't also prepare and make bank deposits. Likewise, the person writing cheques to pay business bills shouldn't be authorised to sign those cheques; to be safe, have one person prepare the cheques based on authorised documentation and a second person sign those cheques, after reviewing the authorised documentation.

When setting up your cash-handling systems, try to think like an embezzler to figure out how someone can take advantage of a system.

✔ **Financial report preparation and analysis:** Involves the actual preparation of the financial reports and any analysis of those reports. Someone who's not involved in the day-to-day entering of transactions in the books needs to prepare the financial reports. For most small businesses, the bookkeeper turns over the raw reports from the computerised accounting system to an outside accountant who reviews the materials and prepares the financial reports. In addition, the accountant does a financial analysis of the business activity results for the previous accounting period.

I realise that you may be just starting up a small business and therefore not have enough staff to separate all these duties. Until you do have that capability, make sure that you stay heavily involved in the inflow and outflow of cash in your business. The following tips tell you how:

✔ **Periodically (once a month) open your business's bank statements and review the transactions.** Someone else can be given the responsibility of reconciling the statement, but you still need to keep an eye on the transactions listed.

✔ **Periodically look at your business cheque book counterfoils to ensure that no cheques are missing.** A bookkeeper who knows that you periodically check the books is less likely to find an opportunity for theft or embezzlement. If you find that a cheque or page of cheques is missing, act quickly to find out if the cheques were used legitimately. If you can't find the answer, call your bank and put a stop on the missing cheque numbers.

✔ **Periodically observe your cashiers and managers handling cash to make sure that they're following the rules you've established.** This practice is known as *management by walking around* – the more often you're out there, the less likely you are to be a victim of employee theft and fraud.

Balancing control costs

As a small-business person, you're always trying to balance the cost of protecting your cash and assets with the cost of adequately separating those duties. Putting in place too many controls, which end up costing you money, can be a big mistake. For example, you may create stock controls that require salespeople to contact one particular person who has the key to your product warehouse. This kind of control may prevent employee theft, but can also result in lost sales, because salespeople can't find the key-holder while dealing with an interested customer. In the end, the customer gets mad, and you lose the sale.

When you put controls in place, talk to your staff both before and after instituting the controls to see how they're working and to check for any unforeseen problems. Be willing and able to adjust your controls to balance the business needs of selling your products, managing the cash flow and keeping your eye on making a profit. Talk to other businesspeople to see what they do and pick up tips from established best practice. Your external accountant can be a good source of valuable information.

Generally, as you make rules for your internal controls, make sure that the cost of protecting an asset is no more than the asset you're trying to protect. For example, don't go overboard to protect office supplies by forcing your staff to wait around for hours to access needed supplies while you and a manager are at a meeting away from the office.

Ask yourself these four questions as you design your internal controls:

- ✔ What exactly do I want to prevent or detect – errors, sloppiness, theft, fraud or embezzlement?
- ✔ Do I face the problem frequently?
- ✔ What do I estimate the loss to be?
- ✔ What is the cost to me of implementing the change in procedures to prevent or detect the problem?

You can't answer all these questions yourself, so consult with your managers and the staff the changes are likely to impact. Get their answers to these questions and listen to their feedback.

When you finish putting together the new internal control rule, ensure that you document why you decided to implement the rule and the information you collected in developing it. After the rule's been in place for a while, test your assumptions. Make sure that you are in fact detecting the errors, theft, fraud or embezzlement that you hoped and expected to detect. Check the costs of keeping the rule in place by looking at cash outlay, employee time and morale, and the impact on customer service. If you find any problems with your internal controls, take the time to fix them and change the rule, again documenting the process. Detailed documentation ensures that, if two or three years down the road someone questions why he or she is doing something, you have the answers and are able to determine whether the problem is still valid, as well as whether the rule is still necessary or needs to be changed.

Insuring Your Cash through Fidelity Bonds

Employers can insure themselves against the loss of money through embezzlement by employees. A *fidelity bond* is a form of insurance that companies can take out to protect themselves against financial loss caused by employee theft or dishonesty. If an employee steals from you or one of your customers, the insurance covers the loss.

This type of insurance is a specialist one and can be packaged up with your normal business insurance. The cost varies greatly depending on the type of business you operate and the amount of cash or other assets that are handled by the employees you want to bond. Ask your insurance broker to get an accurate quotation for your business.

Part III
Recording Day-to-Day Business Operations

'Brother Cedric's doing the abbey's books now – They should be ready for your inspection in five years.'

In this part . . .

Do you want to know every single financial transaction that happens in your business each and every day? You should. Recording every transaction is the only way you can put all the pieces together and see how well your business is doing financially.

This part shows you how to monitor your day-to-day business operations by recording sales and purchases as well as any discounts and returns. Also, because you can't run a business without paying your employees, we guide you through the basics of setting up and managing employee payroll and all the paperwork you need to do after hiring your workforce.

Chapter 8

Planning Your Workload

· ·

· ·

*A*s a bookkeeper, you need to work in an orderly manner and be aware of what jobs need doing on a daily, weekly and monthly basis, which is why checklists are so useful. You need to do certain jobs on a daily basis, for example, perhaps entering invoices, depending on the size of your business, while other jobs are done on a monthly basis, such as reconciling your bank account. Most businesses only receive one statement once a month and wait until they have received this until they reconcile their bank account.

As the company bookkeeper, analyse all the jobs that require completing and decide an appropriate order in which to conduct those tasks. The work must then be allocated to the appropriate person or department, so that everyone in the office is aware of what responsibilities they have. If your business is so small that you are the only person in it, you have to do everything. Nothing like hands on experience!

This chapter offers hints and tips to help you process your transactions in an efficient manner.

Introducing Checklists

Having a list of all the jobs that need to be carried out in a month is always a good idea. That way, you know what you are working towards. In book-keeping, the number of transactions that you deal with varies massively from company to company. You are reacting both to the number of invoices that a business generates itself for customers and also the invoices that it receives from its suppliers. Every business differs in the number of invoices that it handles. Some businesses have entire departments that process just invoices. For example, you may have a department that processes just purchase invoices. The business may receive so many that you have Purchase journal clerks who only process and write up purchase invoices. The bigger the company, the more likely it is that you use a computerised accounting system. However, whether you use computers or not, you still benefit from using checklists to guide you through the monthly bookkeeping routine.

Figure 8-1 is an example of a checklist that I use on a monthly basis.

Bookkeeping Checklist	Apr	May	Jun	Jul	Aug	Sep	Oct	Nov	Dec	Jan	Feb	Mar
Monthly												
Enter Sales Invoices												
Enter Purchase Invoices												
Enter Cheque Payments												
Enter Receipts from paying in book												
Enter prepayment journals												
Enter accruals journals												
Enter wages journals												
Enter stock journal												
Enter depreciation												
Pay Inland Revenue												
Bank Reconciliation												
Quarterly												
VAT Return												

Figure 8-1:
An example
of a monthly
book-
keeping
checklist.

Sorting Out Your Sales Invoices

If your business produces sales invoices for customers who are buying on credit, read on! These invoices may be produced by hand, a word processor or a computerised system. I talk about cash sales and computer-generated invoices in Chapter 10. Here I discuss the filing and management of those invoices after they've been produced.

Referring to the checklist shown in Figure 8-1, you can see that the first job on the list is entering sales invoices. Make sure that the person who produces the sales invoices puts them somewhere you can easily find them, for example, an in-tray simply for sales invoices or a concertina-style file that invoices are kept in prior to being entered into your bookkeeping system.

If you have a computerised system that produces sales invoices automatically, you can skip this step, as those invoices are automatically produced and the Sales journal updated accordingly, as detailed in Chapter 10.

You should find that each sales invoice has already been given an invoice number. Adopt a sequential numbering system that allows you to notice if invoices have been missed or not. The invoice numbers can be alpha-numeric if it helps with your business, but the invoices should be filed in numerical order, so that they are filed and entered into your bookkeeping system in roughly chronological order.

As each invoice is entered into your Sales journal, tick or mark the invoice in some way to indicate that it has been posted into your bookkeeping system so you avoid entering the same invoice twice.

Your invoices can be filed neatly in a lever arch file.

Entering Your Purchases Invoices

You will receive purchase invoices in the post on an almost daily basis. Whoever opens the post needs to know where to put those invoices until it is time to enter them into the bookkeeping system. Again, as with the sales invoices, keep the purchase invoices in one dedicated place until you are ready to enter them into your Purchase journal.

Sequential numbering and coding

Some companies like to keep a separate lever arch file for each supplier, or at least file the invoices in supplier order. Others simply number the purchase invoices sequentially with a stamping machine and use this number within the bookkeeping system. Using this method, you can file all your purchase invoices in one file and just keep them in numerical order.

When you enter the invoice into the bookkeeping system, you need to know into which category or column to enter the invoice. It may not be immediately obvious what the invoice is for. For example, as a bookkeeper, you need to know whether the invoice relates to a direct cost of the business or whether it is simply an overhead of the business.

Some companies use a data-entry stamp, which has spaces to enter vital information such as the date the invoice was posted, nominal code and maybe a space for the data-entry clerk to initial, to confirm the transaction has been entered.

You may find that you are entering invoices on a daily basis. When you begin to enter invoices at the start of each day, check your bookkeeping system to see what the last invoice entered was. You can check the last invoice number used and then you know which invoice number to start with when you enter your next invoice. If you are using a computerised system such as Sage 50 Accounts, you can check the Purchase day book. See Figure 8-2 for an example of the report you can run to check the last purchase invoice entered.

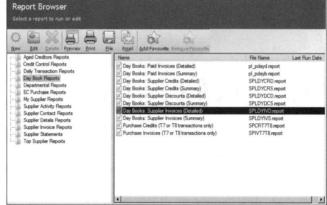

Figure 8-2: Check your Purchase day book to see the last invoice entered.

Notice the Invoice Reference column in Figure 8-3. This column is where the sequential purchases invoice number appears.

Date: 12/09/2010
Time: 20:50:24

Practice Company

Day Books: Supplier Invoices (Detailed)

Page: 1

Date From: 01/01/1980
Date To: 31/12/2019

Supplier From:
Supplier To: ZZZZZZZZ

Transaction From: 1
Transaction To: 99,999,999

N/C From:
N/C To: 99999999

Dept From: 0
Dept To: 999

Tran No.	Type	Date	A/C Ref	N/C	Inv Ref	Dept	Details	Net Amount	Tax Amount	T/C	Gross Amount	V	B
5	PI	01/06/2010	WHOLESAL	5000	1	0	12 reels of cotton	12.00	2.10	T1	14.10	N	-
6	PI	15/06/2010	WHOLESAL	5000	2	0	20 boxes of cotton thread	120.00	21.00	T1	141.00	N	-
7	PI	23/06/2010	WHOLESAL	5000	3	0	5 packets of thread	15.00	2.63	T1	17.63	N	-
14	PI	20/07/2010	PLANT	0020	4	0	Cutting machine	20,000.00	3,500.00	T1	23,500.00	N	-
15	PI	20/07/2010	OFFICE	0030	5	0	Photocopier	5,000.00	875.00	T1	5,875.00	N	-
16	PI	20/07/2010	OFFICE	0040	6	0	Office table & chairs	2,500.00	437.50	T1	2,937.50	N	-
23	PI	15/07/2010	HOBSONS	7100	7	0	Rent of office space	3,000.00	525.00	T1	3,525.00	N	-
24	PI	23/07/2010	DALES	7201	8	0	Gas	500.00	25.00	T5	525.00	N	-
25	PI	07/09/2010	OFFICE	7500	9	0	Leaflet print	1,000.00	175.00	T1	1,175.00	N	-
26	PI	30/07/2010	ELECTRIC	7200	10	0	Electric bill	100.00	17.50	T1	117.50	N	-
							Totals	32,247.00	5,580.73		37,827.73		

Page 1 of 1
100%

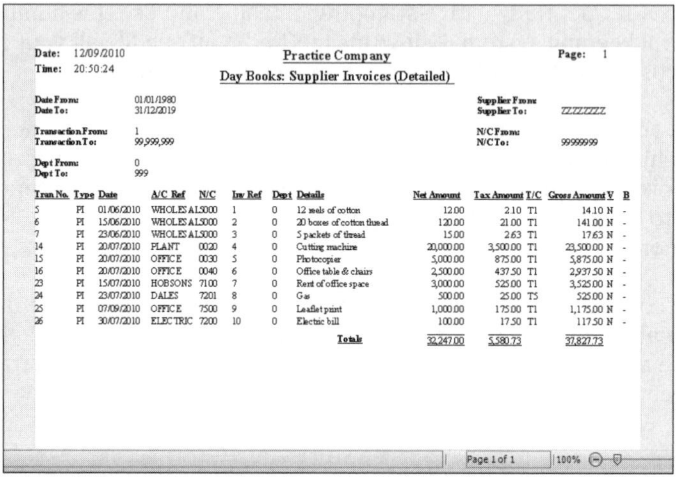

Figure 8-3: Running your day book report.

Paying your suppliers

Although I don't include this on the checklist, paying your suppliers on time is vital to any business. Flip to Chapter 9 to see just why!

You may decide to pay your suppliers at specific times in the month, so add this to your monthly bookkeeping routine.

Checking Cash Payments and Receipts

In Chapter 14, I discuss the importance of ensuring that all banking entries are included in your bookkeeping system, particularly when you need to reconcile your bank account. In this chapter, I discuss the practical ways that you can ensure you include all your data in your system.

Cash payments

Most businesses make payments in several ways. Cash payments include:

- Cash (naturally!) – usually from the petty cash tin
- Cheque
- Bank transfer, CHAPS or BACS, or another form of electronic payment

As a bookkeeper, make sure that you collect all the payment information from all the relevant sources. The bank reconciliation process highlighted in Chapter 14 ensures that you do this; however, here are some more practical tips so that the reconciliation process is made as simple as possible.

An easy way to ensure that you have entered all your petty cash payments is to physically tick or initial the petty cash voucher or cash receipt after entering it into your bookkeeping system. You then avoid entering items twice. You can batch up your petty cash payments and give them a batch reference so that they can be easily retrieved from your filing system.

Look at Figure 8-4 to see an example of a batch entry of petty cash receipts being posted onto Sage 50 Accounts. The batch of receipts has been given the reference PC01. A separate bank account has been set up called Petty Cash.

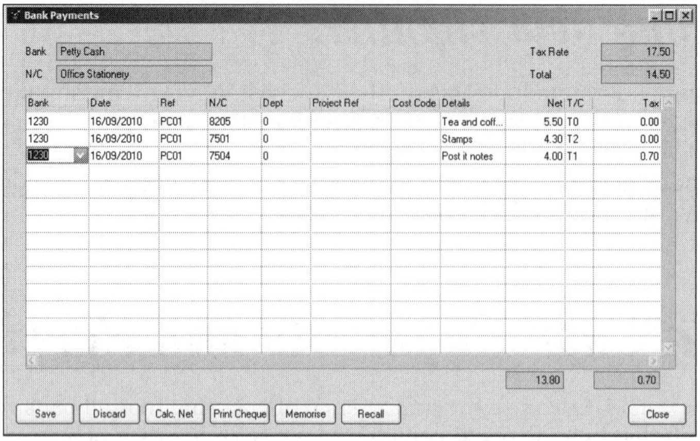

Figure 8-4:
Petty cash payment showing PC01 as a batch reference.

To make life as easy as possible, when you write out cheques, ensure that you include clear information about who you are paying on the cheque stub. Don't attempt to write *War and Peace* here, but include the date, the payee and the amount. Write this information clearly, as it may not be you that ultimately writes up the Cash Payments book or enters the amount into your computerised accounting system. If you have spidery handwriting, spare a thought for the person who needs to read this information! Wrong amounts entered or the wrong account entered lead to problems when trying to reconcile the bank account.

At some point the information written on the cheque stub is entered into the bookkeeping system. After the information has been written up in your Cash Payments book or entered onto your computing system, make sure that you physically tick the cheque stub. That way, you know you have entered that information, and it is very easy to flick through the cheque stubs at a later date and find where you last entered information.

You won't be aware of what electronic payments have been made until you see the bank statements for the month. Most businesses don't receive the previous month's statements until the end of the first week of the following month. For most businesses, this is impractical, so with the advent of Internet banking, most businesses can print out copies of their bank statements on a daily basis if necessary. Therefore you can reconcile your bank account on a much more regular basis than simply once a month, which was the traditional way. You can also identify your electronic payments sooner and enter them accordingly.

Once again, an easy way to ensure that you are entering the information correctly is to physically tick the transaction on your copy of the bank statement.

Avoid printing too many copies of your bank statements, as this is when mistakes can happen with the same information entered twice.

Cash receipts

These transactions include:

- ✔ Items physically paid in at the bank via the paying-in book
- ✔ Electronic receipts via BACS and other electronic methods, including interest earned on the bank account

For items paid in using the paying-in book, make sure that you include as much detail as possible. If you can, include the invoice numbers that the customer is paying, so that you can easily allocate the receipt to the correct invoices. Knowing which invoices the customer is paying is crucial so that the Aged Debtor report is correct. (See Chapter 10 for more on Aged Debtor reports.)

After you've entered the information from the pay-in slip to your bookkeeping system, tick the stub to show it's been entered so that you can see at a glance where you are up to.

Reconciling Your Bank Account

Reconciling your bank account to check that your manual or computerised Cash book matches your bank statement is usually part of your monthly accounting process. Chapter 14 shows you how to carry out the reconciliation process both manually and using computer software, but I want to highlight a practical way to ensure that your reconciliations are as easy as possible.

Follow these steps:

Place a tick against all the items already entered into your bookkeeping system, including all cheques and items paid in via paying-in books.

A number of items remain unticked.

Now enter all the remaining entries into your system, ticking them once after you enter them.

These entries include all your electronic receipts and payments, such as direct debits and BACS payments. You now have a tick placed against all the entries on your bank statement.

Work through each transaction in your Cash book and match them against the bank statement as a double-check.

For manual bookkeeping systems, you mark the Cash book using a tick (or perhaps a *B* for bank statement). All items that are left on the Cash book without a tick are items that have not appeared on the bank statement. These items are your unpresented cheques or outstanding lodgements (deposits in transit). You can now easily write up your bank reconciliation, as shown in Chapter 14.

When you tick each item in the Cash book against the bank statement entry, also place a cross against the original tick on the bank statement. You can then see at a glance on the bank statement that all transactions have been entered and also checked against the Cash book.

Entering Your Journals

Monthly journals always need to be completed. If you refer back to the checklist shown in Figure 8-1, I refer to prepayments, accruals, wages, stock and depreciation. Your business may have some or all of these journals, but you may also have additional ones which are specific to your business. Ensure that all the journals that you need to process are on your checklist so that they aren't missed out.

For more information on accruals and prepayments, depreciation and Stock journals, see Chapter 17.

Getting on a Course

You may decide that you want to learn more about bookkeeping. Many institutions offer courses to help you understand the quirks of the bookkeeping world. The first place to look is local adult education centres, which often run bookkeeping courses, particularly on computerised bookkeeping.

If you feel that you can't get to an organised class, then perhaps learning at home is for you. To find out about all the courses on offer online or by correspondence, simply type 'bookkeeping courses' into Google.

Chapter 9

Buying and Tracking Your Purchases

· ·

In This Chapter

▶ Tracking stock and monitoring costs

▶ Keeping your business supplied

▶ Paying your bills

· ·

*I*n order to make money, your business must have something to sell. Whether you sell products or offer services, you have to deal with costs directly related to the goods or services being sold. Those costs primarily come from the purchase or manufacturing of the products you plan to sell or the items you need in order to provide the services.

All businesses must keep careful watch over the cost of the products to be sold or services to be offered. Ultimately, your business's profits depend on how well you manage those costs because, in most cases, costs increase over time rather than decrease. How often do you find a reduction in the price of needed items? Doesn't happen often. When costs increase but the price to the customer remains unchanged, the profit you make on each sale is less.

In addition to the costs to produce products or services, every business has additional expenses associated with purchasing supplies needed to run the business. The bookkeeper has primary responsibility for monitoring all these costs and expenses as invoices are paid and alerting business owners or managers when suppliers increase prices. This chapter covers how to track purchases and their costs, manage stock, buy and manage supplies, and pay the bills for the items your business buys.

Keeping Track of Stock

Products to be sold are called *stock.* As a bookkeeper, you use two accounts to track stock:

- **Purchases:** Where you record the actual purchase of goods to be sold. This account is used to calculate the *Cost of Goods Sold,* which is an item on the profit and loss statement (see Chapter 18 for more on this statement).

- **Stock:** Where you track the value of stock on hand. This value is shown on the balance sheet as an asset in a line item called *Stock* (Chapter 19 addresses the balance sheet).

Businesses track physical stock on hand using one of two methods:

- **Periodic stock count:** Conducting a physical count of the stock in the stores and in the warehouse. This count can be done daily, monthly, yearly or for any other period that best matches your business needs. (Many businesses close for all or part of a day to count stock.)

- **Perpetual stock count:** Adjusting stock counts as each sale is made. In order to use this method, you must manage your stock using a computerised accounting system tied into your point of sale (usually cash registers).

- Even if you use a perpetual stock method, periodically do a physical count of stock to ensure that the numbers match what's in your computer system. Because theft, damage and loss of stock aren't automatically entered in your computer system, the losses don't show up until you do a physical count of the stock you have on hand in your business.

When preparing your profit and loss statement at the end of an accounting period (whether that period is for a month, a quarter or a year), you need to calculate the Cost of Goods Sold in order to calculate the profit made.

In order to calculate the Cost of Goods Sold, you must first find out how many items of stock were sold. You start with the amount of stock on hand at the beginning of the month (called *Opening Stock*), as recorded in the Stock account, and add the amount of purchases, as recorded in the Purchases account, to find the Goods Available for Sale. Then you subtract the stock on hand at the end of the month *(Closing Stock),* which is determined by counting remaining stock.

Here's how you calculate the number of goods sold:

> Opening Stock + Purchases = Goods Available for Sale − Closing Stock = Items Sold

After you determine the number of goods sold, compare that number to the actual number of items the business sold during that accounting period, which is based on sales figures collected through the month. When the numbers don't match, you have a problem. The mistake may be in the stock count, or items may be unaccounted for because they've been misplaced or damaged and discarded. In the worst-case scenario, you may have a problem with customer or employee theft. These differences are usually tracked within the accounting system in a line item called *Stock Shortages*.

Entering initial cost

When your business first receives stock, you enter the initial cost of that stock into the bookkeeping system based on the shipment's invoice. In some cases, invoices are sent separately, and only a delivery note is included in the order. When that situation applies, you still record the receipt of the goods, because the business incurs the cost from the day the goods are received, and you must be sure that the money is available to pay for the goods when the invoice arrives and the bill comes due. You track outstanding bills in the Trade Creditors (Accounts Payable) account. Where you only have a delivery note, use the price agreed on your purchase order (if you use purchase orders) or the price from your last invoice from that supplier.

Entering the receipt of stock is a relatively easy entry in the bookkeeping system. For example, if your business buys £1,000 of stock to be sold, you make the following record in the books:

	Debit	*Credit*
Purchases	£1,000	
Trade Creditors		£1,000

The Purchases account increases by £1,000 to reflect the additional costs, and the Trade Creditors account increases by the same amount to reflect the amount of the bill that needs to be paid in the future.

When stock enters your business, in addition to recording the actual costs, you need more detail about what was bought, how much of each item was bought and what each item cost. You also need to track:

- How much stock you have on hand
- The value of the stock you have on hand
- When you need to order more stock

Tracking these details for each type of product bought can be a nightmare, especially if you're trying to keep the books for a retail shop, because you need to set up a special Stock journal with pages detailing purchase and sale information for every item you carry. (See Chapter 5 for the low-down on journals.)

However, computerised accounting simplifies this process of tracking stock. Details about stock can be entered initially into your computer accounting system in several ways:

✔ If you pay by cheque or credit card when you receive the stock, you can enter the details about each item on the cheque counter-foil or credit card slip.

✔ If you use purchase orders, you can enter the detail about each item on the purchase order, record receipt of the items when they arrive and update the information when you receive the bill.

✔ If you don't use purchase orders, you can enter the detail about the items when you receive them and update the information when you receive the bill.

To give you an idea of how this information is collected in a computerised accounting software program, Figure 9-1 shows you how to enter the details in Sage 50 Accounts. This particular form is for the receipt of stock without a purchase order and can be used when you receive a supplier invoice.

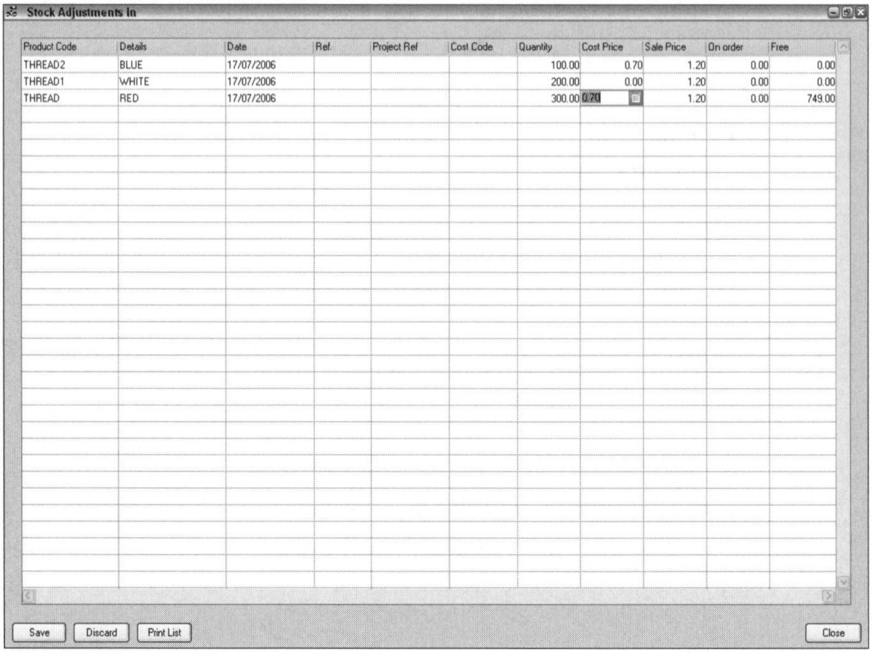

Figure 9-1:
Recording of the receipt of stock using Sage 50 Accounts.

Figure 9-2 shows a stock item record in the computerised accounting system. Note that you must give the item a product code and a description. The product code is a short unique name or code to identify the stock item internally. The longer description is a more user-friendly name that can appear on customer invoices (sales transactions). You can input a cost and sales price if you want, or you can leave them at zero and enter the cost and sales prices with each transaction.

If you have a set contract purchase price or sales price on a stock item, you can enter the price on this form to save time – you don't then have to enter the price each time you record a transaction. But, if the price changes frequently, leave the space blank so that you don't forget to enter the updated price when you enter a transaction.

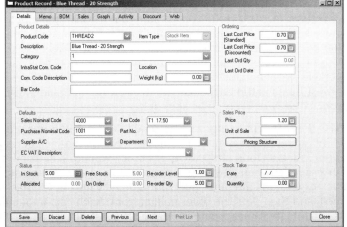

Figure 9-2:
Setting up
a stock
item using
Sage 50
Accounts.

Notice in Figure 9-2 that you can also use this form to give you information about stock on hand and when stock needs to be reordered. To make sure that your shelves are never empty, enter a number for each item that indicates at what point you want to reorder stock. You can indicate the 'Reorder Level' in the section called 'Status'. (A nice feature of Sage 50 Accounts is that you can run a report to see which stock items have fallen below their reorder level and use that to place your next order.)

If you use the Purchase Order Processing routine and save the form that records the receipt of stock in Sage 50 Accounts, the software automatically:

✔ Adjusts the quantity of stock you have in stock

✔ Increases the Asset account called Stock

✔ Lowers the quantity of items on order (if you initially entered the information as a purchase order)

✔ Averages the cost of stock on hand

✔ Increases the Trade Creditor account

Managing stock and its value

After you record the receipt of stock, you have the responsibility of managing the stock you have on hand. You must also know the value of that stock. You may think that as long as you know what you paid for the items, the value isn't difficult to calculate. Well, accountants can't let things be that simple, and so five different ways exist to value stock:

✔ **LIFO (Last In, First Out):** You assume that the last items put on the shelves (the newest items) are the first items to be sold. Retail shops that sell non-perishable items, such as tools, are likely to use this type of system. For example, when a hardware store gets new hammers, workers probably don't unload the hammers on the shelves and put the newest items in the back. Instead, the new hammers are just put in the front, so they're likely to be sold first.

✔ **FIFO (First In, First Out):** You assume that the first items put on the shelves (the oldest items) are sold first. Shops that sell perishable goods, such as food shops, use this stock valuation method most often. For example, when new milk arrives at a shop, the person stocking the shelves unloads the older milk, puts the new milk at the back of the shelf, and then puts the older milk in front. Each carton of milk (or other perishable item) has a date indicating the last day it can be sold, so food shops always try to sell the oldest stuff first, while those items are still sellable. (They try, but how many times have you reached to the back of a food shelf to find items with the longest shelf life?)

✔ **Averaging:** You average the cost of goods received, to avoid worrying about which items are sold first or last. This method of stock is used most often in any retail or services environment where prices are constantly fluctuating and the business owner finds that an average cost works best for managing his or her Cost of Goods Sold.

✔ **Specific Identification:** You maintain cost figures for each stock item individually. Retail outlets that sell big-ticket items, such as cars, which often have a different set of extras on each item, use this type of stock valuation method.

✔ **LCM (Lower of Cost or Market):** You set stock values based on whichever is lower: the amount you paid originally for the stock item (the
cost), or the current market value of the item. Businesses that deal in
precious metals, commodities, or publicly traded securities often use
this method because the prices of their products can fluctuate wildly,
sometimes even in the same day.

After you choose a stock valuation method, you need to use the same method
each year on your financial reports and when you file your accounts. If you
decide you want to change the method, you need to explain the reasons for
the change to both HM Revenue & Customs and to your financial backers. If
you run an incorporated business in which shares have been sold, you need to
explain the change to your shareholders. You also have to go back and show
how the change in stock method impacts your prior financial reporting, and
adjust your profit margins in previous years to reflect the new stock valuation
method's impact on your long-term profit history.

Figuring out the best method for you

I'm sure that you're wondering why the stock valuation method you use matters so much. The key to the choice is the impact on your bottom line as well
as the tax your business pays.

Because FIFO assumes the oldest (and most likely the lowest priced) items
are sold first, this method results in a lower Cost of Goods Sold number.
Because Cost of Goods Sold is subtracted from sales to determine profit, a
lower Cost of Goods Sold number produces a higher profit. (For more on
Cost of Goods Sold, see 'Keeping Track of Stock', earlier in this chapter.)

The opposite is true for LIFO, which uses cost figures based on the last price
paid for the stock (and most likely the highest price). Using the LIFO method,
the Cost of Goods Sold number is higher, which means a larger sum is subtracted from sales to determine profit. Thus, the profit margin is lower. The
good news, however, is that the tax bill is also low.

The Averaging method gives a business the best picture of what's happening
with stock costs and trends. Rather than constantly dealing with the ups and
downs of stock costs, this method smoothes out the numbers used to calculate a business's profits. Cost of Goods Sold, taxes and profit margins for this
method fall between those of LIFO and FIFO. Definitely choose this method
when you're operating a business in which stock prices are constantly going
up and down.

The Averaging method always falls between LIFO and FIFO as regards the
cost of goods sold, taxes and profit margin.

Sage 50 Accounts uses the LIFO method to calculate Cost of Goods Sold and Stock line items on its financial reports, so if you choose this method, you can use Sage 50 Accounts and the financial reports it generates. However, if you choose to use one of the other four stock methods, you can't use the Sage 50 Accounts financial report numbers. Instead, you have to print out a report of purchases and calculate the accurate numbers to use on your financial reports for the Cost of Goods Sold and Stock accounts.

Check with your accountant to see which stock method he or she thinks is best for you given the type of business you're operating and which one will be most acceptable to HM Revenue & Customs.

Comparing the methods

To show you how much of an impact stock valuation can have on profit margin, in this section I compare three of the most common methods: FIFO, LIFO and Averaging. In this example, I assume Business A bought the stock in question at different prices on three different occasions. Opening Stock is valued at £500 (50 items at £10 each).

Here's the calculation to determine the number of items sold (from the earlier 'Keeping Track of Stock' section):

Opening Stock + Purchases = Goods Available for Sale – Closing Stock = Items Sold

50 + 500 = 550 – 75 = 475

Here's what the business paid to purchase the stock:

Date	Quantity	Unit Price
1 April	150	£10
15 April	150	£25
30 April	200	£30

Here's an example of how you calculate the Cost of Goods Sold using the Averaging method:

Category	Quantity (Unit Price)	Total Cost
Opening Stock	50 (£10)	£500
Purchases	150 (£10)	£1,500
	150 (£25)	£3,750
	200 (£30)	£6,000
Total Stock	550	£11,750

Now you can do other calculations:

Average Stock Cost	£11,750 ÷ 550 = £21.36
Cost of Goods Sold	475 × £21.36 = £10,146
Closing Stock	75 @ £21.36 = £1,602

The Cost of Goods Sold number appears on the profit and loss statement and is subtracted from Sales. The Closing Stock number shows up as an asset on the balance sheet. This system applies to all three stock valuation methods.

Now, I demonstrate how you calculate the Cost of Goods Sold using the FIFO method. With this method, you assume that the first items received are the first ones sold, and because the first items received here are those in Opening Stock, I start with them:

Date	*Quantity (Unit Price)*	*Total*
Opening Stock	50 (£10)	£500
1 April	150 (£10)	£1,500
15 April	150 (£25)	£3,750
30 April	125 (£30)	£3,750
Cost of Goods Sold	475	£9,500
Closing Stock	75 @ £30	£2,250

Note: Only 125 of the 200 units purchased on April 30 are used in the FIFO method. Because this method assumes that the first items into stock are the first items sold (or taken out of stock), the first items used are those on April 1. Then the April 15 items are used, and finally the remaining needed items are taken from those bought on April 30. Because 200 were bought on April 30 and only 125 were needed, 75 of the items bought on April 30 are left in Closing Stock. The Cost of Goods Sold figure, which is £9,500, is the sum of the total values of the units above which are deemed to have been sold to arrive at this figure (£500 + £1,500 + £3,750 + £3,750).

Next, I calculate the Cost of Goods Sold using the LIFO method. With this method, you assume that the last items received are the first ones sold, and because the last items received were those purchased on April 30, I start with them:

Date	*Quantity (Unit Price)*	*Total*
30 April	200 (£30)	£6,000
15 April	150 (£25)	£3,750
1 April	125 (£10)	£1,250
Cost of Goods Sold	475	£11,000
Closing Stock	75 @ £10	£750

Note: Because LIFO assumes the last items to arrive are sold first, the Closing Stock includes the 25 remaining units (150 purchased less 125 used/sold) from the 1 April purchase plus the 50 units in Opening Stock.

Here's how the use of stock under the LIFO method impacts the business profits. I assume the items are sold to the customers for £40 per unit, which means total sales of £19,000 for the month (£40 × 475 units sold). In this example, I just look at the *Gross Profit,* which is the profit from Sales before considering expenses incurred for operating the business. I talk more about the different profit types and what they mean in Chapter 18. The following equation calculates Gross Profit:

Sales – Cost of Goods Sold = Gross Profit

Table 9-1 shows a comparison of Gross Profit for the three methods used in this example.

Table 9-1	Comparison of Gross Profit Based on Stock Valuation Method		
Profit and Loss Statement Line Item	*FIFO*	*LIFO*	*Averaging*
Sales	£19,000	£19,000	£19,000
Cost of Goods Sold	£9,500	£11,000	£10,146
Gross Profit	£9,500	£8,000	£8,854

Looking at the comparisons of gross profit, you can see that stock valuation can have a major impact on your bottom line. LIFO is likely to give you the lowest profit because the last stock items bought are usually the most expensive. FIFO is likely to give you the highest profit because the first items bought are usually the cheapest. And the profit that the Averaging method produces is likely to fall somewhere in between the two.

Buying and Monitoring Supplies

In addition to stock, all businesses must buy the supplies used to operate the business, such as paper, pens and paper clips. Supplies that aren't bought in direct relationship to the manufacturing or purchasing of goods or services for sale fall into the category of *expenses.*

Just how closely you want to monitor the supplies you use depends on your business needs. The expense categories you establish may be as broad as Office Supplies and Retail Supplies, or you may want to set up accounts for each type of supply used. Each additional account is just one more thing that needs to be managed and monitored in the accounting system, so you need to determine whether keeping a very detailed record of supplies is worth your time.

Your best bet is to track supplies that make a big dent in your budget carefully with an individual account. For example, if you anticipate paper usage is going to be very high, monitor that usage with a separate account called Paper Expenses.

Many businesses don't use the bookkeeping system to manage their supplies. Instead, they designate one or two people as office managers or supply managers and keep the number of accounts used for supplies to a minimum. Other businesses decide to monitor supplies by department or division, and so they set up a supply account for each one. This system puts the burden of monitoring supplies in the hands of the department or division managers.

Staying on Top of Your Bills

Eventually, you have to pay for both the stock and the supplies you purchase for your business. In most cases, the bills are posted to the Trade Creditors account when they arrive, and they're paid when due. A large chunk of the cash paid out of your Cash account (see Chapters 5 and 7 for more information on the Cash account and handling cash) is in the form of the cheques sent out to pay bills due in Trade Creditors, so you need to have careful controls over the five key functions of Trade Creditors:

- ✔ Entering the bills to be paid into the accounting system
- ✔ Preparing cheques to pay the bills
- ✔ Signing cheques to pay the bills
- ✔ Sending out payment cheques to suppliers
- ✔ Reconciling the bank account

In your business, the person who enters the bills to be paid into the system is likely to be the same person who also prepares the payment cheques. However, you must ensure that someone else does the other tasks: never allow the person who prepares the cheques to review the bills to be paid and sign the cheques, unless of course that person's you, the business owner. (I talk more about cash control and the importance of separating duties in Chapter 7.)

Properly managing Trade Creditors allows you to avoid late fees or interest and take advantage of discounts offered for paying early, therefore saving your business a lot of money. If you're using a computerised accounting system, the bill due date and any discount information needs to be entered at the time you receive the stock or supplies (see Figure 9-1 for how you record this information).

If you're working with a paper system rather than a computerised accounting system, you need to set up some way to ensure that you don't miss bill due dates. Many businesses use two accordion files: one set up by the month, and the other set up by the day. On receipt, a bill is put into the first accordion file according to the due month. On the first day of that month, the Purchase Ledger clerk pulls all the bills due that month and puts them in the daily accordion file based on the date the bill is due. Payment cheques are then posted in time to arrive in the supplier's office by the due date.

In some cases, businesses offer a discount if their bills are paid early. Sage 50 Accounts allows you to set up for each supplier Settlement Due dates and Settlement Discount percentage figures. For example, a supplier set up as 10 days and 2 per cent means that if the bill is paid in 10 days, the purchasing business can take a 2 per cent discount; otherwise, the amount due must be paid in full in 30 days. In addition, many businesses state that interest or late fees are charged if a bill isn't paid in 30 days (although in reality few dare make this charge if they want to retain the business). If the total amount due for a bill is £1,000 and the business pays the bill in 10 days, that business can take a 2 per cent discount, or £20. This may not seem like much, but if your business buys £100,000 of stock and supplies in a month and each supplier offers a similar discount, you can save £1,000. Over the course of a year, discounts on purchases can save your business a significant amount of money and improve your profits.

Chapter 10

Counting Your Sales

· ·

· ·

*E*very business loves to take in money, and this means that you, the bookkeeper, have lots to do to ensure that sales are properly recorded in the books. In addition to recording the sales themselves, you must monitor customer accounts, discounts offered to customers and customer returns and allowances.

If the business sells products on credit, you have to monitor customer accounts carefully in Trade Debtors (Accounts Receivable), including monitoring whether customers pay on time and alerting the sales team when customers are behind on their bills and future purchases on credit need to be declined. Some customers never pay, and in that case, you must adjust the books to reflect non-payment as a bad debt.

This chapter reviews the basic responsibilities of a business's bookkeeping and accounting staff for tracking sales, making adjustments to those sales, monitoring customer accounts and alerting management to slow-paying customers.

Collecting on Cash Sales

Most businesses collect some form of cash as payment for the goods or services they sell. Cash receipts include more than just notes and coins; cheques and credit and debit card payments are also considered cash sales for bookkeeping purposes. In fact, with electronic transaction processing (when a customer's credit or debit card is swiped through a machine), a deposit is usually made to the business's bank account the same day (sometimes within seconds of the transaction, depending on the type of system the business sets up with the bank).

The only type of payment that doesn't fall under the umbrella of a cash payment is purchases made on credit. And by *credit,* I mean credit your business offers to customers directly rather than through a third party, such as a bank credit card or loan. I talk more about this type of sale in the section 'Selling on Credit', later in this chapter.

Discovering the value of sales receipts

Modern businesses generate sales receipts in one of three ways: by the cash register, by the credit or debit card machine or by hand (written out by the salesperson). Whichever of these three methods you choose to handle your sales transactions, the sales receipt serves two purposes:

- ✔ Gives the customer proof that the item was purchased on a particular day at a particular price in your shop in case he or she needs to exchange or return the merchandise.

- ✔ Gives the shop a receipt that can be used at a later time to enter the transaction into the business's books. At the end of the day, the receipts are also used to cash up the cash register and ensure that the cashier has taken in the right amount of cash based on the sales made. (In Chapter 7, I talk more about how to use cash receipts as an internal control tool to manage your cash.)

You're familiar with cash receipts, no doubt, but just to show you how much useable information can be generated for the bookkeeper on a sales receipt, Figure 10-1 shows a sample receipt from a bakery.

Receipts contain a wealth of information that can be collected for your business's accounting system. A look at a receipt tells you the amount of cash collected, the type of products sold, the quantity of products sold and how much Value Added Tax (VAT) was collected. In the example used in Figure 10-1 no VAT is chargeable as most food products are currently exempt from VAT.

Unless your business uses some type of computerised system that integrates the point of sale (usually the cash register) with the business's accounting system, sales information is collected throughout the day by the cash register and printed out in a summary form at the end of the day. At that point, you enter the details of the sales day in the books.

		Item		Qty.	Price		Total	
		White Serving Set	1	£40	£40	—		
		Cheesecake, Marble	1	£20	£20	—		
		Cheesecake, Blueberry	1	£20	£20	—		
							£80	—
					£80	—		
		Cash Paid			£90	—		
		Change			£10	—		

Figure 10-1:
A sales receipt from Ashcroft Bakery.

Sales Receipt
24/4/2010
VAT No.:

Ashcroft Bakery
Clegg Street
Cardiff

If you don't use a computerised system to monitor stock, you use the data collected by the cash register to simply enter into the books the cash received, total sales and VAT collected. Although you're likely to have many more sales and much higher numbers at the end of the day, the entry in the Cash Receipts book for the receipt appears as follows:

	Debit	*Credit*
Bank Account	£80.00	
Sales		£66.66
VAT account		£13.34

Cash receipts for 25 April 2010

In this example entry, Bank Account is an Asset account shown on the balance sheet (see Chapter 19 for more about balance sheets), and its value increases with the debit. The Sales account is a Revenue account on the profit and loss statement (see Chapter 18 for more about profit and loss statements), and its balance increases with a credit, showing additional revenue. (I talk more about debits and credits in Chapter 2.) The VAT Collected account is a Liability account that appears on the balance sheet, and its balance increases with this transaction.

Businesses pay VAT to HM Revenue & Customs monthly or quarterly, depending on rules set by HM Revenue & Customs. Therefore, your business must hold the money owed in a Liability account so that you're certain you can pay the VAT collected from customers when due. I talk more about VAT payments in Chapter 23.

Recording cash transactions in the books

If you're using a computerised accounting system, you can enter more detail from the day's receipts and record stock sold as well. Most of the computerised accounting systems include the ability to record the sale of stock. Figure 10-2 shows you the Sage 50 Accounts Cash Sales screen that you can use to input data from each day's sales. Note that you need the Sage 50 Accounts Professional version to use the Sales Order Processing function to generate cash sales and automatically update your stock.

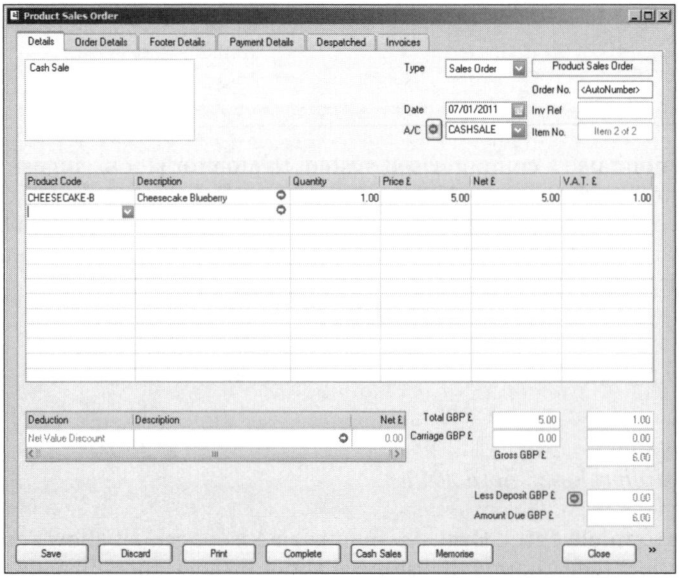

Figure 10-2:
Example of
a cash sale
in Sage 50
Accounts.

In addition to the information included in the Cash Receipts book, note that Sage 50 Accounts also collects information about the items sold in each transaction. Sage 50 Accounts then automatically updates stock information, reducing the amount of stock on hand when necessary. If the cash sale in Figure 10-2 is for an individual customer, you enter his or her name and address in the A/C field. At the bottom of the Cash Sales screen, the Print tab takes you to a further menu where you have the option to print or email the receipt. You can print the receipt and give it to the customer or, for a phone or Internet order, email it to the customer. Using this option, payment can be made by any method such as cheque, electronic payment or credit or debit card.

Sage 50 Accounts also gives you the ability to process card payments from customers over the phone and use real time authorisation and posting. To use Sage Pay, you need a Sage Pay account and a merchant bank account. For more information about this, please see www.sagepay.com.

If your business accepts credit cards, expect sales revenue to be reduced by the fees paid to credit card companies. Usually, you face monthly fees as well as fees per transaction; however, each business sets up individual arrangements with its bank regarding these fees. Sales volume impacts how much you pay in fees, so when researching bank services, ensure that you compare credit card transaction fees to find a good deal.

Selling on Credit

Many businesses decide to sell to customers on credit, meaning credit the business offers and not through a bank or credit card provider. This approach offers more flexibility in the type of terms you can offer your customers, and you don't have to pay bank fees. However, credit involves more work for you, the bookkeeper, and the risk of a customer not paying what he or she owes.

When you accept a customer's bank-issued credit card for a sale and the customer doesn't pay the bill, you get your money; the bank is responsible for collecting from the customer, taking the loss if he or she doesn't pay. This doesn't apply when you decide to offer credit to your customers directly. If a customer doesn't pay, your business takes the loss.

Deciding whether to offer credit

The decision to set up your own credit system depends on what your competition is doing. For example, if you run an office supply store and all other office supply stores allow credit to make it easier for their customers to get supplies, you probably need to offer credit to stay competitive.

You need to set up some ground rules when you want to allow your customers to buy on credit. For personal customers you have to decide:

- ✔ How to check a customer's credit history
- ✔ What the customer's income level needs to be for credit approval
- ✔ How long to give the customer to pay the bill before charging interest or late fees

If you want to allow your trade or business customers to buy on credit, you need to set ground rules for them as well. The decisions you need to make include:

- ✔ Whether to deal only with established businesses. You may give credit only to businesses that have been trading for at least two years.

- ✔ Whether to require *trade references,* which show that the business has been responsible and paid other businesses when they've taken credit. A customer usually provides you with two suppliers that offered them credit. You then contact those suppliers directly to see if the customer has been reliable and on time with their payments.

- ✔ Whether to obtain credit rating information. You may decide to use a third-party credit-checking agency to provide a credit report on the business applying for credit. This report suggests a maximum credit limit and whether the business pays on time. Of course a fee is charged for this service, but using it may help you avoid making a terrible mistake. A similar service is available for individuals.

The harder you make getting credit and the stricter you make the bill-paying rules, the less chance you have of taking a loss. However, you may lose customers to a competitor with lighter credit rules. For example, you may require a minimum income level of £50,000 and make customers pay in 30 days to avoid late fees or interest charges. Your sales staff reports that these rules are too rigid because your direct competitor down the street allows credit on a minimum income level of £30,000 and gives customers 60 days to pay before charging late fees and interest charges. Now you have to decide whether you want to change your credit rules to match those of the competition. If you do lower your credit standards to match your competitor, however, you may end up with more customers who can't pay on time (or at all) because you've qualified customers for credit at lower income levels and given them more time to pay. If you do loosen your qualification criteria and bill-paying requirements, monitor your customer accounts carefully to ensure that they're not falling behind.

The key risk you face is selling products for which you're never paid. For example, if you allow customers 30 days to pay and cut them off from buying goods when their accounts fall more than 30 days behind, the most you can lose is the amount purchased over a two-month period (60 days). But if you give customers more leniency, allowing them 60 days to pay and cutting them off after payment is 30 days late, you're faced with three months (90 days) of purchases for which you may never be paid.

Recording credit sales in the books

When sales are made on credit, you have to enter specific information into the accounting system. In addition to inputting information regarding cash receipts (see 'Collecting on Cash Sales', earlier in this chapter), you update the customer accounts to make sure that each customer is billed and the money is collected. You debit the Trade Debtors account, an Asset account shown on the balance sheet (see Chapter 19), which shows money due from customers.

Here's how a journal entry of a sale made on credit looks:

	Debit	**Credit**
Trade Debtors	£80.00	
Sales		£80.00

Cash receipts for 25 April 2010.

In addition to making this journal entry, you enter the information into the customer's account so that accurate statements can be sent out at the end of the month. When the customer pays the bill, you update the individual customer's record to show that payment has been received and enter the following into the bookkeeping records:

	Debit	**Credit**
Trade Debtors		£80.00
Cash	£80.00	

Payment from Mrs Jolly on invoice 5.

If you're using Sage 50 Accounts, you can enter credit sales on an invoice form like the one in Figure 10-3. Most of the information on the invoice form is similar to the Cash Sales screen (see 'Collecting on Cash Sales', earlier in this chapter), but the invoice form also has space to enter a different address for shipping (the Delivery Address field) and includes payment terms (the Settlement Terms field).

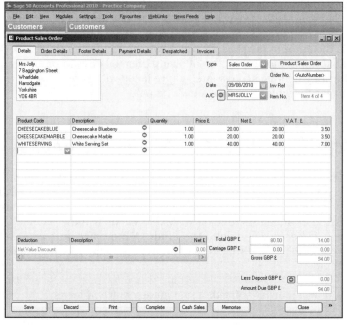

Figure 10-3: Creating a sales invoice using Sage 50 Accounts for goods sold on credit.

Sage 50 Accounts uses the information on the invoice to update the following accounts:

- ✔ Trade Debtors

- ✔ Stock

- ✔ Customer's account

- ✔ Value Added Tax account

Print out the invoice and send it to the customer straight away. Depending on the payment terms you have negotiated with your customer, send out monthly statements to remind customers that their debt to your company is still outstanding. Regular monitoring of your Aged Debtor Report ensures that you know who has not yet paid you. In order to keep these reports up to date, allocate the cash to each customer account on a regular basis.

When you receive payment from a customer, here's what to do:

1. **From the Bank module, click the Customer icon and select the customer account.**

2. **Sage 50 Accounts automatically lists all outstanding invoices. (See Figure 10–4)**

3. **Enter how much the customer is paying in total.**

4. **Select the invoice or invoices paid.**

5. **Sage 50 Accounts updates the Trade Debtors account, the Cash account and the customer's individual account to show that payment has been received.**

If your customer is paying a lot of outstanding invoices, Sage 50 Accounts has two very clever options that may save you some time. The first option, Pay in Full, marks every invoice as paid if the customer is settling up in full. The other option, Wizard, matches the payment to the outstanding invoices by starting with the oldest until it matches up the exact amount of the payment.

If your business uses a point-of-sale program integrated into the computerised accounting system, recording credit transactions is even easier for you. Sales details feed into the system as each sale is made, so you don't have to enter the detail at the end of day. These point-of-sale programs save a lot of time, but they can get very expensive.

Even if customers don't buy on credit, point-of-sale programs provide businesses with an incredible amount of information about their customers and what they like to buy. This data can be used in the future for direct marketing and special sales to increase the likelihood of return business.

Figure 10-4:
In Sage 50 Accounts, recording payments from customers who bought on credit starts with the Customer Receipt form.

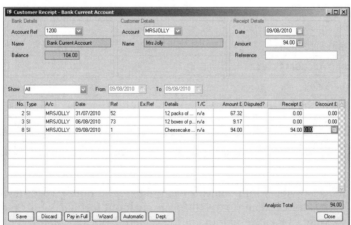

Cashing Up the Cash Register

To ensure that cashiers don't pocket a business's cash, at the end of each day, cashiers must *cash up* (show that they have the right amount of cash in the register based on the sales transactions during the day) the amount of cash, cheques and credit sales they took in during the day.

This process of cashing up a cash register actually starts at the end of the previous day, when cashier John Smith and his manager agree on the amount of cash left in John's register drawer. Cash sitting in cash registers or cash drawers is recorded as part of the Cash on Hand account.

When John comes to work the next morning, he starts out with the amount of cash left in the drawer. At the end of the business day, he or his manager runs a summary of activity on the cash register for the day to produce a report of the total sales taken in by the cashier. John counts the amount of cash in his register as well as totals for the cheques, credit card receipts and credit account sales. He then completes a cash-out form that looks something like Table 10-1:

Table 10-1	Cash Register: John Smith 25/4/2010	
Receipts	*Sales*	*Total*
Opening Cash		£100
Cash Sales	£400	
Credit Card Sales	£800	
Credit Account Sales	£200	
Total Sales		£1,400
Sales on Credit		£1,000
Cash Received		£400
Total Cash in Register		£500

A manager reviews John Smith's cash register summary (produced by the actual register) and compares it to the cash-out form. If John's ending cash (the amount of cash remaining in the register) doesn't match the cash-out form, he and the manager try to pinpoint the mistake. If they can't find a mistake, they fill out a cash-overage or cash-shortage form. Some businesses charge the cashier directly for any shortages, whereas others take the position that the cashier's fired after a certain number of shortages of a certain amount (say, three shortages of more than £10).

The manager decides how much cash to leave in the cash drawer or register for the next day and deposits the remainder. She carries out this task for each of her cashiers and then deposits all the cash and cheques from the day in a night-deposit box at the bank. She sends a report with details of the deposit to the bookkeeper so that the data appears in the accounting system. The bookkeeper enters the data on the cash sales screen (refer to Figure 10-2) if a computerised accounting system is being used, or into the Cash Receipts book if the books are being kept manually.

Monitoring Sales Discounts

Most business offer discounts at some point in time to generate more sales. Discounts are usually in the form of a sale with 10 per cent, 20 per cent or even more off purchases.

When you offer discounts to customers, monitor your sales discounts in a separate account so that you can keep an eye on how much you discount sales in each month. If you find you're losing more and more money to discounting, look closely at your pricing structure and competition to find out why you're having to lower your prices frequently to make sales. You can monitor discount information very easily by using the data found on a standard sales register receipt. Figure 10-5 shows a bakery receipt that includes sales discount details.

Sales Receipt
25/4/2010
VAT No.:

Ashcroft Bakery
Clegg Street
Cardiff

Item	Qty.	Price		Total	
White Serving Set	1	£40	—	£40	—
Cheesecake, Marble	1	£20	—	£20	—
Cheesecake, Blueberry	1	£20	—	£20	—
				£80	—
Sales Discount @ 10%		(8.00)	—		
				£72	—
Cash Paid		£80	—		
Change		£8	—		

Figure 10-5: A sales receipt from Ashcroft Bakery showing sales discount.

From this example, you can see clearly that the business takes in less cash when discounts are offered. When recording the sale in the Cash Receipts book, you record the discount as a debit. This debit increases the Sales Discount account, which is subtracted from the Sales account to calculate the Net Sales. (I walk you through all these steps and calculations when I discuss preparing the profit and loss statement in Chapter 18.) Here's what the bakery's entry for this particular sale looks like in the Cash Receipts book:

	Debit	**Credit**
Bank Account	£72.00	
Sales Discounts	£8.00	
Sales		£80.00

Cash receipts for 25 April 2010

If you use a computerised accounting system, add the sales discount as a line item on the sales receipt or invoice, and the system automatically adjusts the sales figures and updates your Sales Discount account.

Recording Sales Returns and Allowances

Most businesses deal with *sales returns* on a regular basis. Customers regularly return purchased items because the item is defective, they change their minds or for other reasons. Instituting a no-return policy is guaranteed to produce very unhappy customers: ensure that you allow sales returns to maintain good customer relations.

Accepting sales returns can be a complicated process. Usually, a business posts a set of rules for returns that may include:

- ✔ Returns allowed only within 30 days of purchase.
- ✔ You must have a receipt to return an item.
- ✔ When you return an item without a receipt, you can receive only a credit note.

You can set up whatever rules you want for returns. For internal control purposes, the key to returns is monitoring how your staff handles them. In most cases, ensure that a manager's approval is required on returns. Also, make sure that your staff pays close attention to how the customer originally paid for the item being returned. You certainly don't want to give a customer cash when they used credit – you're just handing over your money! After a return's approved, the cashier returns the amount paid by cash or credit card. Customers who bought the items on credit don't get any money back, because they didn't pay anything but expected to be billed later. Instead, a form is filled out so that the amount of the original purchase can be subtracted from the customer's credit account.

You use the information collected by the cashier who handled the return to input the sales return data into the books. For example, a customer returns a £47 item that was purchased with cash. You record the cash refund in the Cash Receipts book like this:

	Debit	*Credit*
Sales Returns and Allowances	£39.17	
Value Added Tax @ 20%	£7.83	
Bank Account		£47.00

To record return of purchase, 30/4/2010.

If the item was bought with a discount, you list the discount as well and adjust the price to show that discount.

In this journal entry:

- ✔ The Sales Returns and Allowances account increases. This account normally carries a debit balance and is subtracted from Sales when preparing the profit and loss statement, thereby reducing revenue received from customers.

- ✔ The debit to the Value Added Tax account reduces the amount in that account because Value Added Tax is no longer due on the purchase.

- ✔ The credit to the Bank Account reduces the amount of cash in that account.

Sales allowances (sales incentive programmes) are becoming more popular with businesses. Sales allowances are most often in the form of a gift card. A sold gift card is actually a liability for the business because the business has received cash, but no merchandise has gone out. For that reason, gift card sales are entered in a Gift Card Liability account. When a customer makes a purchase at a later date using the gift card, the Gift Card Liability account is reduced by the purchase amount. Monitoring the Gift Card Liability account allows businesses to keep track of how much is yet to be sold without receiving additional cash.

Monitoring Trade Debtors

Making sure that customers pay their bills is a crucial responsibility of the bookkeeper. Before sending out the monthly bills, prepare an *Aged Debtor Report* that lists all customers who owe money to the business and the age of each debt. If you keep the books manually, you collect the necessary information from each customer account. If you keep the books in a computerised accounting system, you can generate this report automatically. Either way, your Aged Debtor Report looks similar to this example report from a bakery shown in Table 10-2:

Table 10-2	Aged Debtor Report – as of 1 May 2010			
Customer	*Current*	*31–60 Days*	*61–90 Days*	*>90 Days*
S.Smith	£84.32	£46.15		
J.Smith			£65.78	
H.Harris	£89.54			
M.Man				£125.35
Totals	£173.86	£46.15	£65.78	£125.35

The Aged Debtor Report quickly tells you which customers are behind in their bills. In this example, customers are put on stop when their payments are more than 60 days late, so J. Smith and M. Man can't buy on credit until their bills are paid in full.

Give a copy of your Aged Debtor Report to the sales manager so he or she can alert staff to problem customers. The sales manager can also arrange for the appropriate collections procedures. Each business sets up its own specific collections process, usually starting with a phone call, followed by letters and possibly legal action, if necessary.

Accepting Your Losses

You may encounter a situation in which a customer never pays your business, even after an aggressive collections process. In this case, you have no choice but to write off the purchase as a *bad debt* and accept the loss.

Most businesses review their Aged Debtor Reports every 6 to 12 months and decide which accounts need to be written off as bad debt. Accounts written off are recorded in a Nominal Ledger account called *Bad Debt*. (See Chapter 4 for more information about the Nominal Ledger.) The Bad Debt account appears as an Expense account on the profit and loss statement. When you write off a customer's account as bad debt, the Bad Debt account increases, and the Trade Debtors account decreases.

To give you an idea of how you write off an account, assume that one of your customers never pays £105.75 due. Here's what your journal entry looks like for this debt:

	Debit	*Credit*
Bad Debt	£105.75	
Trade Debtors		£105.75

Sage 50 Accounts has a wizard that helps you write off individual transactions as a bad debt and does all the double entry for you, so you don't need to worry!

If the bad debt included Value Added Tax (VAT), you have suffered a double loss because you've paid over the VAT to HM Revenue & Customs, even though you never received it. Fortunately, you can reclaim this VAT when you do your next VAT return.

Chapter 11

Employee Payroll and Benefits

· ·

· ·

*U*nless your business employs just one person (you, the owner), you probably need to hire employees, and that means you have to pay them, offer benefits and manage a payroll.

Responsibilities for hiring and paying employees are usually shared between the human resources staff and the bookkeeping staff. As the bookkeeper, you must make sure that all HM Revenue & Customs tax-related forms are completed, and you need to manage all payroll responsibilities including paying employees, collecting and paying employee taxes, collecting and managing employee benefit contributions and paying benefit providers.

Before you proceed any further, visit the HM Revenue & Customs website at www.hmrc.gov.uk and click on the Employers link to go to the help area for new employers. Alternatively, phone the New Employer Helpline on 0845-6070143 and let them talk you through the process. You may be surprised at how helpful the people working there are.

This chapter examines the various employee staffing issues that bookkeepers need to be able to manage.

Staffing Your Business

After you decide that you want to hire employees for your business, you must be ready to deal with a lot of official paperwork. In addition to paperwork, you're faced with many decisions about how employees are to be paid and who's going to be responsible for maintaining the paperwork that HM Revenue & Customs requires.

Knowing what needs to be done to satisfy these officials isn't the only issue you must consider before the first person is hired; you also need to decide how frequently you're going to pay employees and what type of wage and salary scales you want to set up.

Completing new starter forms

Even before you pay your first employee, you need to start completing the HM Revenue & Customs forms related to hiring. If you plan to hire staff, you must first make sure that they have a National Insurance number. HM Revenue & Customs uses this number to track your employees, the money you pay them, as well as any PAYE (Pay As You Earn) tax and NICs (National Insurance Contributions) collected and paid on their behalf.

The following sections explain how to deal with each of these situations.

Obtaining an Employer's PAYE Reference

Every business must have an Employer's PAYE Reference in order to hire employees. Without this reference, you can't legally pay staff and deduct PAYE tax and NICs.

Luckily, HM Revenue & Customs makes it very straightforward to obtain an Employer's PAYE Reference, which is typically a three-digit number (to identify the tax office) followed by four alpha characters (to identify the employer). The fastest way is to call HM Revenue & Customs New Employer Helpline on 0845-6070143 and complete the form by telephone. Be prepared to provide the following information:

- ✔ **General business information:** Business name, trading address, name and address of employer, National Insurance number and Unique Taxpayer Reference of employer, contact telephone number, contact e-mail address if registering using e-mail, nature of business

- ✔ **Employee information:** The date you took on (or intend to take on) your first employee(s), how many employees you intend to have, the date you intend to pay them for the first time, how often you intend to pay them

If your business is a partnership or a limited company, you need to give additional information:

- **Partnership:** Names and addresses of any business partners, National Insurance numbers and Unique Taxpayer References of any business partners and your LLP number if you are a Limited Liability Partnership (LLP)
- **Limited company:** The company's registered address, company registration number and date of incorporation, the names, addresses, private telephone numbers, National Insurance numbers and Unique Taxpayer References of the company directors

In addition to your Employer's PAYE Reference, you receive a New Employer's Guide, which includes a CD-ROM with online help and a payroll Tax and National Insurance Calculator, which makes your life so much easier. This guide also includes some samples of the forms you need, which are covered later in this chapter.

As well as tracking pay and taxes, HM Revenue & Customs uses your PAYE Reference to track the payment of PAYE tax and NICs, both of which the employer must pay.

Collecting P45s

Every person you hire should bring a P45 from his or her previous employer. The *P45* is a record of the employee's taxable earnings, PAYE deducted and tax code for the current tax year.

This form, shown in Figure 11-1, gives you the information you need as the new employer to make sure that you can deduct the correct amount of PAYE and National Insurance from the new employee.

Ask a new employee right from the start if he or she has a P45 from a previous employer. If an employee doesn't have a P45, you must deduct income tax out of his or her wage as if it is all taxable. I talk more about deducting taxes in the section 'Collecting Employee Taxes', later in this chapter.

The recently updated P45 is now an A4-sized four-part carbon form:

- **Part 1** shows details of the employee leaving work. The previous employer sends Part 1 to its tax office. This process keeps HM Revenue & Customs informed that the employee has left his or her old job.
- **Part 1A** is an exact copy of Part 1 that the employee keeps for his or her records.

HM Revenue & Customs

P45 Part 1
Details of employee leaving work
Copy for HM Revenue & Customs

File your employee's P45 online at **www.hmrc.gov.uk**

Use capital letters when completing this form

1 Employer PAYE reference
Office number   Reference number

2 Employee's National Insurance number

3 Title – enter MR, MRS, MISS, MS or other title

Surname or family name

First or given name(s)

4 Leaving date *DD MM YYYY*

5 Student Loan deductions

Enter 'Y' if Student Loan deduction is due to be made

6 Tax Code at leaving date

If week 1 or month 1 applies, enter 'X' in the box below.

Week 1/Month 1

7 Last entries on P11 *Deductions Working Sheet*.
Complete only if Tax Code is cumulative. Make no entry if week 1 or month 1 applies, go straight to box 8.

Week number   Month number

Total pay to date
£

Total tax to date
£

8 This employment pay and tax. Leave blank if the Tax Code is cumulative and the amounts are the same as box 7.
Total pay in this employment
£

Total tax in this employment
£

9 Works number/Payroll number and Department or branch (if any)

10 Gender. Enter 'X' in the appropriate box

Male   Female

11 Date of birth *DD MM YYYY*

12 Employee's private address

Postcode

13 I certify that the details entered in items 1 to 11 on this form are correct.
Employer name and address

Postcode

Date *DD MM YYYY*

14 **When an employee dies.** If the employee has died enter 'D' in the box and send all four parts of this form to your HMRC office immediately.

Instructions for the employer
• Complete this form following the 'What to do when an employee leaves' instructions in the Employer Helpbook E13 *Day-to-day payroll.* Make sure the details are clear on all four parts of this form and that your name and address is shown on Parts 1 and 1A.
• Send Part 1 to your HM Revenue & Customs office immediately.
• Hand Parts 1A, 2 and 3 to your employee when they leave.

P45(Manual) Part 1

HMRC 04/08

© Crown Copyright.

Figure 11-1:
All new employees bring form P45 so that you know how much to take out of their wages for PAYE and National Insurance.

✔ **Part 2** contains the information that you (as the new employer) need to have to ensure that you deduct the correct amount for PAYE tax and National Insurance. Keep this part in your records system. The information you need to answer the seven questions here is already filled in as a result of Part 1 being completed, so you have nothing to complete, just keep it.

✔ **Part 3** is filled in by you as the new employer. Again, questions 1 to 7 are already completed for you as a result of Part 1 being completed. You complete the bottom half of the P45 – boxes 8 to 16 – sign the declaration in box 17 and send it on to your local HM Revenue & Customs office. Fortunately this process is very straightforward. The questions you need to answer are:

- Q8: Enter your PAYE Reference.

- Q9: Enter the date the new employee started working for you.

- Q10: Enter details of the new employee's works/payroll number, branch or depot, and tick if you want these details shown on any tax code notifications.

- Q11: Enter P if the employee will not be paid by you between the employment start date and the next 5 April.

- Q12: Enter the tax code in use if different to code at Q6.

- Q13: If the tax figure you are entering on form P11 differs from item shown in Q7, enter your figure.

- Q14: Enter the employee's job title or description.

- Q15: Enter the employee's private address.

- Q16: Enter the employee's gender.

- Q17: Enter the employee's date of birth.

- Q18: Declaration and current employer's name and address.

Starting fresh with employees without a P45

If a worker is new to the job market, he or she must have a National Insurance number. In some cases, however, a new employee may not have a National Insurance number or a P45.

Many new employees don't have P45s, perhaps because they've lost it, or this is their first job, or maybe they are keeping another job as well as working for you. In these cases, your new employee must complete a P46. Essentially, the P46 is a substitute for the P45. The new employee must complete Section 1, shown in Figure 11-2, and the new employer (that's you) completes Section 2, shown in Figure 11-3. You then send the completed form to your local tax office on the employee's first pay day.

P46: Employee without a form P45

Section one To be completed by the employee

Please complete section one and then hand the form back to your present employer. If you later receive a form P45 from your previous employer, hand it to your present employer. Use capital letters when completing this form.

Your details

National Insurance number
This is very important in getting your tax and benefits right

Date of birth *DD MM YYYY*

Title – *enter MR, MRS, MISS, MS or other title*

Address
House or flat number

Surname or family name

Rest of address including house name or flat name

First or given name(s)

Postcode

Gender. Enter 'X' in the appropriate box

Male   Female

Your present circumstances

Read all the following statements carefully and enter 'X' in **the one** box that applies to you.

A – This is my first job since last 6 April and **I have not** been receiving taxable Jobseeker's Allowance, Employment and Support Allowance or taxable Incapacity Benefit or a state or occupational pension.

OR

B – This is now my only job, but since last 6 April **I have** had another job, or have received taxable Jobseeker's Allowance, Employment and Support Allowance or taxable Incapacity Benefit. I do not receive a state or occupational pension.

OR

C – I have another job or receive a state or occupational pension.

Student Loans (advanced in the UK)

If you left a course of UK Higher Education before last 6 April and received your first UK Student Loan instalment on or after 1 September 1998 and you have not fully repaid your Student Loan, enter 'X' in box D. *(Do **not** enter 'X' in box D if you are repaying your UK Student Loan by agreement with the UK Student Loans Company to make monthly payments through your bank or building society account.)*

Signature and date

I can confirm that this information is correct

Signature

Date *DD MM YYYY*

Figure 11-2: Section 1 of the P46, which a new employee must complete if he or she doesn't have a P45.

© Crown Copyright.

Section two   To be completed by the employer

File your employee's P46 online at **www.hmrc.gov.uk**
Use capital letters when completing this form. Guidance on how to fill it in, including what to do if your employee has
not entered their National Insurance number on page 1, is at **www.hmrc.gov.uk/employers/working_out.htm**
and in the E13 Employer Helpbook *Day-to-day payroll.*

Employee's details

Date employment started *DD MM YYYY*

Works/payroll number and department or branch (if any)

Job title

Employer's details

Employer PAYE reference
Office number   Reference number

Address

Building number

Employer name

Rest of address

Postcode

Tax code used
If you do not know the tax code to use or the current National Insurance contributions (NICs)
lower earnings limit, go to **www.hmrc.gov.uk/employers/rates_and_limits.htm**

Enter 'X' in the appropriate box

Box A
Emergency code on a **cumulative** basis   A

Box B
Emergency code on a **non-cumulative**
Week 1/Month 1 basis   B

Box C
Code BR   C

Tax code used

If Week 1 or
Month 1 applies,
enter 'X' in this box

Send this form to your HM Revenue & Customs office on the first pay day.
If the employee has entered 'X' in box A or box B, on page 1, and their earnings are below the
NICs lower earnings limit, **do not send the form until their earnings reach the NICs lower earnings limit.**

Figure 11-3:
Section 2
of the P46,
which an
employer
must
complete
if a new
employee
doesn't
have a P45.

The end result of using a P46 is that the new employee initially pays too much tax and National Insurance until the local HM Revenue & Customs office sends you the correct tax code and cumulative taxable pay and tax paid information. In effect, the HM Revenue & Customs office provides you with what would have been on the P45.

Completing forms for foreign workers

As an employer in the UK, it is your responsibility to verify that any person you hire is a UK citizen or has the right to work in the United Kingdom – you can't just accept his or her word. If you have any doubts, ask to see his or her passport and Home Office Work Permit. Of course, some foreign workers, namely those from the European countries that make up the European Economic Area (EEA), don't need a work permit.

The EU has an agreement with Norway, Iceland and Liechtenstein (countries within the European Economic Area or EEA) and a separate agreement with Switzerland, which confer rights similar to those of EU nationals on nationals of those countries.

The EEA is quite extensive now and comprises older member states who joined before 1 May 2004 and those that joined on 1 May 2004. Table 11-1 shows the countries whose citizens qualify to work in the UK under EEA residence rules. Citizens of the UK, of course, are eligible for jobs here.

Table 11-1   Countries whose Citizens Qualify to Work in the UK

Austria	Greece	Norway
Belgium	Hungary	Poland
Bulgaria	Iceland	Portugal
The Czech Republic	Italy	Republic of Ireland
Cyprus	Latvia	Romania
Denmark	Liechtenstein	Slovakia
Estonia	Lithuania	Slovenia
Finland	Luxembourg	Spain
France	Malta	Sweden
Germany	Netherlands	Switzerland

If you have any doubts, contact your local HM Revenue & Customs office: EEA members are subject to change and some special rules apply to some of the newer signatories.

Picking pay periods

Deciding how frequently to pay your employees is an important point to work out before hiring staff. Most businesses choose one of these two pay periods:

- ✔ **Weekly:** Employees are paid every week, which means you must do payroll 52 times a year.
- ✔ **Monthly:** Employees are paid once a month, which means you must do payroll 12 times a year.

You can choose to use either pay period, and you may even decide to use more than one type. For example, some businesses pay hourly employees (employees paid by the hour) weekly and pay salaried employees (employees paid by a set salary regardless of how many hours they work) monthly.

Determining wage and salary scales

You have a lot of leeway regarding the level of wages and salary that you pay your employees, but you still have to follow some rules laid out by the government. Under the National Minimum Wage Regulations, employers must pay workers a minimum amount as defined by law. These rules apply to businesses of all sizes and in all industries.

The three levels of minimum wage rates from 1 October 2010 are:

- ✔ £5.93 per hour for workers aged 21 years and older.
- ✔ £4.92 per hour for workers aged 18 to 20 years old.
- ✔ £3.64 per hour for workers aged between 16 and 17 years old.

    The government has accepted a recommendation from the Low Pay Commission (LPC) to introduce a new apprentice rate of £2.50 per hour. It will apply to apprentices under the age of 19 and also apprentices aged 19 and over in their first year.

Don't assume that the minimum wage isn't going to change though, and check the HM Revenue & Customs website periodically to get the current wage rates. You can get advice on the minimum wage by contacting the Pay and Work Rights Helpline on 0800-9172368.

Making statutory payments

As well as guaranteeing minimum wage payments for workers, government statutes provide other benefits:

✔ **Sick pay:** Employees who are off sick for more than four consecutive work days are entitled to receive Statutory Sick Pay (SSP). Of course, a sick employee must inform you as soon as possible and supply you with evidence of his or her sickness.

In many cases the business continues to pay employees for short periods of sickness as part of good employment practice. However, if you don't pay employees when they are off sick for more than four days, they can claim SSP, which is based on their average earnings. As an employer, you may be able to recover some of the SSP you have paid against your NIC amounts.

The first three days that the employee is away from work are called *waiting days* and don't qualify for SSP.

✔ **Parental pay:** If employees qualify for Statutory Maternity Pay (SMP), then they are paid for a maximum of 39 weeks. For the first six weeks an employee is entitled to 90 per cent of her average wage. For the other weeks she is entitled to £124.88 per week or 90 per cent of average earnings if this is less than £124.88.

New dads are entitled to Statutory Paternity Pay (SPP) for two weeks, calculated in much the same way as SMP.

Most employees who adopt children are entitled to Statutory Adoption Pay (SAP), which is payable for up to 39 weeks at the lower rate of £124.88 per week or 90 per cent of average weekly wages if this is less.

All these statutory payments are offset against the NICs, which the business has to pay over each month. For example, if the business was due to pay over £1,000 in NICs but paid out recoverable SSP of £108.85, it makes a net payment of £891.15. The payslip has room for you to show this adjustment.

Dealing with the Payroll Administration

Before you start to take on and pay any employees, you need to be up to speed on all the forms you need. Day-to-day payroll involves forms and more forms. The following list gives you an idea of the typical range of HM Revenue & Customs forms you have to deal with during the tax year:

✔ **P45:** You complete this form for each employee who leaves at any time during the tax year and for all new employees starting work for your business. The P45 gives details of earnings, Pay As You Earn (PAYE), National Insurance Contributions (NICs) and the tax code for the tax year.

✔ **P46:** You complete this form for any new-start employees who don't have a P45.

✔ **P46 (Car):** You use this form to notify HM Revenue & Customs when an employee is first provided with a company car or any change occurs to this benefit.

✔ **P6:** Notification from HM Revenue & Customs of a new tax code for an employee. This form is your authority to change an employee's tax code.

✔ **P11 (Deductions Working Sheet):** This form is the record of each individual employee's NICs, earnings, statutory payments, PAYE deductions and student loans.

✔ **P32 (Employer's Payment Record):** Use this form to record details of the total deductions for all employees including PAYE, student loans, NICs, Statutory Sick Pay (SSP), Statutory Maternity Pay (SMP), Statutory Paternity Pay (SPP), Statutory Adoption Pay (SAP) and the reclaims you have received for SSP, SMP, SPP and SAP.

✔ **CA6855:** Use this form to trace a National Insurance number (NINO) if a new employee can't provide one.

A whole range of guides is available from HM Revenue & Customs (www. hmrc.gov.uk) to help you. Here are just a few:

✔ **New Employer Guide Pack:** This pack is an absolute must for any new employer. The pack contains sample P45, P46 and P11 forms, and also a CD-ROM with tutorials and the excellent P11 Calculator, which calculates and records PAYE and NICs.

✔ **P49 (2009) (Paying someone for the first time):** The current guide on how to get your payroll started.

✔ **E13 (Day-to-day payroll):** Similar to P49, but with additional useful information and easier to understand.

✔ **E3 (2010) (Order form):** This form lists all the forms and guides you can possibly want, and you can use it to order each one.

Collecting Employee Taxes

As the bookkeeper you must be familiar with how to calculate the Pay As You Earn (PAYE) tax and National Insurance Contributions (NICs) that you must deduct from each employee's wage or salary.

Although you can run a manual payroll, the calculation of PAYE and NICs is a monumental nightmare, demanding the most accurate and methodical approach to using the tables that HM Revenue & Customs provides each tax year. As well as getting the calculations correct, you have to record this information on a Deductions Working Sheet for each employee, which is very time consuming.

Save yourself a lot of grief and use a payroll bureau to run your weekly and monthly payroll and end-of-tax-year returns. If you employ more than 30 employees, this method saves you a lot of time and the cost isn't all that high. If you employ fewer than 30 employees and have the time to spare, use the P11 Calculator that HM Revenue & Customs gives you as part of the New Employer Guide or buy an off-the-shelf payroll package.

Sorting out National Insurance Contributions

The easiest and quickest way to work out the National Insurance Contributions (NICs) is to use the NICs Calculator on the Employer CD-ROM you receive when you first become an employer, and which is updated each time NICs are changed. However, for those of you who are feeling masochistic or want to know the principles behind the NICs, this section gives a broad outline.

NICs are made up of two elements:

✓ Employee contributions, which you deduct from your employees' pay

✓ Employer contributions, which your business must pay

Several different categories of NICs exist depending on the employee's age and sex. For most men aged 16 to 64 and most women aged 16 to 59, you use Category A, which is referred to later as Table A. If you are unsure about which category your employee falls under, contact your local HM Revenue & Customs or go to the website at www.hmrc.gov.uk.

To calculate Category A NICs, you need booklet *CA38 National Insurance Contributions Tables A & J* from HM Revenue & Customs. Make sure that the tables you have are for the correct year. Start at page 8 of Table A if you are doing weekly pay and page 23 for monthly pay.

The next challenge is using Table A correctly. Look up the employee's gross pay in the left-hand column of the table 'Employee's Earnings up to and including the UEL (Upper Earnings Limit)'. If the exact amount isn't shown in the table, use the next smaller figure. I show an example of both weekly and monthly NICs in the following sections.

If your employee earns more than £97 per week or £421 per month, you must keep a record of his or her earnings even if no NICs are due.

A weekly pay example

In this example, an employee is paid £201.92 on 26 May 2010 for the week. According to Table A, the week is number 8 (based on the fact that this is the eighth week after the start of the tax year, which starts on 6 April). Look at Weekly Table A to find the next smaller figure than the amount being paid, which in this example is £201. Copy the figures from columns 1a to 1f of Weekly Table A to columns 1a to 1f of form P11 (the Deductions Working Sheet). Figure 11-4 shows an extract from Table A as well as where to enter information on form P11.

Each year HM Revenue & Customs sets new Lower Earnings Limits (LEL) below which no NICs are payable by an employee. It also sets an Upper Earnings Limit (UEL) above which no more NICs are payable. There is an Earnings Threshold (ET), below which lower NICs are due and above which higher NICs are due. These are shown above the columns on P11 in Figure 11-5.

A monthly pay example

In this example, an employee is paid £494.50 on 26 May 2010 for the month. According to Table A, the month is number 2 (based on the number of months from the start of the tax year in April). Look at Monthly Table A to find the next smaller figure, which in this example is £493. Copy the figures from columns 1a to 1f of Monthly Table A to columns 1a to 1f of form P11 (the Deductions Working Sheet). Figure 11-5 shows how this information appears.

Figuring out Pay As You Earn tax

Deducting Pay As You Earn (PAYE) tax is a much more complex task for bookkeepers than deducting NICs. You have to worry about an employee's tax code (of which numerous permutations exist) as well as using Table A to calculate the final tax figure to deduct.

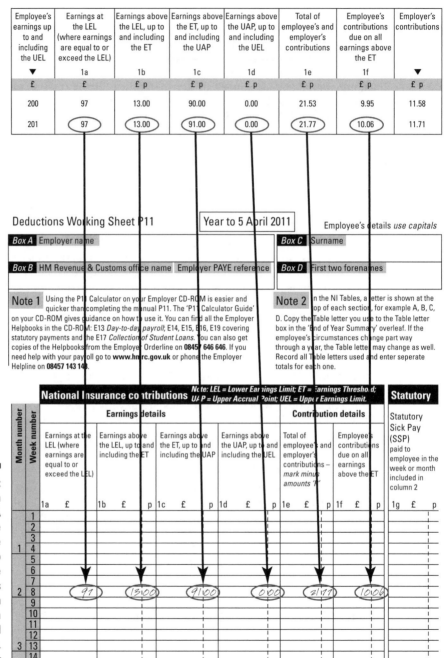

Employee's earnings up to and including the UEL ▼	Earnings at the LEL (where earnings are equal to or exceed the LEL) 1a	Earnings above the LEL, up to and including the ET 1b	Earnings above the ET, up to and including the UAP 1c	Earnings above the UAP, up to and including the UEL 1d	Total of employee's and employer's contributions 1e	Employee's contributions due on all earnings above the ET 1f	Employer's contributions ▼
£	£	£ p	£ p	£ p	£ p	£ p	£ p
200	97	13.00	90.00	0.00	21.53	9.95	11.58
201	97	13.00	91.00	0.00	21.77	10.06	11.71

Deductions Working Sheet P11   Year to 5 April 2011   Employee's details *use capitals*

Box A Employer name

Box C Surname

Box B HM Revenue & Customs office name   Employer PAYE reference

Box D First two forenames

Note 1 Using the P11 Calculator on your Employer CD-ROM is easier and quicker than completing the manual P11. The 'P11 Calculator Guide' on your CD-ROM gives guidance on how to use it. You can find all the Employer Helpbooks in the CD-ROM: E13 *Day-to-day payroll*; E14, E15, E16, E19 covering statutory payments and the E17 *Collection of Student Loans*. You can also get copies of the Helpbooks from the Employer Orderline on **08457 646 646**. If you need help with your payroll go to **www.hmrc.gov.uk** or phone the Employer Helpline on **08457 143 143**.

Note 2 In the NI Tables, a letter is shown at the top of each section, for example A, B, C, D. Copy the Table letter you use to the Table letter box in the 'End of Year Summary' overleaf. If the employee's circumstances change part way through a year, the Table letter may change as well. Record all Table letters used and enter seperate totals for each one.

National Insurance contributions Note: LEL = Lower Earnings Limit; ET = Earnings Threshold; UAP = Upper Accrual Point; UEL = Upper Earnings Limit.   **Statutory**

Month number	Week number	Earnings at the LEL (where earnings are equal to or exceed the LEL) 1a £	Earnings above the LEL, up to and including the ET 1b £ p	Earnings above the ET, up to and including the UAP 1c £ p	Earnings above the UAP, up to and including the UEL 1d £ p	Total of employee's and employer's contributions – mark minus amounts 'R' 1e £ p	Employees contributions due on all earnings above the ET 1f £ p	Statutory Sick Pay (SSP) paid to employee in the week or month included in column 2 1g £ p
1	1							
	2							
	3							
	4							
	5							
	6							
	7							
2	8	91	13.00	91.00	0.00	21.77	10.06	
	9							
	10							
	11							
	12							
3	13							
	14							

Figure 11-4: Extract from Table A showing the NICs due and how to enter the numbers on form P11 for a weekly paid employee.

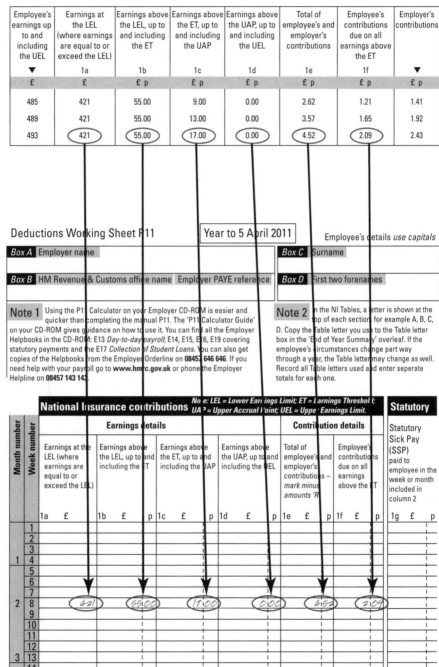

Employee's earnings up to and including the UEL ▼	Earnings at the LEL (where earnings are equal to or exceed the LEL) 1a	Earnings above the LEL, up to and including the ET 1b	Earnings above the ET, up to and including the UAP 1c	Earnings above the UAP, up to and including the UEL 1d	Total of employee's and employer's contributions 1e	Employee's contributions due on all earnings above the ET 1f	Employer's contributions ▼
£	£	£ p	£ p	£ p	£ p	£ p	£ p
485	421	55.00	9.00	0.00	2.62	1.21	1.41
489	421	55.00	13.00	0.00	3.57	1.65	1.92
493	421	55.00	17.00	0.00	4.52	2.09	2.43

Deductions Working Sheet P11   Year to 5 April 2011   Employee's details *use capitals*

Box A Employer name   *Box C* Surname

Box B HM Revenue & Customs office name   Employer PAYE reference   *Box D* First two forenames

Note 1 Using the P11 Calculator on your Employer CD-ROM is easier and quicker than completing the manual P11. The 'P11 Calculator Guide' on your CD-ROM gives guidance on how to use it. You can find all the Employer Helpbooks in the CD-ROM: E13 *Day-to-day payroll*; E14, E15, E16, E19 covering statutory payments and the E17 *Collection of Student Loans*. You can also get copies of the Helpbooks from the Employer Orderline on **08457 646 646**. If you need help with your payroll go to **www.hmrc.gov.uk** or phone the Employer Helpline on **08457 143 143**.

Note 2 In the NI Tables, a letter is shown at the top of each section, for example A, B, C, D. Copy the Table letter you use to the Table letter box in the 'End of Year Summary' overleaf. If the employee's circumstances change part way through a year, the Table letter may change as well. Record all Table letters used and enter seperate totals for each one.

National Insurance contributions *Note: LEL = Lower Earnings Limit; ET = Earnings Threshold; UAP = Upper Accrual Point; UEL = Upper Earnings Limit.*   **Statutory**

Month number	Week number	Earnings details				Contribution details		Statutory Sick Pay (SSP) paid to employee in the week or month included in column 2
		Earnings at the LEL (where earnings are equal to or exceed the LEL) 1a £	Earnings above the LEL, up to and including the ET 1b £ p	Earnings above the ET, up to and including the UAP 1c £ p	Earnings above the UAP, up to and including the UEL 1d £ p	Total of employee's and employer's contributions — mark minus amounts 'R' 1e £ p	Employee's contributions due on all earnings above the ET 1f £ p	1g £ p
	1							
	2							
	3							
1	4							
	5							
	6							
	7							
2	8	421	55.00	17.00	0.00	4.52	2.09	
	9							
	10							
	11							
	12							
3	13							
	14							

Figure 11-5: Extract from Table A showing the NICs due and how to enter the details on form P11 for a monthly paid employee.

Considering the tax codes

A tax code is usually made up of one or more numbers followed by a letter. The number indicates the amount of pay an employee is allowed to earn in a tax year before tax becomes payable. For example, an employee with a tax code of 647L can earn £6,475 in the current tax year before becoming liable to pay any tax at all.

A letter follows the number part of the tax code: L, P, T, V or Y. The letters show how the tax code is adjusted to take account of any budget changes.

If the tax code is followed by week 1/month 1 or an X, instead of keeping a running total of the pay to date, you treat each pay day for that employee as if it is the first week or month of the tax year. For regular employees, you work on a running total basis of 'total pay to date' at each pay day.

Tax codes work on an annual cumulative tax allowance. For example, a tax code of 647L means an employee can earn £6,475 tax free in a complete tax year (52 weeks or 12 months). If they are paid weekly, this tax-free sum adds up as the weeks go by. In this example, in week 1 the employee can earn £124.52 total pay without paying any tax (£6,475 ÷ 52). By week 8, that employee could have earned £996.15 total pay to date that year without paying any tax. Assuming that they have been paid in each of the intervening weeks (1 to 7), these sums earned are deducted from the total year-to-date tax-free-earnings figure to calculate how much is taxable. All this information is provided in the tax tables that you can obtain from HM Revenue & Customs.

Finally, as if all this wasn't confusing enough, an employee may have a totally different BR tax code, which stands for Basic Rate. For an employee with a BR tax code, you must deduct tax from all the pay at the basic rate – currently 20 per cent. The BR code can also be followed by a week 1/month 1 or X, which indicates that you operate the code on a non-cumulative basis. Of course, if week 1/month 1 or X aren't indicated, you work on a running-total basis of total-pay-to-date at each pay day.

The easiest and quickest way to work out the tax deduction is to use the Tax Calculator on your Employer CD-ROM. This calculator provides you with the figures you need for columns 2 to 8 of the P11.

Calculating the PAYE deduction for a weekly paid employee

Looking at the same weekly employee from the previous section 'A weekly pay example', who earned £201.92 in his new employment for tax week 8, you can calculate the PAYE tax that needs to be deducted. The information from the employee's P45 states:

✔ Tax code is 647L

✔ Total pay to date is £1,546.15

✔ Total tax to date is £134.60

Figure 11-6 shows the entries on the form P11 (Deduction Working Sheet).

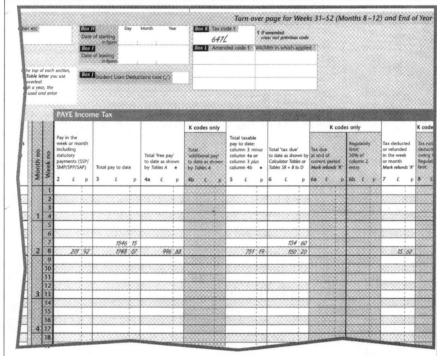

Figure 11-6:
PAYE
entries
on form
P11 for a
weekly paid
employee.

© Crown Copyright.

The following list explains how the numbers in Figure 11-6 are calculated:

✔ **Column 2 (Pay in the week or month):** Enter here the pay that the employee earned in the current week, which is week 8.

✔ **Column 3 (Total pay to date):** This column includes pay from any previous employment during the current tax year. The employee's P45 indicates that this amount is £1,546.15 for week 7 – the week before the current pay week.

As PAYE works on a cumulative basis, you then add the current week's pay – £201.92 – to this figure to get the cumulative or 'Total pay to date' figure, which is £1,748.07. You enter that total on the line for week 8, just below the previous 'Total pay to date' figure.

✓ **Column 4a (Total 'free pay' to date):** Find the page in Table A for the week that includes the pay date (week 8). Next, find your employee's tax code, which in the example is 647L, and read off the table the amount of tax-free pay. In the example (and you have to take my word for this) code 647L gives free pay of £996.88 at week 8, made up of two elements (£769.28 + £227.60), shown in the following list. For codes over 500 you must use the further instructions at the bottom of the page to calculate the full tax-free pay to date:

   • Week 8 figure for code 500 is £769.28

   • Week 8 figure for code 147 (647 – 500) is £227.60

   • Total free pay for week 8 is £996.88 – the sum of the two figures

   • Enter £996.88 on the week 8 line in column 4a.

✓ **Column 5 (Total taxable pay to date):** This column features a straight-forward calculation in which you deduct the column 4a figure from the column 3 figure to see how much pay is taxable. In this example, column 3 is £1,748.07 for week 8 and deducting the column 4a figure of £996.88 for the same week gives you a taxable pay figure of £751.19 for the year to date.

✓ **Column 6 (Total 'tax due' to date):** For this step you need your *Taxable Pay Tables, Calculator Method*. For weekly paid employees, turn to pages 4, 5 and 6. For monthly paid employees, turn to pages 2 and 3. Find the week, in this example for the employee's taxable pay period (week 8), and go to Section A of the Weekly paid – Calculator Tables. Follow the guidance given there.

✓ You can obtain these booklets from HM Revenue & Customs and you definitely need them prior to paying anybody. If you hate using tables, then use the CD-Rom that HM Revenue & Customs send out with the New Employer pack.

✓ In the example, the £751.19 taxable pay figure is rounded down to £751 on which tax is due at 20 per cent (the standard rate), amounting to £150.20 for the year to date. Enter this figure in column 6 against the week 8 line.

✓ **Column 7 (Tax deducted or refunded):** Assuming that the 'Total tax to date' figure from the P45 is correct, you can move on to the final stage. If the figure in column 6 against week 8 (£150.20) is greater than the figure in column 6 week 7 (£134.60), the difference – £15.60 – is tax to be deducted, which you enter in column 7 against week 8.

As a point of interest, if the figure in column 7 for week 8 is the same as in week 7, no tax is deductible. Also, if the figure in column 7 for week 8 is less than in week 7, a tax refund is due to the employee.

After you work out how much PAYE tax and NICs to deduct from your employees' pay and record the amounts on their P11s, you need to work out how much pay to give your employees – the next section tells you how. In fact, by law all your employees are entitled to receive a statement (usually a payslip), which shows the deductions you have made from their pay. The statement must show: gross pay, NICs deducted and tax deducted. At the end of the year you must give all your employees a record showing the details for the whole year. (This record, the P60, is covered in Chapter 21.)

Determining Net Pay

Net pay is the amount a person is paid after subtracting all tax and benefit deductions from his or her gross pay.

After you figure out all the necessary PAYE and NICs to be taken from an employee's wage or salary (see the preceding sections), you can calculate the pay amount, which is shown on his or her payslip. The equation you use is pretty straightforward:

Gross pay – (PAYE + NICs) = Net pay

This formula when used for a sample employee may look like this:

Gross pay = £201.92

Less: PAYE tax deducted – £15.60

Less: Employee NICs – £10.11

Net pay = £176.21

This net pay calculation doesn't include any deductions for benefits. Many businesses offer their employees health, pensions, company cars and other benefits but expect the employees to share a portion of some of those costs. Most benefits are liable to PAYE tax and NICs, whereas employee contributions to pensions and some other benefits are tax deductible. To get full details on which benefits are taxable and which are not, visit the HM Revenue & Customs website (www.hmrc.gov.uk) or ask your tax advisor.

Taxing Benefits

Many businesses offer their employees a range of benefits as well as their wage or salary. These benefits may include perks like a company car, all fuel paid for, health insurance and a business pension scheme. However, most benefits are taxable, so the employee has to pay tax on the money on the value of the benefits received. Very few benefits are non-taxable.

Fortunately the process of collecting this tax on benefits is very straightforward. Your business informs HM Revenue & Customs what benefits each employee receives each tax year, and it adjusts the employee tax code to ensure that you collect the tax due through the payroll.

However, two benefits – company cars and fuel benefits – involve some additional work for you if you're involved in the payroll.

The quickest and simplest way to calculate the value of these benefits is to use the Car and Car Fuel Benefit Calculator, which comes with the New Employer Guide from HM Revenue & Customs. The calculator guides you through the whole process. Also, all the monthly car magazines include the taxable benefit figures in their rating for each car reviewed.

You're responsible for working out the value of the company car benefit and telling HM Revenue & Customs. In simple terms, the car benefit charge is obtained by multiplying the list price of the car plus accessories less any capital contribution by the employee by the appropriate percentage. The *appropriate percentage* is based on the car's approved CO_2 emissions figure. The maximum appropriate percentage is 35 per cent, but this amount can be adjusted depending on the type of fuel used and whether it is electric or a hybrid car. However, just to complicate matters, older cars registered prior to 1 January 1998 don't have an approved CO_2 emissions figure, and so their engine size determines the approved percentage. Low-emission cars also have special rules.

If an employer pays for all the fuel for company car users, they can claim an additional taxable benefit called a fuel benefit charge for the non-business fuel used. Fortunately, this is even simpler to calculate. Since 2008/9, the fuel benefit charge has been a fixed sum of £16,900 to which you apply the appropriate percentage used to calculate the car benefit. So if your car had an appropriate percentage (based on CO_2 emissions) of 24 per cent, for example, then your taxable fuel benefit charge would be £4,056 (£16,900 × 24 per cent).

When you have calculated the taxable value of the company car and fuel benefit, you must inform HM Revenue & Customs so that it can issue you with a revised tax code for that employee to collect the extra PAYE and NICs due each month. You use form P46 (Car) to notify HM Revenue & Customs of any new company cars and fuel benefits, or any changes to these benefits.

Preparing and Posting Payroll

After you deal with deductions and taxes, you have to figure out your employee's gross and net pay and post all the amounts in your journals.

Calculating payroll for hourly employees

When you're ready to prepare payroll for your hourly paid employees, the first thing you need to do is collect time records from each person being paid hourly. Some businesses use time clocks and some use time sheets to produce the required time records, but whatever the method used, usually the manager of each department reviews the time records for each employee that he or she supervises and then sends those time records to you, the bookkeeper.

With time records in hand, you have to calculate gross pay for each employee. For example, if an employee worked 45 hours and is paid £12 an hour, you calculate gross pay as follows:

40 standard hours × £12 per hour = £480

5 overtime hours × £12 per hour × 1.5 overtime rate = £90

£480 + £90 = £570

Doling out funds to salaried employees

You also must prepare payroll for salaried employees. Payments for salaried employees are relatively easy to calculate – all you need to know are their base salaries and pay period calculations. For example, if a salaried employee is paid £15,000 per year and is paid monthly (totalling 12 pay periods), that employee's gross pay is £1,250 for each pay period (£15,000 ÷ 12).

Totalling up for commission payments

Running payroll for employees who are paid based on commission can involve complex calculations. To show you a number of variables, in this section I calculate a commission payment based on a salesperson who sells £60,000 worth of products during one month.

For a salesperson on a straight commission of 10 per cent, you calculate pay using this formula:

Total amount sold × Commission percentage = Gross pay

£60,000 × 0.10 = £6,000

For a salesperson with a guaranteed base salary of £2,000, plus an additional 5 per cent commission on all products sold, you calculate pay using this formula:

Base salary + (Total amount sold × Commission percentage) = Gross pay

£2,000 + (£60,000 × 0.05) = £5,000

Although this salesperson may be happier with a base salary that she can count on each month, in this scenario she actually makes less with a base salary because the commission rate is so much lower. The salesperson makes only £3,000 in commission at 5 per cent if she sells £60,000 worth of products. Without the base pay, she would have made 10 per cent on the £60,000, or £6,000. Therefore, taking into account her base salary of £2,000, she actually receives £1,000 less with a base pay structure that includes a lower commission pay rate.

If a salesperson has a slow sales month of just £30,000 worth of products sold, the pay is:

£30,000 × 0.10 = £3,000 on straight commission of 10 per cent

and

£30,000 × 0.05 = £1,500 plus £2,000 base salary, or £3,500

For a slow month, the salesperson makes more money with the base salary rather than the higher commission rate.

You can calculate commissions in many other ways. One common way is to offer higher commissions on higher levels of sales. Using the figures in this example, this type of pay system encourages salespeople to keep their sales levels over a threshold amount to get the best commission rate.

With a graduated commission scale, a salesperson can make a straight commission of 5 per cent on the first £10,000 in sales, 7 per cent on the next £20,000 and 10 per cent on anything over £30,000. Here's what this salesperson's gross pay calculation looks like using this commission pay scale:

$$(£10,000 \times 0.05) + (£20,000 \times 0.07) + (£30,000 \times 0.10) = £4,900 \text{ Gross pay}$$

One other type of commission pay system involves a base salary plus tips. This method is common in restaurant settings in which servers receive between £2.50 and £5 per hour plus tips.

Businesses that pay less than minimum wage must prove that their employees make at least minimum wage when tips are accounted for. Today, that's relatively easy to prove because most people pay their bills with credit cards and include tips on their bills. Businesses can then come up with an average tip rate using that credit card data.

As an employer, you must report an employee's gross taxable wages based on salary plus tips. Here's how you calculate gross taxable wages for an employee whose earnings are based on tips and wages:

Base wage + Tips = Gross taxable wages

$$(£3 \times 40 \text{ hours per week}) + £300 = £420$$

If your employees are paid using a combination of base wage plus tips, you must be sure that they're earning at least the minimum wage rate appropriate to them (generally £5.93 per hour). Checking this employee's gross wages, the hourly rate earned is £10.50 per hour.

Hourly wage = £10.50 (£420 ÷ 40)

PAYE and NICs are calculated on the base wage plus tips, so the net payment you prepare for the employee in this example is for the total gross wage minus any taxes due.

After calculating the take-home pay for all your employees, you prepare the payroll, make the payments and post the payroll to the books. In addition to Cash, payroll impacts many accounts, including:

- ✔ **Accrued Pay As You Earn (PAYE) Payable,** which is where you record the liability for tax payments

- ✔ **Accrued National Insurance Contributions (NICs) Payable,** which is where you record the liability for NICs payments

When you post the payroll entry, you indicate the withdrawal of money from the Cash account and record liabilities for future cash payments that are due for PAYE and NICs payments. To give you an example of the proper set-up for a payroll journal entry, I assume the total payroll is £10,000 with £1,000 each set aside for PAYE and NICs payable. In reality, your numbers are sure to be very different, and your payments are likely to never all be the same. Table 11-2 shows what your journal entry for posting payroll looks like.

Table 11-2	Payroll Journal Entry for 26 May 2010	
	Debit	Credit
Gross Salaries and Wages Expense	£10,000	
Accrued PAYE Payable		£1,000
Accrued NICs Payable		£1,000
Cash (Net Payment)		£8,000

Table 11-2 shows only the entries that affect the take-home pay of the employees. The business must also make Employer National Insurance Contributions payments. Use the manual tables or the P11 Calculator on the New Employers Guide CD-ROM to calculate this amount. The Employer NIC is a cost of employment and therefore must be treated in the books in exactly the same way as Gross Salaries and Wages. Table 11-3 shows the journal entry to record Employer NICs payments.

Table 11-3	Employer NICs Expenses for May	
	Debit	Credit
Employer NICs Expense	£1,100	
Accrued Employer NICs Payable		£1,100

In this entry, you increase the Expense account for salaries and wages as well as all the accounts in which you accrue future obligations for PAYE and employee NICs payments. You decrease the amount of the Cash account; when cash payments are made for the PAYE and NICs payments in the future, you post those payments in the books. Table 11-4 shows an example of the entry posted to the books after making the PAYE withholding tax payment.

Table 11-4	Recording PAYE Payments for May	
	Debit	Credit
Accrued PAYE and NICs Payable	£3,100	
Current Account		£3,100

Settling up with HM Revenue & Customs

Every month you need to pay over to HM Revenue & Customs all the PAYE and NIC amounts you deduct from your employees. To work out what you have to pay HM Revenue & Customs, add together:

- ✔ Employee NICs
- ✔ Employer NICs
- ✔ PAYE tax
- ✔ Student loan repayments

These payments must be made to HM Revenue & Customs by the 19th of the following month if paying by cheque, or on the 22nd of the following month if paying electronically. If you employ more than 250 employees, you must make monthly electronic payments. Contact Banking Operations Cumbernauld (Tel: 01236-783361) for further help on setting up this facility. A special concession exists for small businesses to pay quarterly (5 July, 5 October, 5 January and 5 April) if the average monthly payment of PAYE and NICs is less than £1,500.

To help you keep track of these payments, HM Revenue & Customs sends you a payslip booklet in which you record details of your total payments. In addition, you're sent a P32 Employment Record to work out and record your total monthly payments.

Outsourcing Payroll and Benefits Work

If you don't want to take on payroll and benefits, you can also pay for a monthly payroll service from the software company that provides your accounting software. For example, Sage provides various levels of payroll services. The Sage payroll features include calculating earnings and deductions, printing cheques or making direct deposits, providing updates to the tax tables and supplying the data needed to complete all HM Revenue & Customs forms related to payroll. The advantage of doing payroll in-house in this manner is that you can more easily integrate payroll into the business's books.

Part IV
Preparing the Books for Year- (Or Month-) End

'I hate the end of the financial year.'

In this part . . .

*E*ventually, every accounting period comes to an end. You need to check your work and get ready to close down the period, whether at the end of a month, a quarter, or a year.

This part introduces you to the process of preparing your books for closing an accounting period. You find out about the key adjustments needed to record depreciation of your assets, such as cars and buildings. This part also shows you how to calculate and record your interest payments and income in your books.

To round off the closing process, we show you how to check your books by reconciling your cash, testing your book's balance, and making any needed adjustments or corrections.

Chapter 12

Depreciating Your Assets

. . . .

. . . .

*A*ll businesses use equipment, furnishings and vehicles that last more than a year. Any asset that has a lifespan of more than a year is called a *fixed asset*. They may last longer than other assets, but even fixed assets eventually get old and need replacing.

And because your business needs to match expenses with revenue, you don't want to *write off* (set off against profits) the full expense of a fixed asset in one year. After all, you're sure to make use of the asset for more than one year.

Imagine how bad your profit and loss statement looks when you write off the cost of a £100,000 piece of equipment in just one year. You can give the impression that your business isn't doing well. Imagine the impact on a small business – £100,000 can eat up its entire profit or maybe even put the business in the position of reporting a loss.

Instead of writing off the full amount of a fixed asset in one year, you use an accounting method called *depreciation* to write off the asset as it gets used up. In this chapter, I introduce you to the various ways you can depreciate your assets and explain how to calculate depreciation, how depreciation impacts the profit and loss statement and how to record depreciation in your books.

Defining Depreciation

You may think of depreciation as something that happens to your car as it loses value. In fact, most new cars depreciate 20 to 30 per cent or even more as soon as you drive them off the garage forecourt. But when you're talking about accounting, the definition of depreciation is a bit different.

Essentially, accountants use *depreciation* as a way to allocate the costs of a fixed asset over the period in which the asset is useable to the business. You, the bookkeeper, record the full transaction when the asset is bought, but then subtract a portion of that value as a depreciation expense each year to reduce the value of the asset gradually. Depreciation expenses don't involve the exchange of cash; they're solely done for accounting purposes. Most businesses enter depreciation expenses into the books once a year just before preparing their annual reports, but others calculate depreciation expenses monthly or quarterly.

Although you can decide how much depreciation to charge your business and thereby reduce your business profits, HM Revenue & Customs isn't quite so obliging. Instead, it gives you Capital Allowances (which are a bit like depreciation), but strict rules exist about how you can write off assets as tax-deductible expenses. I talk more about HM Revenue & Customs rules in the section 'Tackling Taxes and Depreciation', later in this chapter.

Knowing what you can and can't depreciate

Businesses don't depreciate all assets. Low-cost items or items that aren't expected to last more than one year are recorded in Expense accounts rather than Asset accounts. For example, office supplies are expense items and not depreciated, but the office copier, which you're going to use for more than one year, is recorded in the books as a fixed asset and depreciated each year.

Lifespan isn't the deciding factor for depreciation, however. Some assets that last many years suffer very low depreciation. One good example is land and buildings; you can always make use of these, so their value seldom depreciates (you always hope that property prices will go up, but they can and do go down as well). You also can't depreciate any property that you lease or rent, but if you make improvements to leased property, you can depreciate the cost of those improvements. In that case, you write off the lease or rent as an expense item and depreciate the lease improvements over their estimated useful life.

You can't depreciate any items that you use outside your business, such as your personal car or home computer. However, if you use these assets for both personal needs and business needs, you can claim a proportion of their Capital Allowances on your tax return. I talk more about this subject in the section 'Tackling Taxes and Depreciation', later in this chapter. If you drive your car a total of 12,000 miles in a year and have records showing that 6,000 of those miles were for business purposes, you can claim Capital Allowances for that car.

Figuring out the useful life of a fixed asset

You're probably wondering how you figure out the useful life of a fixed asset. Your accountant can advise you about common practice and any peculiarities of your business or trade. As one example, computer equipment is usually depreciated at a rate of 33.3 per cent per annum. However, if your computers have to be replaced every year, the appropriate depreciation rate is 100 per cent.

Table 12-1 gives you some initial guidance on common depreciation rates.

Table 12-1	Depreciation Rates for Business Assets
Life/Depreciation Rate	*Business Equipment*
40 years/2.5% per annum	Land and buildings
10 years/10% per annum	Long-life plant and machinery
5 years/20% to 4 years/25% per annum	Office furniture and fixtures, equipment, motor vehicles
3 years/33.3% per annum	Computer equipment

Delving into cost basis

In order to calculate depreciation for an asset, you need to know the cost basis of that asset. The equation for cost basis is:

Cost of the fixed asset + Disallowed VAT + Shipping and delivery costs + Installation charges + Other costs = Cost basis

✔ **Cost of the fixed asset:** What you paid for the equipment, furniture, structure, vehicle or other asset.

✔ **Disallowed Value Added Tax:** Any VAT charged on the purchase of the asset that you're unable to reclaim.

- ✔ **Shipping and delivery:** Any shipping or delivery charges you paid to get the fixed asset.

- ✔ **Installation charges:** Any charges you paid in order to have the equipment, furniture or other fixed asset installed on your business's premises.

- ✔ **Other costs:** Any other charges you need to pay to make the fixed asset usable for your business. For example, if you buy a new computer and need to set up certain hardware in order to use that computer for your business, those set-up costs can be added as part of the cost basis of the fixed asset (the computer).

Depreciating the Value of Assets

After you decide on the useful life of an asset and calculate its cost basis (see the preceding sections), you have to decide how to go about reducing the asset's value according to accounting standards.

Evaluating your depreciation options

When calculating depreciation of your assets each year, you have a choice of two main methods: Straight-Line and Reducing Balance. In this section, I explain these methods as well as the pros and cons of using each one.

Although other methods of calculating depreciation are available, for accounting purposes the two main methods are Straight-Line and Reducing Balance. Either method is acceptable, and it does not matter to HM Revenue & Customs which you use. In practice, a business chooses one method and sticks with it. Straight-Line suits those businesses that want to write off their assets more quickly.

To show you how the methods handle assets differently, I calculate the first year's depreciation expense using the purchase of a piece of equipment on 1 January 2010, with a cost basis of £25,000. I have assumed the equipment has a useful life of five years, so the annual depreciation rate is 20 per cent.

Straight-Line

When depreciating assets using the *Straight-Line method,* you spread the cost of the asset evenly over the number of years the asset is to be used. Straight-Line is the most common method used for depreciation of assets, and the easiest one to use. The formula for calculating Straight-Line depreciation is:

Cost of fixed asset × Annual depreciation rate = Annual depreciation expense

For the piece of equipment in this example, the cost basis is £25,000 and the annual depreciation rate is 20 per cent. With these figures, the calculation for finding the annual depreciation expense of this equipment based on the Straight-Line depreciation method is:

£25,000 × 20% = £5,000 per annum

Each year, the business's profit and loss statement includes £5,000 as a depreciation expense for this piece of equipment. You add this £5,000 depreciation expense to the accumulated depreciation account for this asset. This accumulated depreciation account is shown below the asset's original value on the balance sheet. You subtract the accumulated depreciation from the value of the asset to show a net asset value, which is the value remaining on the asset.

Reducing Balance

The *Reducing Balance method* of depreciation works well because it comes closest to matching the calculation of Capital Allowances, HM Revenue & Customs' version of depreciation.

The peculiarity of this method is that, unlike Straight-Line, the annual depreciation expense varies, and in theory the asset is never fully depreciated. Each year the calculated depreciation figure is deducted from the previous year's value to calculate the new brought-forward figure. As time goes on, the annual depreciation figure gets smaller and the new brought-forward figure for the asset gets gradually smaller and smaller – but the item never fully depreciates.

Using the same asset as in the preceding section at a cost of £25,000 and depreciating at an annual rate of 20 per cent, calculating depreciation using the Reducing Balance method is as follows:

Cost	25,000
First Year: depreciation (20%)	5,000
Balance	**20,000**
Second Year: depreciation (20% of £20,000)	4,000
Balance	**16,000**
Third Year: depreciation (20% of £16,000)	3,200
Balance	**12,800**
Fourth Year: depreciation (20% of £12,800)	2,560
Balance	**10,240**

And so on, for ever.

Using Sage 50 Accounts to calculate depreciation

With two different methods for depreciating your business's assets, you're probably wondering which method to use. Your accountant is the best person to answer that question. He or she can look at the way your business operates and determine which method makes the most sense for presenting your financial data.

Depreciation doesn't involve the use of cash. When talking about accounting, depreciation's purely a way to show how quickly you're using up an asset.

If you're using Sage 50 Accounts, the good news is that you don't have to calculate depreciation expense amounts manually. The Fixed Asset Record section of Sage 50 Accounts has a function called 'Depreciation Method' and 'Depreciation Rate', into which you can enter the required method and rate. When you set up your asset records on Sage 50 Accounts, you enter how you want to depreciate each asset and every month the computerised system does everything for you as part of the month-end routine. Figure 12-1 shows the Depreciation menu.

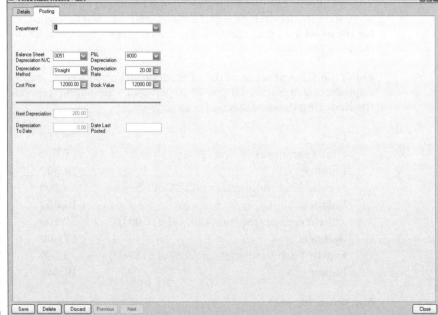

Figure 12-1:
You can enter information about your fixed assets in Sage 50 Accounts.

After you enter asset information, the system automatically calculates the depreciation expense using the Straight-Line method or the Reducing Balance method, as shown in Figure 12-2. You select the method you want to use and save the information about each asset, which you can then refer to at the end of each year when you need to record the depreciation expense for that year.

Figure 12-2:
Sage 50
Accounts
calculates
the depre-
ciation
expense
using your
chosen
method.

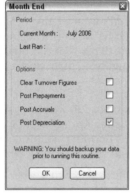

Make sure that you check on how to enter data correctly based on your system. I don't give you lengthy instructions for Sage 50 Accounts here because it depends on how you or your accountant initially set up the system.

Tackling Taxes and Depreciation

Depreciation calculations for tax purposes are a completely different animal compared with the calculations used to record depreciation for accounting purposes.

HM Revenue & Customs doesn't recognise depreciation as a valid business expense because a business can set the rates it wants for any category of asset. In an extreme example, a business may chose to depreciate 100 per cent of a very expensive computer in one year. In fact HM Revenue & Customs *adds back* your depreciation figures to your profit as their starting point for calculating your business tax bill.

The good news is that HM Revenue & Customs gives Capital Allowances instead of depreciation, which you can set off against your business profits. Capital Allowances are a simplified (just one asset categorisation) tax allowance you can offset against profits and thereby reduce your taxable profits.

HM Revenue & Customs keeps things simple. All assets are described as plant and machinery, including vans, cars, tools, furniture and computers. The only distinction is how long the items last.

You can also include items of plant and machinery that you used privately before using them in your business and items that you only partly use for business purposes.

Most businesses have an Annual Investment Allowance (AIA) of £50,000 for plant and machinery that has been purchased between the beginning of the 2008–2009 tax year and the end of the 2009–2010 tax year. Companies are able to write off 100 per cent of the cost of qualifying plant and machinery up to the value of £50,000 against their taxable profits.

Companies have been given an Annual Investment Allowance (AIA) of £100,000 for plant and machinery purchased after April 2010. For businesses whose accounting period spans the increased period, transitional rules apply. See the HM Revenue & Customs' website (www.hmrc.gov.uk) for further details.

For expenditure over this amount, the standard rate of capital allowance is 20 per cent, although other rates may apply, depending on the type of expenditure.Special rates apply for certain assets, for example, cars. Except for cars used for both business and private use, which must be allocated to a single asset pool, qualifying expenditure on cars must be allocated to one of two general plant and machinery pools:

Special-rate pool for cars with CO_2 emissions over 160 grams per kilometre. These cars have a writing-down allowance of 10 per cent per annum.

Main pool for cars with CO_2 emissions of 160 grams per kilometre or less. These cars have a writing-down allowance of 20 per cent per annum.

Note: If you buy a new, unused car that has CO_2 emissions lower than 110grams per kilometre, it qualifies for 100 per cent first-year allowance. Please refer to www.businesslink.gov.uk for detailed guidance on capital allowances, including case studies and methods of calculation.

Setting up Depreciation Schedules

In order to keep good accounting records, you need to track how much you depreciate each of your assets in some form of a schedule. After all, your financial statements only include a total value for all your assets and a total accumulated depreciation amount. Most businesses maintain depreciation schedules in some type of spreadsheet program that exists outside their accounting systems. Usually, one person is responsible for managing assets and their depreciation. However, in a large business, these tasks can turn into full-time jobs for several people.

The best way to keep track of depreciation is to prepare a separate schedule for each Asset account that you depreciate. For example, set up depreciation schedules for Buildings, Furniture and Fixtures, Office Equipment and so on. Your depreciation schedule must include all the information you need to determine annual depreciation, such as the original purchase date, original cost basis and recovery period. You can add columns to track the actual depreciation expenses and calculate the current value of each asset. Table 12-2 shows a sample depreciation schedule for vehicles.

Table 12-2	Depreciation Schedule: Vehicles			
Date Put in Service	**Description**	**Cost**	**Useful Life**	**Annual Depreciation**
1/5/2009	Black car	£30,000	5 years	£6,000
1/1/2010	Blue van	£25,000	5 years	£5,000

Depreciation can be more than just a mathematical exercise. Keeping track of depreciation is a good way to monitor the age of your assets and know when to plan for their replacement. As your assets age, they incur greater repair costs, so keeping depreciation schedules can help you plan repair and maintenance budgets as well.

Recording Depreciation Expenses

Recording a depreciation expense calls for a rather simple entry into your accounting system.

After calculating your depreciation expense, no matter which method you use, you record a depreciation expense the same way. Recording a depreciation expense of $4,000 for a vehicle (or vehicles) looks like this:

	Debit	*Credit*
Depreciation Expense	$4,000	
Accumulated Depreciation: Vehicles		$4,000

The Depreciation Expense account increases by the amount of the debit, and the Accumulated Depreciation: Vehicles account increases by the credit. On the profit and loss statement, you subtract the Depreciation Expense from Sales, and on the balance sheet, you subtract the Accumulated Depreciation: Vehicles from the value of Vehicles.

Chapter 13

Paying and Collecting Interest

· ·

· ·

*F*ew businesses can make major purchases without taking out loans. Whether the loans are for vehicles, buildings or other business needs, businesses must pay *interest,* a percentage of the amount loaned, to whoever loans them the money.

Some businesses loan their own money and receive interest payments as income. In fact, a savings account can be considered a type of loan because by placing your money in the account, you're giving the bank the opportunity to loan that money to others. So the bank pays you for the use of your money by paying interest, which is a type of income for your business.

This chapter reviews different types of loans and how to calculate and record interest expenses for each type. In addition, I discuss how you calculate and record interest income in your business's books.

Deciphering Types of Interest

Any time you make use of someone else's money, such as a bank's, you have to pay interest for that use – whether you're buying a house, a car or some other item. The same applies to someone else using your money. For example, when you buy an investment bond or deposit money in a savings account, you're paid interest for allowing the use of that money.

The financial institution with your money is likely to combine your deposit with other depositors' money and loan to other people in order to make more interest than they're paying you. Therefore, when the interest rates you have to pay on loans are low, the interest rates you can earn on savings are even lower.

Banks actually use two types of interest calculations:

- ✔ **Simple interest** is calculated only on the principal amount of the loan.

- ✔ **Compound interest** is calculated on the principal and on interest earned.

Working out simple interest

Simple interest is simple to calculate. The formula, in which n represents the number of years of the loan, is:

Principal $\times$ Interest rate $\times n$ = Interest

To show you how interest is calculated, assume that you deposit £10,000 in a savings account earning 3 per cent (0.03) interest for three years (this may seem a little optimistic at the moment, but bear with us!). The interest earned over three years is therefore:

£10,000 $\times$ 0.03 $\times$ 3 = £900

Calculating compound interest

Compound interest is computed on both the principal and any interest earned. You must calculate the interest each year and add it to the balance before you can calculate the next year's interest payment, which is based on both the principal and interest earned.

Here's how you calculate compound interest:

Principal $\times$ Interest rate = Interest for Year One

(Principal + Previous year's interest) $\times$ Interest rate = Interest for Year Two

(Principal + Previous year's interest) $\times$ Interest rate = Interest for Year Three

You repeat this calculation for every year of the deposit or loan. However, with a loan, if you pay the total interest due each month or year (depending on when your payments are due), no previous year's interest exists to compound.

To show you how compound interest impacts earnings, I now calculate the three-year deposit of £10,000 at 3 per cent (0.03):

£10,000 × 0.03 = £300 Year One interest

(£10,000 + 300) × 0.03 = £309 Year Two Interest

(£10,000 + 300 +309) × 0.03 = £318.27 Year Three Interest

Total interest earned = £927.27

You earn an extra £27.27 during the first three years of that deposit if the interest is compounded. When working with much larger sums or higher interest rates for longer periods of time, compound interest can make a big difference to how much you earn or how much you pay on a loan.

Ideally, you want to find a savings account, certificate deposit or other savings instrument that earns compound interest. But, if you want to borrow money, look for a simple interest loan.

Also, not all accounts earning compound interest are created equal. Watch carefully to see how frequently the interest is compounded. Although the preceding example shows an account for which interest is compounded annually, if you can find an account where interest is compounded monthly, the interest you earn is even higher. Monthly compounding means that interest earned is calculated each month and added to the principal each month before calculating the next month's interest, which results in a lot more interest than an account that compounds interest just once a year.

Handling Interest Income

The income your business earns from its savings accounts, certificates of deposits or other investment vehicles is called *Interest Income*. As the bookkeeper, you're rarely required to calculate interest income using the simple interest or compounded interest formulas described in the preceding sections. In most cases, the financial institution sends you a monthly, quarterly or annual statement with a separate line item reporting interest earned.

When you get your statement, you then reconcile the books. *Reconciliation* is a process in which you prove whether the amount the bank says you have in your account is equal to what you think you have in your account.

I talk more about reconciling bank accounts in Chapter 14. The reason I mention it now is that the first step in the reconciliation process involves recording any interest earned or bank fees in the books so that your balance matches what the bank shows. Figure 13-1 shows you how to record £15 in Interest Income.

© 2010 Sage (UK) Limited. All rights reserved.

If you're keeping the books manually, a journal entry to record interest looks similar to this:

	Debit	**Credit**
Cash	£15	
Interest Income		£15

To record interest income from HSBC Bank.

When preparing financial statements, you show Interest Income on the profit and loss statement (see Chapter 18 for more information about the profit and loss statement) in a section called Other Income. Other Income includes any income your business earned that was not directly related to your primary business activity – selling your goods or services.

Delving into Loans and Interest Expenses

Businesses borrow money for both *short-term periods* (periods of less than 12 months) and *long-term periods* (periods of more than one year). Short-term debt usually involves some form of credit card debt or overdraft. Long-term debt can include a five-year car loan, 20-year mortgage or any other type of debt paid over more than a year.

Writing up short-term debt

Any money due in the next 12-month period is shown on the balance sheet as short-term or current liability. Any interest paid on that money is shown as an Interest Expense on the profit and loss statement.

In most cases, you don't have to calculate your interest due. The financial institution sends you a bill giving you a breakdown of the principal and interest to be paid.

Looking at how credit card interest is calculated

The credit card bill you receive at home contains lines showing you new charges, the amount to pay in full to avoid all interest and the amount of interest charged during the current period on any money not paid from the previous bill. If you don't pay your balance in full, interest on most cards is calculated using a daily periodic rate of interest, which is compounded each day based on the unpaid balance. Yes, credit cards charge a type of compound interest. When not paid in full, interest is calculated on the unpaid principal balance plus any unpaid interest. Table 13-1 shows what a typical interest calculation looks like on a credit card.

Table 13-1	Credit Card Interest Calculation				
				Finance Charges	
	Average Daily Balance	Daily Periodic Rate	Corresponding Annual Rate	Daily Rate	Transaction Fees
Purchases	£500	0.034076%	12.40%	£5.28	£0
Cash	£1,000	0.0452%	16.49%	£14.01	£25

On many credit cards, you start paying interest on new purchases immediately, if you haven't paid your balance due in full the previous month. When opening a credit card account for your business, ensure that you understand how interest is calculated and when the bank starts charging on new purchases. Some credit card companies give a grace period of 20 to 30 days before charging interest, but others don't give any grace period at all.

In Table 13-1, the Finance Charges include the daily rate charged in interest based on the daily periodic rate plus any transaction fees. For example, if you take a cash advance from your credit card, many credit card companies charge a transaction fee of 2 to 3 per cent of the total amount of cash taken. This fee can also apply when you transfer balances from one credit card to another. Although the credit card company entices you with an introductory rate of 1 or 2 per cent to get you to transfer the balance, make sure that you read the fine print. You may have to pay a 3 per cent transaction fee on the full amount transferred, which makes the introductory rate much higher.

Using bank loans

As a small-business owner, you get better interest rates using a bank loan rather than a credit card. Interest rates are usually lower on loans. Typically, you use a credit card for purchases, but if you can't pay the bill in full, you utilise your bank loan rather than carry over the credit card balance.

When the money is first received from the bank, you record the cash receipt and the liability. Just to show you how this transaction works, I record the receipt of a bank loan of £1,500. Here is what the journal entry looks like:

	Debit	*Credit*
Cash	£1,500	
Bank Loan		£1,500

To record receipt of cash from bank loan.

In this entry, you increase the Cash account and the Bank Loan account balances. If you're using a computerised accounting program, you record the transaction as a bank receipt, as shown in Figure 13-2.

When you make your first payment, you must record the use of cash, the amount paid on the principal of the loan and the amount paid in interest. That journal entry looks like this:

	Debit	*Credit*
Bank Loan	£150	
Interest Expense	£10	
Cash		£160

To make monthly payment on bank loan.

This journal entry reduces the amount due in the Bank Loan account, increases the amount paid in the Interest Expense account and reduces the amount in the Cash account.

If you're using a computerised system, you enter the transaction as a Bank Payment, making sure that you select the appropriate bank account. The system updates the accounts automatically. Figure 13-3 shows you how to record a loan payment in Sage 50 Accounts.

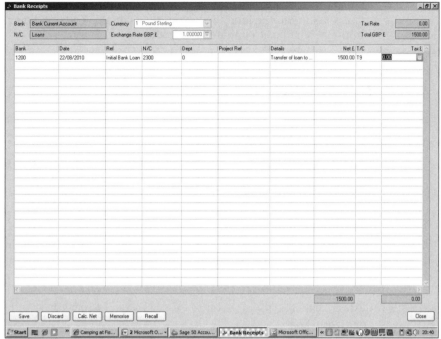

Figure 13-2:
Recording
receipt of
cash from a
bank loan.

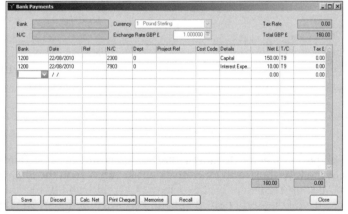

Figure 13-3:
Recording
a loan pay-
ment in
Sage 50
Accounts.

As shown in Figure 13-3, you can enter the accounts that the payment
impacts by splitting the detailed expense information. You indicate that £150
of that payment needs to be recorded in the Bank Loan account and £10

needs to be recorded as Interest Income. Sage 50 Accounts then posts the relevant amounts to the identified expense accounts. You don't need to do any additional postings to update your books.

Looking at long-term debt

Most businesses take on some form of debt that is to be paid over a period of time longer than 12 months. This debt may include car loans, mortgages or promissory notes. A *promissory note* is a written agreement in which you agree to repay someone a set amount of money at some point in the future at a particular interest rate, which can be monthly, yearly or some other term specified in the note. Most instalment loans are types of promissory notes.

Recording a debt

When the business first takes on the debt, you record that debt in the books in much the same way as a short-term debt:

	Debit	*Credit*
Cash	£10,000	
Long-Term Loan		£10,000

To record receipt of cash from Barclays Bank.

Payments are also recorded in a manner similar to short-term debt:

	Debit	*Credit*
Long-Term Loan	£75	
Interest Expense	£30	
Cash		£105

To record payment on Barclays Bank Loan.

You record the initial long-term debt and make payments the same way in Sage 50 Accounts as you do for short-term debt.

Although how you enter the initial information is similar, a big difference exists in the way short- and long-term debt are shown on the financial statements. All short-term debt is shown in the Current Liability section of the balance sheet. Long-term debt is split and shown in different line items. The portion of the debt due in the next 12 months is shown in the Current Liability section, which is usually a line item named something like 'Current Portion of Long-Term Debt'. The remaining balance of the long-term debt due beyond the next 12 months appears in the Long-Term Liability section of the balance sheet as Loans.

Making major purchases and taking on long-term debt

Sometimes a long-term liability is set up at the same time as you make a major purchase. You may pay some portion of the amount due in cash as a down-payment and the remainder as a loan. To show you how to record such a transaction, I assume that a business has purchased a van for £25,000, made a down-payment of £5,000 and borrowed the balance at an interest rate of 6 per cent. Here's how you record this purchase in the books:

	Debit	*Credit*
Vehicles	£25,000	
Cash		£5,000
Bank Loan – Vehicles		£20,000

To record payment for the purchase of the blue van.

You then record payments on the loan in the same way as any other loan payment:

	Debit	*Credit*
Bank Loan – Vehicles	£1,000	
Interest Expense	£250	
Cash		£1,250

To record payment for the purchase of the blue van.

When recording the payment on a long-term debt for which you have a set instalment payment, you may not get a breakdown of interest and principal with every payment. For example, often when you take out a car loan, you get an agreement with just the total payment due each month. Each payment includes both principal and interest, but you don't get any breakdown detailing how much goes towards interest and how much goes towards principal.

Let's assume that you know the split between interest and capital; here is how you record it in the books.

	Debit	*Credit*
Bank Loan – Vehicles	286.66	
Interest Expense	100.00	
Cash		386.66

To record payment on loan for blue van.

Chapter 14

Checking the Books

. . . .

. . . .

*A*ll business owners – whether the business is a small family-owned shop or a major international conglomerate – periodically like to test how well their businesses are doing. They also want to make sure that the numbers in their accounting systems actually match what's physically in their shops and offices. After they check out what's in the books, these business owners can prepare financial reports to determine the business's financial success or failure during the last month, quarter or year. This process of verifying the accuracy of your books is called *checking the books*.

The first step in checking the books involves counting the business's cash and verifying that the cash numbers in your books match the actual cash on hand at a particular point in time. This chapter explains how you can test that the cash counts are accurate, finalise the cash books for the accounting period, reconcile the bank accounts and post any adjustments or corrections to the Nominal Ledger.

Checking the Books: Why Bother?

You're probably thinking that checking the books sounds like a huge task that takes lots of time. And you're right – but checking the books every now and then is essential to ensure that what's recorded in your accounting system realistically measures what's actually going on in your business.

Mistakes can be made with any accounting system and, unfortunately, any business can fall victim to theft or embezzlement. The only way to be sure that none of these problems exist in your business is to check the books periodically. Most businesses do this every month.

The process of checking the books is a big part of the accounting cycle, which I discuss in detail in Chapter 2. The first three steps of the accounting cycle – recording transactions, making journal entries and posting summaries of those entries to the Nominal Ledger – involve following the flow of cash throughout the accounting period. All three steps are part of the process of recording a business's financial activities throughout the entire accounting period. The rest of the steps in the accounting cycle are conducted at the end of the period and are part of the process of checking the accuracy of your books. They include running a trial balance (see Chapter 16), creating a worksheet (see Chapter 16), adjusting journal entries (see Chapter 17), creating financial statements (see Chapters 18 and 19) and closing the books (see Chapter 21).

Of course, you don't want to shut down your business for a week while you check the books, so select a day during each accounting period on which to take a financial snapshot of the state of your accounts. For example, if you prepare monthly financial reports at the end of the month, count the amount of cash your business has on hand as of that certain time and day, such as 6 p.m. on the last day of the month after your business closes for the day. The rest of the testing process – running a trial balance, creating a worksheet, adjusting journal entries, creating financial statements and closing the books – is based on what happened before that point in time. When you open the next day and sell more products and buy new things to run your business, those transactions and any others that follow the point in time of your cash count become part of the next accounting cycle.

Making Sure that the Closing Cash Is Right

Checking your books starts with counting your cash. Why start with cash? Because the accounting process starts with transactions, and transactions occur when cash changes hands to buy things you need to run the business or to sell your products or services. Before you can even begin to test whether the books are right, you need to know if your books have captured what's happened to your business's cash and if the amount of cash shown in your books actually matches the amount of cash you have on hand.

I'm sure that you've heard the well-worn expression, 'Show me the money!' Well, in business, that idea is the core of your success. Everything relies on the cash profits you can take out of your business or use to expand your business.

In Chapter 10, I discuss how a business cashes up the money taken in by each cashier. That daily process gives a business good control of the point at which cash comes into the business from customers who buy the business's products or services. The process also measures any cash refunds given to customers who returned items.

The points of sale and return aren't the only times that cash comes into or goes out of the business. If your business sells products on credit (see Chapter 10), bookkeeping staff responsible for monitoring customer credit accounts collect some of the cash from customers at a later point in time. And when your business needs something, whether products to be sold or supplies for various departments, you must pay cash to suppliers and contractors. Sometimes cash is paid out on the spot, but often the bill is recorded in the Trade Creditors (Accounts Payable) account and paid at a later date. All these transactions involve the use of cash, so the amount of cash on hand in the business at any one time includes not only what's in the cash registers, but also what's on deposit in the business's bank accounts. You need to know the balances of those accounts and test those balances to ensure that they're accurate and match what's in your business's books. I talk more about how to do that in the section 'Reconciling Bank Accounts', later in this chapter.

So your snapshot in time includes not only the cash on hand in your cash registers, but also any cash you may have in the bank. Some departments may also have petty cash accounts, which you count as well. The total cash figure is what you show as an asset named 'Cash' in your business's financial statement, the _balance sheet._ The balance sheet shows all that the business owns (its assets) and owes (its liabilities) as well as the capital the owners have in the business. (I talk more about the balance sheet and how you prepare one in Chapter 19.)

The actual cash you have on hand is just one tiny piece of the cash moving through your business during the accounting period. Your cash books contain the full details of the cash that flowed into and out of the business. Closing those journals is the next step in the process of figuring out how well your business did.

Closing the Cash Books

As I explain in Chapter 5, if you keep the books manually, you can find a record of every transaction that involves cash in one of two cash books: the Cash Receipts book (cash that comes into the business) and the Cash Payments book (cash that goes out of the business). If you use a computerised accounting system, you don't have these cash books, but you have many different ways to find out the same detailed information. You can run reports of sales by customer, by item or by sales representative.

Figure 14-1 shows the types of sales reports Sage 50 Accounts can automatically generate for you. You can also run reports that show you all the business's purchases by supplier, how much you owe any particular supplier, how much you bought so far this year from each supplier and a lot more. Figure 14-2 shows the various purchase reports that Sage 50 Accounts can automatically run for you. These reports can be run by the week, the month, the quarter or the year, or you can customise the reports to show a particular period of time that you're analysing. For example, if you want to know what sales occurred between 5 June and 10 June, you can run a report specifying those exact dates.

Figure 14-1:
Generate reports using Sage 50 Accounts that show your business's top customers, those owing you money, disputed invoices or items sold.

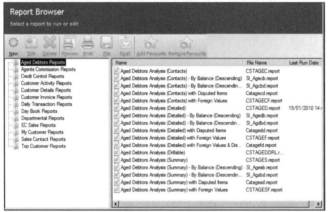

Figure 14-2:
Using Sage 50 Accounts, you can produce reports showing your business's cash payments by supplier or by items bought.

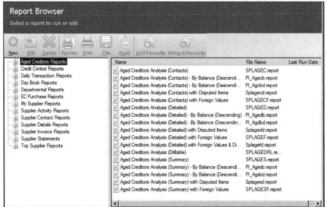

Finalising cash receipts

If your books are up to date, when you summarise the Cash Receipts book on whatever day and time you choose to check them, the result should be a total of all cash received by the business at that time. Unfortunately, in the real world of bookkeeping, things don't always come out so nice and neat. In fact, you probably don't even start entering the transactions from that particular day into the books until the next day, when you enter the cash reports from all cashiers and others who handle incoming cash (such as the Trade Debtors staff who collect money from customers buying on credit) into the Cash Receipts book.

After entering all the transactions from the day in question, the books for the period you're looking at may still be incomplete. Sometimes, adjustments or corrections must be made to the closing cash numbers. For example, monthly credit card fees and interest received from the bank may not yet be recorded in your cash books. As the bookkeeper, you must make sure that all bank fees related to cash receipts as well as any interest earned are recorded in the Cash Receipts book before you summarise the journals for the period you're analysing.

Remembering credit card fees

When your business allows customers to use credit cards, you must pay fees to the bank that processes these transactions, which is probably the same bank that handles all your business accounts. These fees actually lower the amount you take in as cash receipts, so the amount you record as a cash receipt must be adjusted to reflect those costs of doing business. Monthly credit card fees vary greatly depending upon the bank you're using, but here are some of the most common fees your business may be charged:

- ✔ **Address verification service (AVS) fee** is a fee businesses pay if they want to avoid accepting fraudulent credit card sales. This provides a means of comparing the address given by the shopper against the address held by the credit card company. Banks charge this fee for every verified transaction.

- ✔ **Discount rate** is a fee all businesses using credit cards must pay, based on a percentage of the sale or return transaction. The rate your business may be charged varies greatly depending on the type of business you conduct and the volume of your monthly sales. Businesses that use a terminal to swipe cards and electronically send transaction information usually pay lower fees than businesses that use paper credit card transactions, because the electronic route creates less work for the bank and eliminates the possibility of key-entry errors by employees.

✔ **Secure payment gateway fee,** which allows the merchant to process transactions securely, is charged to businesses that transact business over the Internet. If your business sells products online, you can expect to pay this fee based on a set monthly amount.

✔ **Customer support fee** is charged to businesses that want 24 hours a day, 365 days a year, bank support for credit card transactions. Businesses such as mail-order catalogues that allow customers to place orders 24 hours a day look for this support. Sometimes businesses even want this support in more than one language if they sell products internationally.

✔ **Monthly minimum fee** is the least a business is required to pay for the ability to offer its customers the convenience of using credit cards to buy products. This fee usually varies between £10 and £30 per month.

✔ Even if your business doesn't generate any credit card sales during a month, you're still required to pay this minimum fee. As long as enough sales are generated to cover the fee, you shouldn't have a problem. For example, if the fee is £10 and your business pays 2 per cent per sale in discount fees, you need to sell at least £500 worth of products each month to cover that £10 fee. When deciding whether to accept credit cards as a payment option, ensure that you're going to generate enough business through credit card sales to cover that fee. If not, you may find that accepting credit cards costs you more than the sales you generate by offering that convenience.

✔ **Transaction fee** is a standard fee charged to your business for each credit card transaction you submit for authorisation. You pay this fee even if the cardholder is denied and you lose the sale.

✔ **Equipment and software fees** are charged to your business based on the equipment and computer software you use in order to process credit card transactions. You have the option of buying or leasing credit card equipment and related software.

✔ **Chargeback and retrieval fees** are charged if a customer disputes a transaction.

When deciding whether to accept credit cards as a form of payment, you must consider what your competition is doing. When all your competitors offer the convenience of using credit cards and you don't, you may lose sales if customers take their business elsewhere.

Reconciling your credit card statements

Each month, the bank that handles your credit card sales sends you a statement listing:

✔ All your business's transactions for the month

✔ The total amount your business sold through credit card sales

✔ The total fees charged to your account

If you find a difference between what the bank reports was sold on credit cards and what the business's books show regarding credit card sales, you need to play detective and find the reason for the difference. In most cases, the error involves the charging back of one or more sales because a customer disputes the charge. In this case, the Cash Receipts book is adjusted to reflect that loss of sale, and the bank statement and business books match up.

For example, suppose £200 in credit card sales were disputed. The original entry of the transaction in the books looks like this:

	Debit	**Credit**
Sales	£200	
Cash		£200

To reverse disputed credit sales recorded in June.

This entry reduces the total Sales for the month as well as the amount of the Cash account. If the dispute is resolved and the money is later retrieved, the sale is then re-entered when the cash is received.

You also record any fees related to credit card fees in the Cash Payments book. For example, if credit card fees for the month of June total £200, the entry in the books looks like this:

	Debit	**Credit**
Credit Card Fees	£200	
Cash		£200

To post credit card fees for the month of June.

Summarising the Cash Receipts book

When you're sure that all cash receipts as well as any corrections or adjustments to those receipts are properly entered in the books (see the previous two sections), you summarise the Cash Receipts book as explained in detail in Chapter 5. After summarising the Cash Receipts book for the accounting period you're analysing, you know the total cash that was taken into the business from sales as well as from other channels.

In the Cash Receipts book, sales usually appear in two columns:

✔ **Sales:** The cash shown in the Sales column is cash received when the customer purchases the goods using cash, cheque or bank credit card.

✔ **Trade Debtors:** The Trade Debtors column is for sales in which no cash was received when the customer purchased the item. Instead, the customer bought on credit and intends to pay cash at a later date. (Trade Debtors and collecting money from customers is covered in Chapter 10.)

After you add all receipts to the Cash Receipts book, entries for items bought on credit can be posted to the Trade Debtors journal and the individual customer accounts. You then send bills to customers that reflect all transactions from the month just closed as well as any payments still due from previous months. Billing customers is a key part of the closing process that occurs each month.

In addition to the Sales and Trade Debtors columns, your Cash Receipts book needs at least two other columns:

✔ **General:** The General column lists all other cash received, such as owner investments in the business.

✔ **Cash:** The Cash column contains the total of all cash received by the business during an accounting period.

Finalising cash outlays

After you close the Cash Receipts book (see the preceding section), the next step is to close the Cash Payments book. Any adjustments related to outgoing cash receipts, such as bank credit card fees, must be added to the Cash Payments book.

Before you close the book, be certain that any bills paid at the end of the month have been added to the Cash Payments book.

Bills that are related to financial activity for the month being closed but that haven't yet been received have to be *accrued,* which means recorded in the books, so that they can be matched to the revenue for the month. These accruals are necessary only if you use the accrual accounting method. If you use the cash-based accounting method, you need to record the bills only when cash is actually paid. For more on the accrual and cash-based methods, flip to Chapter 2.

You accrue bills yet to be received. For example, suppose that your business prints and mails flyers to advertise a sale during the last week of the month. A bill for the flyers totalling £500 hasn't been received yet. Here's how you enter the bill in the books:

	Debit	*Credit*
Advertising	£500	
Accruals		£500

To accrue the bill from Jack's Printing for June sales flyers.

This entry increases advertising expenses for the month and increases the amount due in the Accruals account. When you receive and pay the bill later, the Accruals account is debited rather than the Advertising account (to reduce the liability), and the Cash account is credited (to reduce the amount in the Cash account). You make the actual entry in the Cash Payments book when the cash is paid out.

When checking out the cash, also review any accounts in which expenses are accrued for later payment, such as Value Added Tax Collected, to ensure that all accrual accounts are up to date. This tax account is actually a Liability account for taxes that need to be paid in the future. If you use the accrual accounting method, the expenses related to these taxes must be matched to the revenues collected for the month in which they're incurred.

Using a Temporary Posting Journal

Some businesses use a Temporary Posting journal to record payments made without full knowledge of how the cash outlay is to be posted to the books and which accounts are impacted. For example, a business using a payroll service probably has to give that service a certain amount of cash to cover payroll even if the amount needed for taxes and other payroll-related costs is not yet known.

In this payroll example, cash must be paid, but transactions can't be entered into all affected accounts until the payroll is done. Suppose a business's payroll is estimated to cost £15,000 for the month of May. The business sends a cheque to cover that cost to the payroll service and posts the payment to the Temporary Posting journal, and after the payroll is calculated and completed, the business receives a statement of exactly how much was paid to employees and how much was paid in taxes. After the statement arrives, allocating the £15,000 to specific accounts such as Payroll Expenses or Pay As You Earn Tax, the information is posted to the Cash Payments book.

If you decide to keep a Temporary Posting journal to monitor cash coming in or going out, before summarising your Cash Payments book and closing the books for an accounting period, make sure that you review the transactions listed in this Temporary Posting journal that may need posting in the Cash Payments book.

Reconciling Bank Accounts

Part of checking out the cash involves checking that what you have in your bank accounts actually matches what the bank thinks you have in those accounts. This process is called *reconciling* the accounts.

Before you tackle reconciling your accounts with the bank's records, make sure that you've made all necessary adjustments to your books. When you make adjustments to your cash accounts, you identify and correct any cash transactions that may not have been properly entered into the books. You also make adjustments to reflect interest income or payments, bank fees and credit card chargebacks.

If you've done everything right, your accounting records match the bank's records of how much cash you have in your accounts. The day you close your books probably isn't the same date as the bank sends its statements, so do your best at balancing the books internally without actually reconciling your bank account. Correcting any problems during the process minimises problems you may face reconciling the cash accounts when that bank statement actually arrives.

You've probably reconciled your personal bank account at least a few times over the years, and the good news is that reconciling business accounts is a similar process. Table 14-1 shows one common format for reconciling your bank account:

Table 14-1	Bank Reconciliation			
Transactions	*Beginning Balance*	*Deposits*	*Disbursements*	*Ending Balance*
Balance per bank statement	£	£	£	£
Deposits in transit (those not shown on statement)		£		£
Outstanding cheques (cheques that haven't shown up yet)			(£)	(£)
Total	£	£	£	£
Balance per cash book or bank account (which should be the same)				£

Tracking down errors

Ideally, your balance and the bank's balance, adjusted by transactions not yet shown on the statement, match. If they don't, you need to find out why.

✔ **If the bank balance is higher than your balance,** check to ensure that all the deposits listed by the bank appear in the Cash account in your books. If you find that the bank lists a deposit that you don't have, you need to do some detective work to work out what that deposit was for and add the detail to your accounting records. Also, check to make sure that all cheques you have issued have cleared. Your balance may be missing a cheque that should have been listed in outstanding cheques.

✔ **If the bank balance is lower than your balance,** check to ensure that all cheques listed by the bank are recorded in your Cash account. You may have missed one or two cheques that were written but not properly recorded. You also may have missed a deposit that you have listed in your Cash account and thought the bank should already have shown as a deposit, but that isn't yet on the statement. If you notice a missing deposit on the bank statement, make sure that you have your proof of deposit and check with the bank to ensure that the cash is in the account.

✔ **If all deposits and cheques are correct but you still see a difference,** your only option is to check your maths and make sure that all cheques and deposits were entered correctly.

Sometimes, you have to decide whether rooting out every little difference is really worthwhile. When the amount is just a few pence, don't waste your time trying to find the error, just adjust the balance in your books. But when the difference is a significant amount for your business, try to track it down. You never know exactly what accounts are impacted by an error or how that difference may impact your profit or loss.

Using a computerised system

If you use a computerised accounting system, reconciliation is much easier than if you keep your books manually. In Sage 50 Accounts, for example, when you start the reconciliation process, a screen pops up in which you can add the ending bank statement balance and any bank fees or interest earned. Figure 14-3 shows you that screen. In this example, £149,996.82 is the ending balance and bank fees are £10. (The bank fees are automatically added to the Bank Charges Expense account.)

Figure 14-3: When you start the reconciliation process in Sage 50 Accounts, you indicate the bank's ending balance and any bank service charges or interest earned on a particular account.

After you click OK, you get a screen that lists all cheques written since the last reconciliation as well as all deposits. Double-click on all the items listed in the top part of your Sage screen that are also shown on your bank statement, as in Figure 14-4. Ensure that the matched balance and the statement balance are the same and the difference is zero (see the bottom right corner of the Sage screen), and then click Reconcile.

Figure 14-4: To reconcile cheques using Sage 50 Accounts, double-click all the cheques and deposits that have cleared the account and click Reconcile.

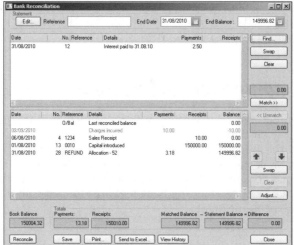

If you enter a Statement Reference in your statement summary, as shown in Figure 14-3, Sage 50 Accounts automatically provides a Bank Reconciliation report, which it saves as a PDF file in the History archive. This report is shown in Figure 14-5. You can also run reports showing unreconciled items at the month-end.

Date: 08/09/2010   **Page:** 1

Time: 12:54:10   **Bank Reconciliation**

1200
Bank Current Account
Currency: Pound Sterling

Bank Balance: £ 99784.32

Figure 14-5:
After reconciling your accounts, Sage 50 Accounts automatically provides a Bank Reconciliation report.

Statement Ref: August 2010   **Statement Date:** 31/08/2010   **Reconciliation Date:** 08/09/2010

Date	Ref.	Details	Payments	Receipts
		Opening Balance	10.00	
08/09/2010		Charges incurred		150,000.00
01/08/2010	0010.	Capital introduced	3.18	
31/08/2010	REFUND	Allocation – 52		10.00
06/08/2010	1234	Sales Receipt		
		Totals:	13.18	150,010.00
		Closing Balance:		149996.82

Posting Adjustments and Corrections

After you close out the Cash Receipts and Cash Payments books as well as reconcile the bank account with your accounting system, you post any adjustments or corrections that you uncover to any other journals the change impacts, such as the Trade Debtors or Trade Creditors. If you make changes that don't impact any journal accounts, you post them directly to the Nominal Ledger.

For example, when you find that several customer payments haven't been entered in the Cash Receipts book, post those payments to the Trade Debtors journal and the customers' accounts. The same is true when you find payments on outstanding bills that haven't been entered into the books. In this case, post the payments to the Trade Creditors journal as well as to the individual suppliers' accounts.

Chapter 15

Closing the Journals

In This Chapter

▶ Making sure that your journals are correct

▶ Gathering journal information for closing

▶ Posting adjustments to the Nominal Ledger

▶ Examining your journals in a computerised system

*A*s the old saying goes, 'The devil is in the detail.' And when it comes to your bookkeeping – especially if you keep your books manually – the small details that can catch you out are in the journals you keep.

This chapter focuses primarily on how to check your journals and close them at the end of an accounting period. (Chapter 14 looks at this process for Cash books in particular, if you're interested.) You also find out how to post all corrections and adjustments to the Nominal Ledger after you make them in the appropriate journal. (To find out how to set up your journals, flip to Chapter 5.)

You don't need to close your journals if you use a computerised accounting system to do your books. But running a series of reports to verify that all the information in the computer accounting system matches what you have on paper is a good idea, and so I talk briefly about how to do this as well.

Prepping to Close: Checking for Accuracy and Tallying Things Up

As you prepare to close the books, you first need to total what is in your journals, a process called *summarising the journals*. As you do this summarising, keep a look out for blatant errors and ensure that the entries accurately reflect the transactions during the accounting period.

Even the smallest error in a journal can cause a lot of frustration when you try to run a trial balance and close your books, so make sure that you do a thorough search for errors as you close each journal for the month. Finding an error at this point in the closing process is much easier than trying to track it back through all your various accounts.

Paying attention to initial transaction details

Do a quick check to ensure that the transaction details in your journals are accurate. Chapter 14 tells you how to do this type of check with the Cash books, but when you follow the rules of accrual accounting, not all transactions involve cash. In accrual accounting, non-cash transactions can include customer purchases made on credit, which you record in the Trade Debtors (Accounts Receivable) journal and bills you're going to pay in the future, which you record in the Trade Creditors (Accounts Payable) journal. You may also have created other journals to record transactions in your most active accounts, and you probably also keep details about sales in the Sales journal and payroll in the Payroll journal.

In the Payroll journal, make sure that all payrolls for the month have been added with all the proper details about salaries, wages and taxes. Also verify that you've recorded all employment taxes that need to be paid. These taxes include the employer's portion of Pay As You Earn (PAYE) and National Insurance. (I talk more about employer tax obligations in Chapter 11.)

Summarising journal entries

The first step in checking for accuracy in your journals is summarising them (as I explain in Chapter 5), which is primarily totalling all the columns in the journal. This summary process gives you totals for the accounts being recorded by each journal. For example, summarising the Trade Debtors journal gives you a grand total of all transactions for that period that involved customer credit accounts. Figure 15-1 shows a summary of a Trade Debtors journal.

The Trade Debtors journal includes transactions from the Sales journal (where customer purchases on credit first appear) and the Cash Receipts book (where customers' payments toward their credit accounts first appear) as well as any credit memos for customer returns. The example in Figure 15-1 is only a few lines long, but in most businesses the Trade Debtors journal is very active with transactions posted every day that the business is open during the month. When you summarise the Trade Debtors journal, you get a *closing balance,* which shows the total of all financial activity recorded in that journal. Figure 15-1 shows a closing balance of £2,240, which is the amount outstanding from customers.

	Rachel & Zoe's Sewing Shop								
	Debtors								
	June 2010								
Date	Description		Ref. No.	Debit	Credit				Balance
1/6	Opening Balance								2,000 —
30/6	From Cash Receipts Jnl		Jnl Page 1		500 —				
30/6	From Sales Jnl		Jnl Page 3	800 —					
3/6	Credit Memo 124 Gen. Jnl		Jnl Page 5		60 —				
	Closing Balance								2,240 —

Figure 15-1:
A sample of the Trade Debtors journal summary.

Each transaction in the journal needs to have a reference number next to it to tell you where the detail for that transaction first appears in the books. You may need to review this information later when you're checking the books. When you check for errors in the journal, you may need to review the original source information used to enter some transactions in order to double-check that entry's accuracy.

In addition to the Trade Debtors journal, you also have individual journal pages for each customer; these pages detail each customer's purchases on credit and any payments made toward those purchases. At the end of an accounting period, prepare an *Aged Debtor Report* detailing all outstanding customer accounts. This report shows you how much money is due from customers and for how long. (I talk more about managing customer accounts in Chapter 10.)

For the purpose of checking the books, the Aged Debtor Report is a quick summary that ensures that the customer accounts information matches what's in the Trade Debtors journal. Table 15-1 shows what an Aged Debtor Report looks like for the time period.

Table 15-1	Aged Debtor Report: Trade Debtors as of 31 March 2010			
Customer	*Current*	*31–60 Days*	*61–90 Days*	*>90 Days*
H. Harris	£500	£240		
Mrs Jolly	£100	£300	£200	
M. Man	£400	£200		
S. Smith	£300			
Total	**£1,300**	**£740**	**£200**	

In this sample Aged Debtor Report, the total amount outstanding from customers matches the balance total in the Trade Debtors journal. Therefore, all customer accounts have been accurately entered in the books, and the bookkeeper needn't encounter any errors related to customer accounts when running a trial balance, which I explain in Chapter 16.

If you find a difference between the information in your journal and your Aged Debtor Report, review your customer account transactions to find the problem. An error may be the result of:

✔ Recording a sales transaction without recording the details of that transaction in the customer's account

✔ Recording a sale directly into the customer's account without adding the sales amount to the Trade Debtors journal

✔ Recording a customer's payment in the customer's account without recording the cash receipt in the Trade Debtors journal

✔ Recording a customer's payment in the Trade Debtors journal without recording the cash receipt in the customer's account record

The process of summarising and closing the Trade Creditors journal is similar to that of the Trade Debtors journal. For Trade Creditors, you can prepare an Aged Creditor Report for your outstanding bills as well. That summary looks something like Table 15-2.

Table 15-2	Aged Creditor Report: Trade Creditors as of 31 March 2010			
Supplier	**Current**	**31–60 Days**	**61–90 Days**	**>90 Days**
Barclays Bank	£150			
Carol's Estate Agents	£800			
Helen's Paper Goods		£250		
Henry's Bakery Supplies		£500		
Plates Unlimited	£400	£200		
Total	£1,350	£950		

The total of outstanding bills on the Aged Creditor Report needs to match the total shown on the Trade Creditors journal summary for the accounting period. If yours match, you're ready for a trial balance. If they don't, you must work out the reason for the difference before closing the Trade Creditors journal. The problem may be the result of:

✔ Recording a bill due in the Trade Creditors journal without recording it in the supplier's account

✔ Recording a bill due in the supplier's account without recording it in the Trade Creditors journal

✔ Making a payment to the supplier without recording it in the Trade Creditors journal

✔ Making a payment to the supplier and recording it in the Trade Creditors journal but neglecting to record it in the supplier's account

Correct any problems you find before closing the journal. If you know that you may be working with incorrect data, you don't want to do a trial balance because you know that balance is going to be filled with errors and you're going to be able to generate accurate financial reports. Also, if you know that errors exist, the books don't balance anyway, so doing a trial balance is just a wasted exercise.

Analysing summary results

You may be wondering how you can find problems in your records by just reviewing a page in a journal. Well, that skill comes with experience and practice. As you summarise your journals each month, you become familiar with the expected level of transactions and the types of transaction that occur month after month. If you don't see a transaction that you expect to find, take the time to investigate the transaction to find out why. The transaction may not have taken place, but equally someone may have forgotten to record it.

For example, suppose that when summarising the Payroll journal, you notice that the payroll for the 15th of the month seems lower than normal. As you check your details for that payroll, you find that the amount paid to hourly employees was recorded, but someone didn't record the amount paid to salaried employees. For that particular payroll, the payroll company experienced a computer problem after running some salary cheques and as a result sent the final report on two separate pages. The person who recorded the payroll numbers didn't know about the separate page for salaried employees, so the final numbers entered into the books didn't reflect the full amount paid to employees.

As you close the books each month, you get an idea of the numbers you can expect for each type of journal. After a while, you can pick out problems just by scanning a page – no detailed investigation required!

Planning for cash flow

The process you go through each month as you prepare to close your books helps you plan for future cash flow. Reviewing the Aged Debtor Report and Aged Creditor Report tells you what additional cash you can expect from customers during the next few months and how much cash you need in order to pay bills for the next few months.

If you notice that your Aged Creditor Report indicates that more and more bills are slipping into past-due status, you may need to find another source for cash, such as an overdraft facility from the bank. For example, the Aged Creditor Report reveals that three key suppliers – Helen's Paper Goods, Henry's Bakery Supplies and Plates Unlimited – haven't been paid on time. Late payments can hurt your business's working relationship with suppliers, who may refuse to deliver goods unless cash is paid upfront. And if you can't get the raw materials you need, you may have trouble filling customer orders on time. The lesson here is to act quickly and find a way to improve cash flow before your suppliers put you on stop. (For more on Trade Creditor management, check out Chapter 9.)

You may also find that your Aged Debtor Report reveals that certain previously good customers are gradually becoming slow or non-paying customers. For example, some portion of Mrs Jolly's account is overdue by more than 60 days. The bookkeeper dealing with these accounts may need to consider putting that account on stop until payment is received in full. (For more on Trade Debtors management, check out Chapter 10.)

Posting to the Nominal Ledger

An important part of closing your books is posting to the Nominal Ledger any corrections or adjustments you find as you close the journals. This type of posting consists of a simple entry that summarises any changes you found.

For example, suppose you find that a customer purchase was recorded directly in the customer's account record but not in the Trade Debtors journal. You have to investigate how that transaction was originally recorded. If the only record was a note in the customer's account, both the Sales account and the Trade Debtors account are affected by the mistake, and the correcting entry looks like this:

	Debit	*Credit*
Trade Debtors	£100	
Sales		£100

To record sale to Mrs Jolly on 15/3/2010 –
corrected 31/03/2010.

If you find this type of error, the Sales transaction record for that date of sale isn't accurate, which means that someone bypassed your standard bookkeeping process when recording the sale. You may want to investigate that part of the issue as well, because something more than a recording problem may be behind this incident. Someone in your business may be allowing customers to take products, purposefully not recording the sale appropriately in your books and pocketing the money instead. Or a salesperson may have recorded a sale for a customer that never took place. If you bill the customer in this latter case, he or she is likely to question the bill, and you find out about the problem then.

The process of checking your journals, or any other part of your bookkeeping records, is a good opportunity to review your internal controls as well. As you find errors during the process of checking the books, keep an eye out for errors (probably similar frequent errors) that may indicate bigger problems than just bookkeeping mistakes. Repeat errors may call for additional staff training to ensure that your bookkeeping rules are being followed to a *T*. Or such errors may be evidence that someone in the business is deliberately recording false information. Whatever the explanation, you need to take corrective action. (I cover internal controls in depth in Chapter 7.)

Checking Out Computerised Journal Records

Although you don't have to close journal pages when you keep your books using a computerised accounting system, running a spot-check (at the very least) of what you have in your paper records against what you have on your computer is a sensible move. Simply run a series of reports using your computerised accounting system and then check to make sure that those computer records match what you have in your files.

For example, in Sage 50 Accounts, go to Suppliers and click Change View and select Supplier Dashboard. Figure 15-2 shows this screen, which has four separate reports: Supplier Cash Overview, Aged Creditors (graphical format), Today's Diary Events and Promised Payments.

Figure 15-2: The Supplier Dashboard in Sage 50 Accounts allows you to see how much money your business owes to others.

Figure 15-3 shows you the kind of detail you get when you select the Detailed Aged Creditor Analysis report. This report is divided into:

- Current bills (up to 29 days old)
- Bills dated 30 days to 59 days (Period 1)

✔ Bills dated 60 days to 89 days (Period 2)

✔ Bills dated 90 days to 119 days (Period 3)

✔ Bills dated more than 120 days (Older)

Obviously, anything in the last two columns – over 90 days old – is bad news. You can expect a supplier whose bills appear in these columns to soon cut you off from any more credit until your account is up to date.

Date: 08/09/2010
Time: 20:23:22

Practice Company
Aged Creditors Analysis (Detailed)

Page: 1

Date From: 01/01/1980
Date To: 08/09/2010

Supplier From:
Supplier To: ZZZZZZZZ

Include future transactions: No
Exclude later payments: No

** NOTE: All report values are shown in Base Currency, unless otherwise indicated **

A/C: DALES   **Name:** Dales   **Contact:**   **Tel:**

No:	Type	Date	Ref	Details	Balance	Future	Current	Period 1	Period 2	Period 3	Older
24	PI	23/07/2010	4	Gas	525.00	0.00	0.00	525.00	0.00	0.00	0.00
				Totals:	525.00	0.00	0.00	525.00	0.00	0.00	0.00

Turnover: 0.00
Credit Limit £   0.00

A/C: HOBSONS   **Name:** Hobsons   **Contact:**   **Tel:**

No:	Type	Date	Ref	Details	Balance	Future	Current	Period 1	Period 2	Period 3	Older
23	PI	15/07/2010	3	Rent of office space	3,525.00	0.00	0.00	3,525.00	0.00	0.00	0.00
				Totals:	3,525.00	0.00	0.00	3,525.00	0.00	0.00	0.00

Turnover: 0.00
Credit Limit £   0.00

A/C: OFFICE   **Name:** Office 2 Go   **Contact:**   **Tel:**

No:	Type	Date	Ref	Details	Balance	Future	Current	Period 1	Period 2	Period 3	Older
16	PI	20/07/2010		Office table & chairs	2,937.50	0.00	0.00	2,937.50	0.00	0.00	0.00
25	PI	07/09/2010		Leaflet print	1,175.00	0.00	1,175.00	0.00	0.00	0.00	0.00
				Totals:	4,112.50	0.00	1,175.00	2,937.50	0.00	0.00	0.00

Turnover: 1,000.00
Credit Limit £   0.00

| | | | | Grand Totals: | 8,162.50 | 0.00 | 1,175.00 | 6,987.50 | 0.00 | 0.00 | 0.00 |

Figure 15-3:
An Aged Creditors Analysis report in Sage 50 Accounts, listing all outstanding bills, the dates the bills were received and the dates they're due.

In addition to locating your bill-paying problem areas, you can also use the information in the Detail report to verify that the paper bills waiting to be paid in supplier files match what you have on your computer. You don't need to check each and every bill, but doing a spot-check of several bills is a good idea. The goal is to verify the accuracy of your records as well as make sure that no one's entering and paying duplicate or non-existent bills.

When it comes to cash flow out of the business, keep tight controls on who can actually sign cheques and how the information that explains those cheques is recorded. In Chapter 7, I talk more about the importance of separating duties to protect each aspect of your bookkeeping system from corruption.

You can also run reports showing the information recorded in your Trade Debtors account. Figure 15-4 shows you a list of possible reports to run from the Customer Reports page. In addition to a full range of outstanding debtor reports covering detailed, summary and disputed items, you can generate a report that shows customer activity and a report on your top customers.

Figure 15-4: You can run reports in Sage 50 Accounts that summarise customer accounts.

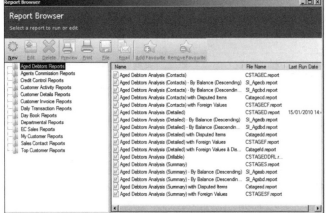

Again, running spot-checks on a few customer accounts to make sure that your paper records of their accounts match the information in your computerised system is a good idea. If, by chance, a customer's purchase has been entered in error in the computer, you can avoid sending a bill to the wrong person.

Some businesses double-check their Trade Debtors bookkeeping for accuracy by sending surveys to customers periodically (usually twice a year) to see whether their accounts are correct. If you choose to double-check in this way, include a postage-paid card with the customer's bill asking if the account is correct and giving the customer room to indicate any account problems before posting the card back to your business. In most cases, an incorrectly billed customer contacts you soon after getting that bill – especially if he or she was billed for more than anticipated.

In addition to keeping actual accounts, such as Trade Creditors or Trade Debtors, your computerised accounting system keeps a journal of all your business's transactions. This journal contains details about all your transactions over a specified time period and the accounts impacted by each transaction. Figure 15-5 shows a sample computerised journal page. Sage 50 Accounts calls this a Nominal Activity Report, as it records all the transactions in each Nominal account.

Figure 15-5:
A computerised accounting system keeps a journal of all transactions, which you can review during the closing process.

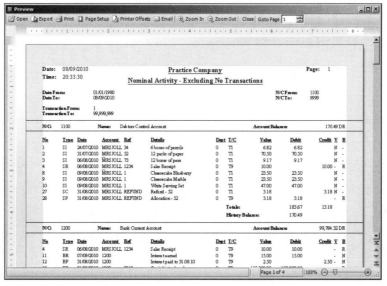

If you want to investigate a specific nominal code, for example, to see why expenditure is so high in Motor Expenses, you can run a Nominal Activity report to see which transactions have been posted to that account. You can select specific dates to narrow down the search. Running a report by date can be a helpful tool when you're trying to locate the source of an error in your books; if you find a questionable transaction, you can open the detail of that transaction and see how it was entered and where you can find the original source material.

Chapter 16

Checking Your Accuracy – By Trial and Hopefully Not Error

. . . .

. . . .

*A*fter you close all your journals and do your best to catch any and all errors (flip back to Chapter 15 for instructions on how to do this), the time comes to test your work. If you've entered all double-entry transactions in the books correctly, the books balance, and your trial's a success!

Unfortunately, few bookkeepers get their books to balance on the first try. And in some cases, the books balance, but errors still exist. This chapter explains how you do a trial balance of your books and gives tips on finding any errors that may be lurking. You also find out how to take your first step to developing financial reports, which I explain in Part V, by creating a worksheet.

Working with a Trial Balance

When you first start entering transactions in a double-entry accounting system, you may think, 'This is a lot of work, and I don't know how I'm ever going to use all this information.' Trust me, after you close your journals and prepare your first set of financial reports, you truly begin to see the value of double-entry accounting.

The first step towards useable reports that help you interpret your financial results is doing a *trial balance*. Basically, a trial balance is a worksheet, prepared manually or produced by your computer accounting system, which lists all the accounts in your Nominal Ledger at the end of an accounting period (whether that's at the end of a month, the end of a quarter or the end of a year).

Conducting your trial balance

If you've been entering transactions manually, you create a trial balance by listing all the accounts with their closing debit or credit balances. (I talk more about debits and credits in Chapter 2.) After preparing the list, you total both the debit and credit columns. If the totals at the bottom of the two columns are the same, the trial is a success, and your books are in balance.

The primary purpose of the trial balance is to prove, at least mathematically, that your debits and credits are equal. If any errors exist in your calculations, or in how you summarised the journals or posted the summaries to the Nominal Ledger, they're uncovered in the trial balance when the columns don't come out equal. Also, if you entered any transactions out of balance, you see the mistake when you add the columns of the trial balance.

The four basic steps to developing a trial balance are:

1. **Prepare a worksheet with three columns: one for account titles, one for debits and one for credits.**

2. **Fill in all the account titles and record their balances in the appropriate debit or credit columns.**

3. **Total the debit and credit columns.**

4. **Compare the column totals.**

Figure 16-1 shows a sample trial balance for a business as of 30 June 2010. Note that the debit column and the credit column both equal $57,850, making this a successful trial balance.

A successful trial balance is no guarantee that your books are totally free of errors; it just means that all your transactions have been entered in balance. You may still have errors in the books related to how you entered your transactions, including:

- ✔ You forgot to put a transaction in a journal or in the Nominal Ledger.

- ✔ You forgot to post a journal entry to the Nominal Ledger.

- ✔ You posted a journal entry twice in the Nominal Ledger or in the journal itself.

✔ You posted the wrong amount.

✔ You posted a transaction to the wrong account.

Account	Debit	Credit
Trial Balance		
Rachel & Zoe's Sewing Shop		
30/6/2010		
Cash	2,500 —	
Petty Cash	500	
Accounts Receivable	1,000	
Stock	1,200	
Equipment	5,050	
Motor Vehicle	25,000	
Furniture	5,600	
Accounts Payable		2,200 —
Loans Payable		29,150 —
Capital		5,000 —
Sales		20,000 —
Sales Discounts	1,000 —	
Purchases	8,000 —	
Purchase Discounts		1,500 —
Credit Card Fees	125 —	
Advertising	1,500 —	
Bank Charges	120 —	
Interest	100 —	
Legal & Accounting	300 —	
Office Expenses	250 —	
P.A.Y.E. & N.I.	350 —	
Postage	75 —	
Rent	800 —	
Salaries & Wages	3,500 —	
Sundry Expenses	300 —	
Telephone	200 —	
Utilities	255 —	
	57,850 —	57,850 —

Figure 16-1:
A sample trial balance.

If the errors listed here somehow slip through the cracks, a good chance exists that someone is going to notice the discrepancy when the financial reports are prepared.

Even with these potentially lurking errors, the trial balance is a useful tool and the essential first step in developing your financial reports.

Dealing with trial balance errors

If your trial balance isn't correct, you need to work backwards in your closing process to find the source of the mathematical error. When you need to find errors after completing a trial balance that fails, follow these four basic steps to identify and fix the problem. And remember, this process is why all bookkeepers and accountants work with pencils, not pens – pencils make rubbing out mistakes and making corrections much easier.

1. **Check your additions.** Keep your fingers crossed and add up your columns again to make sure that the error isn't just one of addition, the simplest kind of error to find. Correct the addition mistake and re-total your columns.

2. **Compare your balances.** Double-check the balances on the trial balance worksheet by comparing them to the totals from your journals and your Nominal Ledger. Ensure that you didn't make an error when transferring the account balances to the trial balance. Correcting this type of problem isn't very difficult or time-consuming. Simply correct the incorrect balances and add up the trial balance columns again.

3. **Check your journal summaries.** Double-check the additions in all your journal summaries, making sure that all totals are correct and that any totals you posted to the Nominal Ledger are correct. Running this kind of a check, of course, is somewhat time-consuming, but still better than re-checking all your transactions. If you do find errors in your journal summaries, correct them, re-enter the totals correctly, change the numbers on the trial balance worksheet to match your corrected totals and re-test your trial balance.

4. **Check your journal and Nominal Ledger entries.** Unfortunately, if Steps 1, 2 and 3 fail to fix your problem, nothing's left but to go back and check your actual transaction entries. The process can be time-consuming, but the information in your books isn't useful until your debits equal your credits. Going back to the original entries in the journals is the only way of finding the more stubborn mistakes. You have to hope you find your mistake early on!

If this step is your last resort, scan through your entries looking specifically for ones that appear questionable. For example, if an entry for office supplies looks much larger or much smaller than you normally expect, check the original source material to make sure that the entry's correct. If you carefully checked the Trade Creditors and Trade Debtors journals, as I explain in Chapters 14 and 15, you can concentrate your efforts on accounts with separate journals. After you find and correct the error or errors, run another trial balance. If things still don't match up, repeat the steps listed here until your debits and credits equal out.

You can always go back and correct the books and do another trial balance before you prepare the financial reports. Don't close the books for the accounting period until the financial reports are completed and accepted. I talk more about the closing process in Chapter 24.

Testing Your Balance Using Computerised Accounting Systems

When you use a computerised accounting system, your trial balance is automatically generated for you. Because the system allows you to enter only transactions that are in balance, the likelihood is that your trial balance is going to be successful. But that doesn't mean your accounts are guaranteed to be error-free.

Remember the saying, 'Garbage in, garbage out'? If you make a mistake when you enter transaction data into the system, the information that comes out is going to be in error, even if the data is in balance. Although you don't have to go through the correction steps covered in the earlier section 'Dealing with trial balance errors' to reach a successful trial balance, you may still have errors lurking in your data.

In Sage 50 Accounts, the trial balance report is the second report at the top of the Financials page, which appears in Figure 16-2. In addition to the trial balance, you can request a report showing the profit and loss, balance sheet and a wide range of reports grouped under the title *Reports*.

Your business's accountant is likely to use many of the report options on this page to double-check that your transactions were entered correctly and that no one is playing with the numbers. In particular, the accountant may use a report option called *Audit Trail,* which reveals what changes impacted the business's books during an accounting period and who made those changes. This report is one of the many within the Reports option.

Although it doesn't match the trial balance done manually in Figure 16-1, the Sage 50 Accounts trial balance shown in Figure 16-3 gives you an idea of what a computerised accounting trial balance looks like.

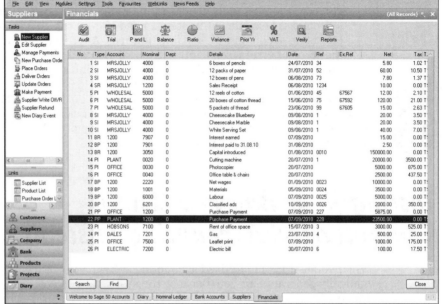

Figure 16-2: The Financials page of Sage 50 Accounts provides the option of creating many useful reports.

Date: 07/09/2010 **Time:** 10:50:04

Practice Company

Period Trial Balance

Page: 1

To Period: Month 1, August 2010

N/C	Name	Debit	Credit
0020	Plant and Machinery	20,000.00	
0030	Office Equipment	5,000.00	
0040	Furniture and Fixtures	2,500.00	
1100	Debtors Control Account	170.49	
1200	Bank Current Account	150,007.50	
2100	Creditors Control Account		36,652.73
2200	Sales Tax Control Account		26.89
2201	Purchase Tax Control Account	5,405.73	
3050	Capital Introduced		150,000.00
4000	Sales Type A		153.60
5000	Materials Purchased	147.00	
7100	Rent	3,000.00	
7200	Electricity	100.00	
7201	Gas	500.00	
7901	Bank Charges	2.50	
	Totals:	186,833.22	186,833.22

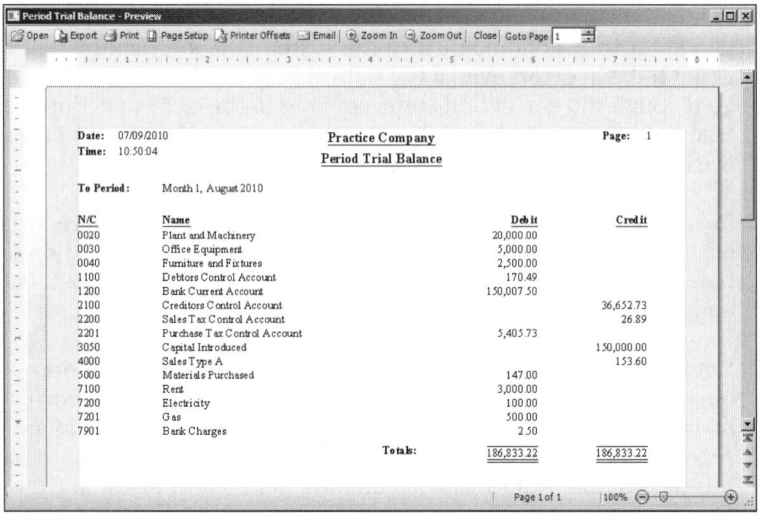

Figure 16-3: A sample trial balance report produced by Sage 50 Accounts.

Developing a Financial Statement Worksheet

After your accounts successfully pass a trial balance test (see 'Conducting your trial balance', earlier in this chapter), you can then take your first stab at creating *financial statements,* including balance sheets and profit and loss statements. The first step in producing these statements is using the information from the trial balance and its corrections to develop a *worksheet* that includes the initial trial balance, the accounts that are shown on a balance sheet and, finally, the accounts that are normally shown on a profit and loss statement.

Create a worksheet that includes these seven columns:

- ✔ **Column 1:** Account list

- ✔ **Columns 2 and 3:** Trial balance (one column for debits, one column for credits)

- ✔ **Columns 4 and 5:** Balance sheet (one column for debits, one column for credits)

- ✔ **Columns 6 and 7:** Profit and loss statement (one column for debits, one column for credits)

Figure 16-4 shows a sample of a worksheet developed from trial balance numbers. Note that the numbers of the trial balance are transferred to the appropriate financial statement; for example, the Cash account, which is an Asset account, is shown in the debit column of the balance sheet. (I talk more about developing financial statements in Chapters 18 and 19.)

After you transfer all the accounts to their appropriate balance sheet or profit and loss statement columns, you total the worksheet columns. Don't panic when you see that the totals at the bottom of your columns aren't equal – the discrepancy is because the net income hasn't been calculated yet. However, the difference between the debits and credits in both the balance sheet and the profit and loss statement totals needs to be the same. That amount should represent the net income that appears on the profit and loss statement. (You see this in practice in Chapter 18, which deals with developing a profit and loss statement.)

In Figure 16-4, the £4,500 difference for the balance sheet is shown as a credit, representing an increase in Retained Earnings. The Retained Earnings account reflects the profits that have been reinvested into the business's assets in order to grow the business. (You can find more about Retained Earnings in Chapter 19.)

Work Sheet
Rachel & Zoe's Sewing Shop
30/6/2010

Account	Trial Balance Debit	Trial Balance Credit	Balance Sheet Debit	Balance Sheet Credit	Profit Loss Debit	Profit Loss Credit
Cash	2,500 —		2,500 —			
Petty Cash	500 —		5,00 —			
Accounts Receivable	1,000 —		1,000 —			
Stock	1,200 —		1,200 —			
Equipment	5,050 —		5,050 —			
Motor Vehicle	25,000 —		25,000 —			
Furniture	5,600 —		5,600 —			
Accounts Payable		2,200 —		2,200 —		
Loans Payable		29,150 —		29,150 —		
Capital		5,000 —		5,000 —		
Sales		20,000 —				20,000 —
Sales Discounts	1,000 —				1,000 —	
Purchases	8,000 —				8,000 —	
Purchase Discounts		1,500 —				1,500 —
Credit Card Fees	125 —				125 —	
Advertising	1,500 —				1,500 —	
Bank Charges	120 —				120 —	
Interest	100 —				100 —	
Legal & Accounting	300 —				300 —	
Office Expenses	250 —				250 —	
P.A.Y.E. & N.I.	350 —				350 —	
Postage	75 —				75 —	
Rent	800 —				800 —	
Salaries & Wages	3,500 —				3,500 —	
Sundry Expenses	300 —				300 —	
Telephone	200 —				200 —	
Utilities	255 —				255 —	
	57,850 —	57,850 —	40,850 —	36,350 —	17,000 —	21,500 —
Net Income			—	4,500 —	4,500 —	
			40,850 —	40,850 —	21,500 —	21,500 —

Figure 16-4: This sample worksheet shows the first step in developing a business's financial statements.

In some limited companies, part of the earnings is taken out in the form of dividends paid to shareholders. *Dividends* are a portion of the earnings divided up among shareholders. The board of directors of the limited company set a certain amount per share to be paid to shareholders.

Many other small businesses that haven't incorporated (gone limited) pay out earnings to their owners using a *Drawings account,* which shows any cash the owners take out. Each owner needs to have his or her own Drawings account so that you have a history of how much each owner withdraws from the business's resources.

Replacing Worksheets with Computerised Reports

When you use a computerised accounting system, you don't have to create a worksheet at all. Instead, the system gives you the option of generating many different types of reports to help you develop your profit and loss statement and balance sheet.

One of the advantages of your computerised system's reports is that you can easily look at your numbers in many different ways. For example, Figure 16-2 shows the Financials screen that shows a range of reports, including the balance sheet and the profit and loss statement. To get the report you want, all you need to do is click the Report icon.

You can obtain additional reports by clicking on the Financial Reports option on the Links list within the Nominal Ledger. For more information about Sage 50 Accounts, read *Sage 50 Accounts For Dummies* by Jane Kelly.

However, if you really want a snapshot of the business's financial position, go to the Company Dashboard, shown in Figure 16-5. The dashboard shows four key statements:

- ✔ **Trading Headlines:** Top-selling products, top customers and the stock position.

- ✔ **Financial Headlines:** Total sales to date, gross profit to date, net profit to date, total debtors and total creditors.

- ✔ **Bank Balances:** A summary of all the businesses bank accounts, loans and credit cards.

- ✔ **Company Overview:** The headline figures for Sales, Purchases, Direct expenses and Overheads. In addition, it shows the headline balance sheet figures for Fixed Assets, Current Assets, Current Liabilities, Long Term Liabilities and Capital & Reserves.

Figure 16-5:
The
Company
Dashboard
with a
high-level
snapshot
of six key
areas.

Computerised accounting systems provide you with the tools to manipulate your business's numbers in whatever way you find useful for analysing your business's results. And if a report isn't quite right for your needs, you can customise it. For example, if you want to see the profit and loss results for a particular week during an accounting period, you can set the dates for only that week and generate the report. You can also produce a report looking at data for just one day, one month, one quarter or any combination of dates.

You can also take the time to design customised reports that meet your business's unique financial information needs. Many businesses produce customised reports to collect information by department or division. You're limited only by your imagination!

When you work with your computerised system, you're asked for information not easily found using standardised reports. The first few times you pull that information together, you may need to do so manually. But as you get used to your computerised accounting system and its report functions, you're able to design customised reports that pull together information in just the way you need it.

Chapter 17

Adjusting the Books

. . . .

In This Chapter

▶ Making adjustments for non-cash transactions

▶ Taking your adjustments for a trial (balance) run

▶ Adding to and deleting from the Chart of Accounts

. . . .

During an accounting period, your bookkeeping duties focus on your business's day-to-day transactions. When the time comes to report those transactions in financial statements, you must make some adjustments to your books. Your financial reports are supposed to show your business's financial health, so your books must reflect any significant change in the value of your assets, even if that change doesn't involve the exchange of cash.

If you use cash-based accounting, these adjustments aren't necessary because you only record transactions when cash changes hands. I talk about accrual and cash-based accounting in Chapter 2.

This chapter reviews the types of adjustments you need to make to the books before preparing the financial statements, including calculating asset depreciation, dividing up prepaid expenses, updating stock figures, dealing with bad debt and recognising salaries and wages not yet paid. You also find out how to add and delete accounts.

Adjusting All the Right Areas

Even after testing your books using the trial balance process that I explain in Chapter 16, you still need to make some adjustments before you can prepare accurate financial reports with the information you have. These adjustments don't involve the exchange of cash but rather involve recognising the use of assets, loss of assets or future asset obligations that aren't reflected in day-to-day bookkeeping activities.

The key areas in which you're likely to need to adjust the books include:

- ✔ **Asset depreciation:** To recognise the use of assets during the accounting period.
- ✔ **Prepaid expenses:** To match a portion of expenses that were paid at one point during the year, but for which the benefits are used throughout the year, such as an annual insurance premium. The benefit needs to be apportioned out against expenses for each month.
- ✔ **Stock:** To update stock to reflect what you have on hand.
- ✔ **Bad debts:** To acknowledge that some customers never pay and to write off those accounts.
- ✔ **Unpaid salaries and wages:** To recognise salary and wage expenses that have been incurred but not yet paid.

Depreciating assets

The largest non-cash expense for most businesses is *depreciation.* Depreciation is an important accounting exercise for every business to undertake because it reflects the use and ageing of assets. Older assets need more maintenance and repair, and eventually need to be replaced. As the depreciation of an asset increases and the value of the asset dwindles, the need for more maintenance or replacement becomes apparent. (For more on depreciation and why you do it, check out Chapter 12.)

The actual time to make this adjustment to the books is when you close the books for an accounting period. (Some businesses record depreciation expenses every month to match monthly expenses with monthly revenues more accurately, but most business owners only worry about depreciation adjustments on a yearly basis, when they prepare their annual financial statements.)

Depreciation doesn't involve the use of cash. By accumulating depreciation expenses on an asset, you're reducing the value of the asset as shown on the balance sheet (see Chapter 19 for the low-down on balance sheets).

Readers of your financial statements can get a good idea of the health of your assets by reviewing your accumulated depreciation. If a financial report reader sees that assets are close to being fully depreciated, he knows that you probably need to spend significant funds on replacing or repairing those assets soon. As he evaluates the financial health of the business, he takes that future obligation into consideration before making a decision to lend money to the business or possibly invest in it.

Usually, you calculate depreciation for accounting purposes using the *Straight-Line depreciation method*. This method is used to calculate an equal amount to be depreciated each year, based on the anticipated useful life of the asset. For example, suppose your business purchases a car for business purposes that costs £25,000. You anticipate that the car is going to have a useful lifespan of five years and be worth £5,000 after five years. Using the Straight-Line depreciation method, you subtract £5,000 from the total car cost of £25,000 to find the value of the car during its five-year useful lifespan (£20,000). Then, you divide £20,000 by five to find your depreciation charge for the car (£4,000 per year). When adjusting the assets at the end of each year in the car's five-year lifespan, your entry to the books looks like this:

	Debit	*Credit*
Depreciation Charge	£4,000	
Accumulated Depreciation: Vehicles		£4,000

To record depreciation for Vehicles.

This entry increases depreciation charges, which appear on the profit and loss statement (see Chapter 18). The entry also increases Accumulated Depreciation, which is the use of the asset and appears on the balance sheet directly under the Vehicles asset line. The Vehicles asset line always shows the value of the asset at the time of purchase.

You can accelerate depreciation if you believe that the asset is not going to be used evenly over its lifespan – namely, that the asset is going to be used more heavily in the early years of ownership. I talk more about alternative depreciation methods in Chapter 12.

If you use a computerised accounting system as opposed to keeping your books manually, you may or may not need to make this adjustment at the end of an accounting period. If your system is set up with an asset register feature, depreciation is automatically calculated, and you don't have to worry about it. Check with your accountant (the person who sets up the asset register feature) before calculating and recording depreciation expenses.

Allocating prepaid expenses

Most businesses have to pay certain expenses at the beginning of the year even though they benefit from that expense throughout the year. Insurance is a prime example of this type of expense. Most insurance businesses require you to pay the premium annually at the start of the year even though the value of that insurance protects the business throughout the year.

For example, suppose your business's annual car insurance premium is £1,200. You pay that premium in January in order to maintain insurance cover throughout the year. Showing the full cash expense of your insurance when you prepare your January financial reports greatly reduces any profit that month and makes your financial results look worse than the actually are, which is no good.

Instead, you record a large expense such as insurance or prepaid rent as an asset called *Prepaid Expenses,* and then you adjust the value to reflect that the asset is being used up. Your £1,200 annual insurance premium is actually valuable to the business for 12 months, so you calculate the actual expense for insurance by dividing £1,200 by 12, giving you £100 per month. At the end of each month, you record the use of that asset by preparing an adjusting entry that looks like this:

	Debit	*Credit*
Insurance Expenses	£100	
Prepaid Expenses		£100

To record insurance expenses for March.

This entry increases insurance expenses on the profit and loss statement and decreases the asset Prepaid Expenses on the balance sheet. No cash changes hands in this entry because cash was laid out when the insurance bill was paid, and the Asset account Prepaid Expenses was increased in value at the time the cash was paid.

Counting stock

Stock is a balance sheet asset that needs to be adjusted at the end of an accounting period. During the accounting period, your business buys stock and records those purchases in a Purchases account without indicating any change to stock. When the products are sold, you record the sales in the Sales account but don't make any adjustment to the value of the stock. Instead, you adjust the stock value at the end of the accounting period because adjusting with each purchase and sale is much too time-consuming.

The steps for making proper adjustments to stock in your books are as follows:

1. **Determine the stock remaining.**

   In addition to calculating closing stock using the purchases and sales numbers in the books, also do a physical count of stock to make sure that what's on the shelves matches what's in the books.

2. **Set a value for that stock.**

   The value of closing stock varies depending on the method your business chooses for valuing stock. I talk more about stock value and how to calculate the value of closing stock in Chapter 9.

3. **Adjust the number of items remaining in stock in the Stock account and adjust the value of that account based on the information collected in Steps 1 and 2.**

If you record stock using your computerised accounting system, the system makes adjustments to stock as you record sales. At the end of the accounting period, the value of your business's closing stock is already adjusted in the books. Although the work's done for you, still do a physical count of the stock to make sure that your computer records match the physical stock at the end of the accounting period.

Allowing for bad debts

No business likes to accept that money owed by some of its customers is never going to be received, but this happens to most businesses that sell items on credit. When your business determines that a customer who bought products on credit is never going to pay for them, you record the value of that purchase as a _bad debt._ (For an explanation of credit, check out Chapter 10.)

At the end of an accounting period, list all outstanding customer accounts in an _Aged Debtor Report,_ which is covered in Chapter 10. This report shows which customers owe how much and for how long. After a certain amount of time, you have to admit that some customers simply aren't going to pay. Each business sets its own policy of how long to wait before tagging an account as a bad debt. For example, your business may decide that when a customer is six months late with a payment, you're unlikely to ever see the money.

After you decide that an account is a bad debt, don't include its value as part of your assets in Trade Debtors (Accounts Receivable). Including bad debt value doesn't paint a realistic picture of your situation for the readers of your financial reports. Because the bad debt is no longer an asset, you adjust the value of your Trade Debtors to reflect the loss of that asset.

You can record bad debts in a couple of ways:

✔ **By customer:** Some businesses identify the specific customers whose accounts are bad debts and calculate the bad debt expense each accounting period based on specified customer accounts.

✔ **By percentage:** Other businesses look at their bad-debts histories and develop percentages that reflect those experiences. Instead of taking the time to identify each specific account that may be a bad debt, these businesses record bad debt expenses as a percentage of their Trade Debtors.

✔ **By using a bit of both:** You can identify specific customers and write them off and apply a percentage to cover the rest.

However you decide to record bad debts, you need to prepare an adjusting entry at the end of each accounting period to record bad debt expenses. Here's an adjusting entry to record bad debt expenses of £1,000:

	Debit	Credit
Bad Debt Expense	£1,000	
Trade Debtors		£1,000

To write off customer accounts.

You can't have bad debt expenses if you don't sell to your customers on credit. You only need to worry about bad debt if you offer your customers the convenience of buying your products on credit.

If you use a computerised accounting system, check the system's instructions for how to write off bad debts. To write off a bad debt using Sage 50 Accounts, follow these steps:

1. **Open the Customers screen and select Write Off/Refund from the Tasks on the left-hand side of the screen. This brings up the Write Offs, Refunds and Returns Wizard (see Figure 17-1). Select Write Off Customer Accounts and click Next.**

2. **Select the customer account you want to write off and click Next (see Figure 17-2).**

3. **Highlight the invoices you're writing off and click Next (see Figure 17-3).**

4. **Select the bank account to post the journal to – usually the Bank Current account. Click Next.**

5. **Choose a date for the transaction to occur – usually the current month. Click Next.**

6. **Confirm the write-off shown on the screen by clicking Finish (see Figure 17-4).**

7. **Double-click on the customer account and click the Activity tab to check that the write-off has been done (see Figure 17-5).**

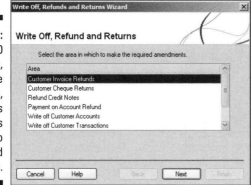

Figure 17-1: In Sage 50 Accounts, use the Write Offs, Refunds and Returns Wizard to write off bad debts.

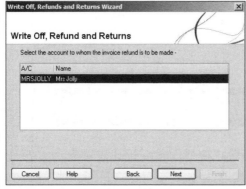

Figure 17-2: Selecting the customer account in which you're writing off debt in Sage 50 Accounts.

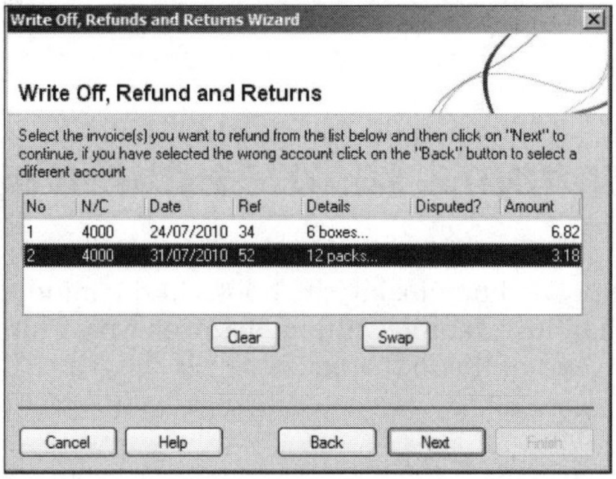

Figure 17-3: Selecting and highlighting the invoices you're writing off in Sage 50 Accounts.

Figure 17-4:
Confirming
the details
of the
write-off
in Sage 50
Accounts.

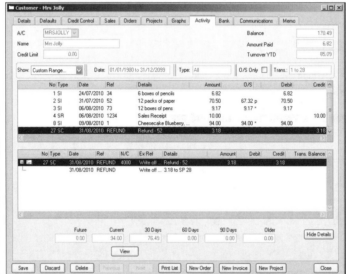

Figure 17-5:
Check that
the write-off
has been
posted
properly by
viewing the
Customer
Activity
screen.

Recognising unpaid salaries and wages

Not all pay periods fall at the end of a month. If you pay your employees
every two weeks, you may end up closing the books in the middle of a pay
period, which means that, for example, employees aren't paid for the last
week of March until the end of the first week of April.

When your pay period hits before the end of the month, you need to make an adjusting entry to record the payroll expense that was incurred but not yet paid. You estimate the amount of the adjustment based on what you pay every two weeks. The easiest thing to do is just accrue the expense of half of your payroll (which means you enter the anticipated expense as an accrual in the appropriate account; when the cash is actually paid out, you then reverse that accrual entry, which reduces the amount in the Liability account, Accrued Payroll expenses and the Cash account, to reflect the outlay of cash). If that expense is £3,000, you make the following adjusting entry to the books to show the accrual:

	Debit	*Credit*
Payroll Expenses	£3,000	
Accrued Payroll Expenses		£3,000

To record payroll expenses for the last week of March.

This adjusting entry increases both the Payroll Expenses reported on the profit and loss statement and the Accrued Payroll Expenses that appear as a liability on the balance sheet. The week's worth of unpaid salaries and wages is actually a liability that you have to pay in the future even though you haven't yet spent the cash. When you finally do pay out the salaries and wages, you reduce the amount in Accrued Payroll Expenses with the following entry:

	Debit	*Credit*
Accrued Payroll Expenses	£3,000	
Cash		£3,000

To record the cash payment of salaries and wages for the last week of March.

Note that when the cash is actually paid, you don't record any expenses; instead, you decrease the Accrued Payroll Expense account, which is a liability. The Cash account, which is an asset, also decreases.

Doing these extra entries may seem like a lot of extra work, but if you don't match the payroll expenses for March with the revenues for March, your profit and loss statements don't reflect the actual state of your affairs. Your profit at the end of March looks very good because your salary and wage expenses aren't fully reflected in the profit and loss statement, but your April profit and loss statement looks very bad given the extra expenses actually incurred in March.

Testing Out an Adjusted Trial Balance

In Chapter 16, I explain why and how you run a trial balance on the accounts in your Nominal Ledger. Adjustments to your books call for another trial balance, the *adjusted trial balance,* to ensure that your adjustments are correct and ready to be posted to the Nominal Ledger. You track all the adjusting entries on a worksheet similar to the one shown in Chapter 16.

You need to do this worksheet only if you're doing your books manually, and not if you're using a computerised accounting system.

The key difference in the worksheet for the Adjusted Trial Balance is that you must add four additional columns to the worksheet for a total of 11 columns. Columns include:

- ✔ **Column 1:** Account titles.

- ✔ **Columns 2 and 3:** Unadjusted trial balance. The trial balance before the adjustments are made with column 2 for debits and column 3 for credits.

- ✔ **Columns 4 and 5:** Adjustments. All adjustments to the trial balance are listed in column 4 for debits and column 5 for credits.

- ✔ **Columns 6 and 7:** Adjusted trial balance. A new trial balance is calculated that includes all the adjustments. Make sure that the credits equal the debits when you total that new trial balance. If they don't, find any errors before adding entries to the balance sheet and profit and loss statement columns.

- ✔ **Columns 8 and 9:** Balance sheet. Column 8 includes all the balance sheet accounts that have a debit balance, and column 9 includes all the balance sheet accounts with a credit balance.

- ✔ **Columns 10 and 11:** Profit and loss statement. Column 10 includes all the profit and loss statement accounts with a debit balance, and column 11 includes all the profit and loss statement accounts with a credit balance.

When you're confident that all the accounts are in balance, post your adjustments to the Nominal Ledger so that all the balances in that ledger include the adjusting entries. With the adjustments, the Nominal Ledger matches the financial statements you prepare.

Changing Your Chart of Accounts

After you finalise your Nominal Ledger for the year, you may want to make changes to your Chart of Accounts, which lists all the accounts in your accounting system. (For the full story on the Chart of Accounts, see Chapter 3.) You may need to add accounts if you think you need additional ones or delete accounts if you think they're no longer needed.

Delete accounts from your Chart of Accounts only at the end of the year. If you delete an account in the middle of the year, your annual financial statements don't reflect the activities in that account prior to its deletion. So even if you decide halfway through the year not to use an account, leave it on the books until the end of the year and then delete it.

You can add accounts to your Chart of Accounts throughout the year, but if you decide to add an account in the middle of the year in order to more closely track certain assets, liabilities, revenues or expenses, you may need to adjust some related entries.

Suppose that you start the year recording paper expenses in the Office Supplies Expenses account, but paper usage and its expense keeps increasing and you decide to track the expense in a separate account beginning in July.

First, you add the new account, Paper Expenses, to your Chart of Accounts. Then you prepare an adjusting entry to move all the paper expenses that were recorded in the Office Supplies Expenses account to the Paper Expenses account. In the interest of space and to avoid boring you, the adjusting entry below is an abbreviated one. In your actual entry, you probably detail the specific dates on which paper was bought as an office supplies expense rather than just tally one summary total.

	Debit	*Credit*
Paper Expenses	£1,000	
Office Supplies Expenses		£1,000

To move expenses for paper from the Office Supplies Expenses account to the Paper Expenses account.

Moving beyond the catchall
Miscellaneous Expenses account

When new accounts are added to the Chart of Accounts, the account most commonly adjusted is the Miscellaneous Expenses account. In many cases, you may expect to incur an expense only one or two times during the year, therefore making it unnecessary to create a new account specifically for that expense. But after a while, you find that your 'rare' expense is adding up, and you'd be better off with a designated account, meaning that you need to create some adjusting entries to move expenses out of the Miscellaneous Expenses account.

For example, suppose you think that you're going to need to rent a car for the business just once before you buy a new vehicle, and so you enter the rental cost in the books as a Miscellaneous Expense. However, after renting cars three times, you decide to start a Rental Expense account mid-year. When you add the Rental Expense account to your Chart of Accounts, you need to use an adjusting entry to transfer any expenses incurred and recorded in the Miscellaneous Expense account prior to the creation of the new account.

Part V
Reporting Results and Starting Over

'Good heavens – this tax investigation must be _really_ serious – You're the _third_ tax inspector to visit my little taxidermist business this month.'

In this part . . .

Now's the time to show off all the hard work you and your employees have put into keeping your business operating and making a profit. This part instructs you in how to use all the information you collect throughout the accounting period to prepare financial reports that give investors, lenders, suppliers, HM Revenue & Customs, and your employees a clear picture of how well your business did during the month, the quarter, or the year.

This part also covers the year-end government reports as well as forms that you need to file with HM Revenue & Customs. Finally, we guide you through the process of closing the books at year-end and getting ready for the next year.

Chapter 18

Producing a Profit and Loss Statement

· ·

· ·

*W*ithout one very important financial report tool, you can never know for sure whether or not your business is making a profit. This tool is called the *profit and loss statement,* and most businesses prepare this statement on a monthly basis, as well as quarterly and annually, in order to get periodic pictures of how well the business is doing financially.

Analysing the profit and loss statement and the details behind it can reveal lots of useful information to help you make decisions for improving your profits and business overall. This chapter covers the various parts of a profit and loss statement, how you develop one and examples of how you can use it to make business decisions.

Lining Up the Profit and Loss Statement

Did your business make any profit? You can find the answer in your *profit and loss statement,* the financial report that summarises all the sales activities, costs of producing or buying the products or services sold and expenses incurred in order to run the business.

Profit and loss statements summarise the financial activities of a business during a particular accounting period (which can be a month, quarter, year or some other period of time that makes sense for a business's needs).

Normal practice is to include two accounting periods on a profit and loss statement: the current period plus the year to date. The five key lines that make up a profit and loss statement are:

- ✔ **Sales or Revenue:** The total amount of invoiced sales taken in from selling the business's products or services. You calculate this amount by totalling all the sales or revenue accounts. The top line of the profit and loss statement is sales or revenues; either is okay.

- ✔ **Cost of Goods Sold:** How much was spent in order to buy or make the goods or services that were sold during the accounting period under review. The section 'Finding Cost of Goods Sold' below shows you how to calculate Cost of Goods Sold.

- ✔ **Gross Profit:** How much a business made before taking into account operations expenses; calculated by subtracting the Cost of Goods Sold from the Sales or Revenue.

- ✔ **Operating Expenses:** How much was spent on operating the business; these expenses include administrative fees, salaries, advertising, utilities and other operations expenses. You add all your expenses accounts on your profit and loss statement to get this total.

- ✔ **Net Profit or Loss:** Whether or not the business made a profit or loss during the accounting period in review; calculated by subtracting total expenses from Gross Profit.

Formatting the Profit and Loss Statement

Before you actually create your business's profit and loss statement, you have to pick a format in which to organise your financial information. You have two options to choose from: the single-step format or the multi-step format. They contain the same information but present it in slightly different ways.

The *single-step format* groups all data into two categories: revenue and expenses. The *multi-step format* divides the profit and loss statement into several sections and offers some key subtotals to make analysing the data easier.

You can calculate the same subtotals from the single-step format in the multi-step format, although it means more work. Therefore, most businesses choose the multi-step format to simplify profit and loss statement analysis for those who read their external financial reports.

The following is an example of a basic profit and loss statement prepared in the single-step format:

Revenues

Net Sales	£1,000
Interest Income	£100
Total Revenue	£1,100

Expenses

Cost of Goods Sold	£500
Depreciation	£50
Advertising	£50
Salaries	£100
Supplies	£100
Interest Expenses	£50
Total Expenses	£850
Net Profit	£250

Using the same numbers, the following is an example of a basic profit and loss statement prepared in the multi-step format.

Revenues

Sales	£1,000
Cost of Goods Sold	£500
Gross Profit	£500

Operating Expenses

Depreciation	£50
Advertising	£50
Salaries	£100
Supplies	£100
Interest Expenses	£50
Total Operating Expenses	£350
Operating Profit	£150

Other Income

Interest Income	£100
Total Profit	£250

Of course, in both examples you end up with the same profit, but the second profit and loss statement provides the reader with a better analysis of what happened in the business.

Preparing the Profit and Loss Statement

Before you can prepare your profit and loss statement, you have to calculate Net Sales and Cost of Goods Sold using information that appears on your worksheet, which is explained in Chapter 16.

Finding Net Sales

Net Sales is a total of all your sales minus any discounts. In order to calculate Net Sales, you look at the line items regarding sales, discounts and any sales fees on your worksheet. For example, suppose that your worksheet lists Total Sales at £20,000 and discounts given to customers at £1,000. Also, according to your worksheet, your business paid £125 in credit card fees on sales. To find your Net Sales, you subtract the discounts and credit card fees from your Total Sales amount, leaving you with £18,875.

Finding Cost of Goods Sold

Cost of Goods Sold is the total amount your business spent to buy or make the goods or services that you sold. To calculate this amount for a business that buys its finished products from another business in order to sell them to customers, you start with the value of the business's Opening Stock (the amount in the Stock account at the beginning of the accounting period), add all purchases of new stock and then subtract any Closing Stock (stock that's still on the shelves or in the warehouse; it appears on the balance sheet, which is covered in Chapter 19).

The following is a basic Cost of Goods Sold calculation:

Opening Stock + Purchases = Goods Available for Sale

£100 + £1,000 = £1,100

Goods Available for Sale – Closing Stock = Cost of Goods Sold

£1,100 – £200 = £900

To simplify the example for calculating Cost of Goods Sold, these numbers assume the Opening (the value of the stock at the beginning of the accounting period) and Closing Stock (the value of the stock at the end of the accounting period) values are the same. See Chapter 9 for details about calculating stock value. So to calculate Cost of Goods Sold you need just two key lines:

the purchases made and the discounts received to lower the purchase cost, as in the following example.

Purchases – Purchases Discounts = Cost of Goods Sold

£8,000 – £1,500 = £6,500

Drawing remaining amounts from your worksheet

After you calculate Net Sales and Cost of Goods Sold (see the preceding sections), you can use the rest of the numbers from your worksheet to prepare your business's profit and loss statement. Figure 18-1 shows a sample profit and loss statement.

Profit and Loss Statement

May 2010

Month Ended	May
Revenues:	
Net Sales	£ 18,875
Cost of Goods Sold	(£ 6,500)
Gross Profit	£ 12,375
Operating Expenses:	
Advertising	£ 1,500
Bank Service Charges	£ 120
Insurance Expenses	£ 100
Interest Expenses	£ 125
Legal & Accounting Fees	£ 300
Office Expenses	£ 250
Payroll Taxes Expenses	£ 350
Postage Expenses	£ 75
Rent Expenses	£ 800
Salaries	£ 3,500
Supplies	£ 300
Telephone Expenses	£ 200
Utilities	£ 255
Total Operating Expenses	£ 7,875
Net Profit	£ 4,500

Figure 18-1: A sample profit and loss statement.

You and anyone else in-house are likely to want to see the type of detail shown in the example in Figure 18-1, but most business owners prefer not to show all their operating detail to outsiders: they like to keep the detail private. Fortunately, if you operate as a sole trader or partnership, only HM Revenue & Customs needs to see your detailed profit and loss figures. If your turnover is less than £68,000 per annum HM Revenue & Customs allow you to file an abbreviated set of accounts for the purpose of completing your Self Assessment Tax return, only requesting the following headings:

- Turnover

- Other Income

- Cost of Goods Sold

- Car, Van and Travel Expenses (after private-use deduction)

- Wages, Salaries and Other Staff Costs

- Rent, Rates, Power and Insurance Costs

- Repairs and Renewals of Property and Equipment

- Accountancy, Legal and Other Professional Fees

- Interest, Bank and Credit Card Financial Charges

- Phone, Fax, Stationery and Other Office Costs

- Other Allowable Business Expenses

Also, if you are a small limited company, when you file your accounts at Companies House you can file abbreviated accounts, which means that you can keep your detailed profit and loss figures secret. Speak with your external accountant about whether you qualify as a small company because the exemption levels do change from time to time.

Gauging Your Cost of Goods Sold

Businesses that make their own products rather than buy them for future sale must record stock at three different levels:

- **Raw materials:** This line item includes purchases of all items used to make your business's products. For example, a fudge shop buys all the ingredients to make the fudge it sells, so the value of any stock on hand that hasn't been used to make fudge yet needs to appear in the raw materials line item.

- **Work-in-progress stock:** This line item shows the value of any products being made but that aren't yet ready for sale. A fudge shop is unlikely to have anything in this line item because fudge doesn't take more than a few hours to make. However, many manufacturing businesses take weeks or months to produce products and therefore usually have some portion of the stock value in this line item.

Valuing work in progress can be very complex. As well as the raw material content, you need to add in direct wages and production overheads consumed to produce the products to the stage they're at. In reality most small businesses do not attempt to value work in progress.

✔ **Finished-goods stock:** This line item lists the value of stock that's ready for sale. (For a business that doesn't make its own products, finished-goods stock is the same as the stock line item.)

If you keep the books for a business that manufactures its own products, you can use a computerised accounting system to record the various stock accounts described here. However, your basic accounting system software won't cut it – you need a more advanced package in order to record multiple stock types. One such system is Sage 50 Accounts.

Deciphering Gross Profit

Business owners must carefully watch their Gross Profit trends on monthly profit and loss statements. Gross Profit trends that appear lower from one month to the next can mean one of two things: sales revenue is down, or Cost of Goods Sold is up.

If revenue is down month to month, you may need to find out quickly why and fix the problem in order to meet your sales goals for the year. Or, by examining sales figures for the same month in previous years, you may determine that the drop is just a normal sales slowdown given the time of year and isn't cause to hit the panic button.

If the downward trend isn't normal, it may be a sign that a competitor's successfully drawing customers away from your business, or it may indicate that customers are dissatisfied with some aspect of the products or services you supply. Whatever the reason, preparing a monthly profit and loss statement gives you the ammunition you need to find and fix a problem quickly, thereby minimising any negative hit to your yearly profits.

The other key element of Gross Profit, Cost of Goods Sold, can also be a big factor in a downward profit trend. For example, if the amount you spend to purchase products that you sell goes up, your Gross Profit goes down. As a business owner, you need to do one of five things if the Cost of Goods Sold is reducing your Gross Profit:

✔ Find a new supplier who can provide the goods cheaper.

✔ Increase your prices, as long as you don't lose sales because of the increase.

✔ Find a way to increase your volume of sales so that you can sell more products and meet your annual profit goals.

✔ Find a way to reduce other expenses to offset the additional product costs.

✔ Accept the fact that your annual profit is going to be lower than expected.

The sooner you find out that you have a problem with costs, the faster you can find a solution and minimise any reduction in your annual profit goals.

Monitoring Expenses

The Expenses section of your profit and loss statement gives you a good summary of how much you spent to keep your business operating that wasn't directly related to the sale of an individual product or service. For example, businesses usually use advertising both to bring customers in and with the hopes of selling many different types of products. That's why you need to list advertising as an Expense rather than a Cost of Goods Sold. After all, rarely can you link an advertisement to the sale of an individual product. The same is true of all the administrative expenses that go into running a business, such as rent, wages and salaries, office costs and so on.

Business owners watch their expense trends closely to be sure that they don't creep upwards and lower the business's bottom lines. Any cost-cutting you can do on the expense side is guaranteed to increase your bottom-line profit.

Using the Profit and Loss Statement to Make Business Decisions

Many business owners find it easier to compare their profit and loss statement trends using percentages rather than the actual numbers. Calculating these percentages is easy enough – you simply divide each line item by Net Sales. Figure 18-2 shows a business's percentage breakdown for one month.

Profit and Loss Statement

May 2010

Month Ended	May	
Net Sales	£ 18,875	100.0%
Cost of Goods Sold	(£ 6,500)	34.4%
Gross Profit	£ 12,375	65.6%
Operating Expenses:		
Advertising	£ 1,500	7.9%
Bank Service Charges	£ 120	0.6%
Insurance Expenses	£ 100	0.5%
Interest Expenses	£ 125	0.7%
Legal & Accounting Fees	£ 300	1.6%
Office Expenses	£ 250	1.3%
Payroll Taxes Expenses	£ 350	1.9%
Postage Expenses	£ 75	0.4%
Rent Expenses	£ 800	4.2%
Salaries	£ 3,500	18.5%
Supplies	£ 300	1.6%
Telephone Expenses	£ 200	1.1%
Utilities	£ 255	1.4%
Total Operating Expenses	£ 7,875	41.7%
Net Profit	£ 4,500	23.8%

Figure 18-2: Percentage breakdown of a profit and loss statement.

Looking at this percentage breakdown, you can see that the business had a gross profit of 65.6 per cent, and its Cost of Goods Sold, at 34.4 per cent, accounted for just over one-third of the revenue. If the prior month's Cost of Goods Sold was only 32 per cent, the business owner needs to find out why the cost of the goods used to make this product seems to have increased. If this trend of increased Cost of Goods Sold continues through the year without some kind of fix, the business makes at least 2.2 per cent less net profit.

You may find it helpful to see how your profit and loss statement results compare to industry trends for similar businesses with similar revenues, a process called *benchmarking*. By comparing results, you can find out if your costs and expenses are reasonable for the type of business you operate, and you can identify areas with room to improve your profitability. You also may spot some red flags for line items upon which you spend much more than the national average.

To find industry trends for businesses similar to yours with similar revenues, visit www.bvdinfo.com. The FAME database contains full financial data on approximately two million companies in the UK and Ireland that file their accounts at Companies House. A word of warning though: small companies are required to file very little financial information – typically just a balance sheet. This means that if you want to see detailed profit and loss information you have to look at the big businesses with turnover above £5.6 million and a balance sheet greater than £2.8 million.

However, the information available for all the companies on this database is useful and can be searched in a number of ways. For example, you can compile industry-average statistics, which can be a useful way to see how your business compares with others in the same line of business. You can take this a stage farther and compare your business to other businesses that you already know or have found on this database.

You can also find out how your business looks to the outside world if you use FAME to dig out the financials for your business. A credit rating, details of any court judgements and other interesting information are all included in the reports.

FAME is available by subscription, which may make it expensive for the occasional user. You may find that a regional library has FAME available to the public on a free basis or through a per-session cost. Most of the UK universities have FAME, so if you can access one of their library services you can also use this facility. This service may be available through an annual library subscription.

Another source of financial information is your local business link (www.businesslink.gov.uk). Business link acts as a signpost to help small and medium-sized businesses. They can help you access your trade association and other business support agencies and consultancies that run benchmarking.

Testing Profits

With a completed profit and loss statement, you can do a number of quick ratio tests of your business's profitability. You certainly want to know how well your business did compared to other similar businesses. You also want to be able to measure your *return* (the percentage you made) on your business.

Three common tests are Return on Sales, Return on Assets and Return on Shareholders' Capital. These ratios have much more meaning if you can find industry averages for your particular type of business, so that you can compare your results. Check with your local Chamber of Commerce to see whether it has figures for local businesses or order a report for your industry online from FAME.

Return on Sales

The Return on Sales (ROS) ratio tells you how efficiently your business runs its operations. Using the information on your profit and loss statement, you can measure how much profit your business produced per pound of sales and how much extra cash you brought in per sale.

You calculate ROS by dividing net profit before taxes by sales. For example, suppose your business had a net profit of £4,500 and sales of £18,875. The following shows your calculation of ROS.

Net profit before taxes ÷ Sales = Return on Sales

£4,500 ÷ £18,875 = 23.8%

As you can see, your business made 23.8 per cent on each pound of sales. To determine whether that amount calls for celebration, you need to find the ROS ratios for similar businesses. You may be able to get such information from your local Chamber of Commerce, or you can order an industry report online from FAME.

Return on Assets

The Return on Assets (ROA) ratio tests how well you're using your business's assets to generate profits. If your business's ROA is the same or higher than other similar companies, you're doing a good job of managing your assets.

To calculate ROA, you divide net profit by total assets. You find total assets on your balance sheet, which you can read more about in Chapter 19. Suppose that your business's net profit was £4,500 and total assets were £40,050. The following shows your calculation of ROA.

Net profit ÷ Total assets = Return on Assets

£4,500 ÷ £40,050 = 11.2%

Your calculation shows that your business made 11.2 per cent on each pound of assets it held.

ROA can vary significantly depending on the type of industry in which you operate. For example, if your business requires you to maintain lots of expensive equipment, such as a manufacturing firm, your ROA is much lower than a service business that doesn't need as many assets. ROA can range from below 5 per cent, for manufacturing businesses that require a large investment in machinery and factories, to as high as 20 per cent or even higher for service businesses with few assets.

Return on Shareholders' Capital

To measure how successfully your business earned money for the owners or investors, calculate the Return on Shareholders' Capital (ROSC) ratio. This ratio often looks better than Return on Assets (see the preceding section) because ROSC doesn't take debt into consideration.

You calculate ROSC by dividing net profit by shareholders' or owners' capital. (You find capital amounts on your balance sheet; see Chapter 19.) Suppose your business's net profit was £4,500 and the owners' capital was £9,500. Here is the formula:

Net profit ÷ Shareholders' or owners' capital = Return on Shareholders' Capital

£4,500 ÷ £9,500 = 47.3%

Most business owners put in a lot of cash upfront to get a business started, so seeing a business whose liabilities and capital are split close to 50 per cent each is fairly common.

Branching Out with Profit and Loss Statement Data

The profit and loss statement you produce for external use – financial institutions and investors – may be very different from the one you produce for in-house use by your managers. Most business owners prefer to provide the minimum amount of detail necessary to satisfy external users of their financial statements, such as summaries of expenses instead of line-by-line expense details, a Net Sales figure without reporting all the detail about discounts and fees, and a cost of goods number without reporting all the detail about how that was calculated.

Internally, the contents of the profit and loss statement are a very different story. With more detail, your managers are better able to make accurate business decisions. Most businesses develop detailed reports based on the data collected to develop the profit and loss statement. Items such as discounts, returns and allowances are commonly pulled out of profit and loss statements and broken down into more detail:

- ✔ **Discounts** are reductions on the selling price as part of a special sale. They may also be in the form of volume discounts provided to customers who buy large amounts of the business's products. For example, a business may offer a 10 per cent discount to customers who buy 20 or more of the same item at one time. In order to put their Net Sales numbers in perspective, business owners and managers must monitor how much they reduce their revenues to attract sales.

- ✔ **Returns** are transactions in which the buyer returns items for any reason – not the right size, damaged, defective and so on. If a business's number of returns increases dramatically, a larger problem may be the cause; therefore business owners need to monitor these numbers carefully in order to identify and resolve any problems with the items they sell.

- ✔ **Allowances** cover gifts cards and other accounts that customers pay for upfront without taking any merchandise. Allowances are actually a liability for a business because the customer (or the person who was given the gift card) eventually comes back to get merchandise and doesn't have to pay any cash in return.

Another section of the profit and loss statement that you're likely to break down into more detail for internal use is the Cost of Goods Sold. Basically, you take the detail collected to calculate that line item, including Opening Stock, Closing Stock, purchases and purchase discounts, and present it in a separate report. (I explain how to calculate Cost of Goods Sold in the section 'Finding Cost of Goods Sold', earlier in this chapter.)

No limit exists to the number of internal reports you can generate from the detail that goes into your profit and loss statement and other financial statements. For example, many businesses design a report that looks at month-to-month trends in revenue, Cost of Goods Sold and profit. In fact, you can set up your computerised accounting system (if you use one) to generate this and other custom-designed reports automatically. Using your computerised system, you can produce these reports at any time during the month if you want to see how close you are to meeting your month-end, quarter-end or year-end goal.

Many businesses also design a report that compares actual spending to the budget. On this report, each of the profit and loss statement line items appear with their accompanying planned budget figures and the actual figures. When reviewing this report, you flag any line item that's considerably higher or lower than expected and then research them to find a reason for the difference.

Chapter 19

Developing a Balance Sheet

In This Chapter

▶ Tackling the balance sheet

▶ Pulling together your balance sheet accounts

▶ Choosing a format

▶ Drawing conclusions from your balance sheet

▶ Polishing electronically produced balance sheets

*P*eriodically, you want to know how well your business is doing. Therefore, at the end of each accounting period, you draw up a balance sheet – a snapshot of your business's condition. This snapshot gives you a picture of where your business stands – its assets, its liabilities and how much the owners have invested in the business at a particular point in time.

This chapter explains the key ingredients of a balance sheet and tells you how to pull them all together. You also find out how to use some analytical tools called ratios to see how well your business is doing.

Breaking Down the Balance Sheet

Basically, creating a balance sheet is like taking a picture of the financial aspects of your business.

The business name appears at the top of the balance sheet along with the ending date for the accounting period being reported. The rest of the report summarises:

✔ **The business's assets,** which include everything the business owns in order to stay in operation

✔ **The business's debts,** which include any outstanding bills and loans that must be paid

✔ **The owners' capital,** which is basically how much the business owners have invested in the business

Assets, liabilities and capital probably sound familiar – they're the key elements that show whether or not your books are in balance. If your liabilities plus capital equal assets, your books are in balance. All your bookkeeping efforts are an attempt to keep the books in balance based on this formula, which I talk more about in Chapter 2.

Gathering Balance Sheet Ingredients

You can find most of the information you need to prepare a balance sheet on your trial balance worksheet, the details of which are drawn from your final adjusted trial balance. (I show you how to develop a trial balance in Chapter 16 and how to adjust that trial balance in Chapter 17.)

To keep this example simple, I assume that the fictitious business has no adjustments for the balance sheet as of 31 May 2010. In the real world, every business needs to adjust something (usually stock levels at the very least) every month.

To prepare the example trial balances in this chapter, I use the key accounts listed in Table 19-1; these accounts and numbers come from the fictitious business's trial balance worksheet.

Table 19-1	Balance Sheet Accounts	
Account Name	**Balance in Account**	
	Debit	Credit
Cash	£2,500	
Petty Cash	£500	
Trade Debtors (Accounts Receivable)	£1,000	
Stock	£1,200	
Equipment	£5,050	
Vehicles	£25,000	
Furniture	£5,600	
Drawings	£10,000	
Trade Creditors (Accounts Payable)		£2,200
Loans Payable		£29,150
Capital		£5,000
Net Profit for the Year		£14,500
Total	£50,850	£50,850

Dividing and listing your assets

The first part of the balance sheet is the Assets section. The first step in developing this section is dividing your assets into two categories: current assets and fixed assets.

Current assets

Current assets are things your business owns that you can easily convert to cash and expect to use in the next 12 months to pay your bills and your employees. Current assets include cash, Trade Debtors (money due from customers), marketable securities (including shares, bonds and other types of securities) and stock. (I cover Trade Debtors in Chapter 10 and stock in Chapter 9.)

When you see cash as the first line item on a balance sheet, that account includes what you have on hand in the tills and what you have in the bank, including current accounts, savings accounts, money market accounts and certificates of deposit. In most cases, you simply list all these accounts as one item, Cash, on the balance sheet.

The current assets for the fictional business are:

Cash	£2,500
Petty Cash	£500
Trade Debtors	£1,000
Stock	£1,200

You total the Cash and Petty Cash accounts, giving you £3,000, and list that amount on the balance sheet as a line item called Cash.

Fixed assets

Fixed assets are things your business owns that you expect to have for more than 12 months. Fixed assets include land, buildings, equipment, furniture, vehicles and anything else that you expect to have for longer than a year.

The fixed assets for the fictional business are:

Equipment	£5,050
Vehicles	£25,000
Furniture	£5,600

Most businesses have more items in the fixed assets section of a balance sheet than the few fixed assets I show here for the fictional business. For example:

- ✔ A manufacturing business that has a lot of tools, dies or moulds created specifically for its manufacturing processes needs to have a line item called Tools, Dies and Moulds.

- ✔ A business that owns one or more buildings needs to have a line item labelled Land and Buildings.

- ✔ A business that leases a building with an option to purchase it at some later date considers that *capitalised lease* to be a fixed asset, and lists it on the balance sheet as a Capitalised Lease. An example of a capitalised lease is where you pay a premium for a lease and regard that premium as a fixed asset rather than an expense. The premium becomes a capitalised lease and set against profits over the life of the lease.

- ✔ A business may lease its business space and then spend lots of money doing it up. For example, a restaurant may rent a large space and then furnish it according to a desired theme. Money spent on doing up the space becomes a fixed asset called Leasehold Improvements and is listed on the balance sheet in the fixed assets section.

Everything mentioned so far in this section – land, buildings, capitalised leases, leasehold improvements and so on – is a *tangible asset.* These items are ones that you can actually touch or hold. Another type of fixed asset is the *intangible asset.* Intangible assets aren't physical objects; common examples are patents, copyrights and trademarks.

- ✔ A **patent** gives a business the right to dominate the markets for the patented product. When a patent expires (usually after 20 years), competitors can enter the marketplace for the product that was patented, and the competition helps to lower the price to consumers. For example, pharmaceutical businesses patent all their new drugs and therefore are protected as the sole providers of those drugs. When your doctor prescribes a brand-name drug, you're getting a patented product. Generic drugs are products whose patents have run out, meaning that any pharmaceutical business can produce and sell its own version of the same product.

- ✔ A **copyright** protects original works, including books, magazines, articles, newspapers, television shows, movies, music, poetry and plays, from being copied by anyone other than the creator(s). For example, this book is copyrighted, so no one can make a copy of any of its contents without the permission of the publisher, John Wiley & Sons, Ltd.

- ✔ A **trademark** gives a business ownership of distinguishing words, phrases, symbols or designs. For example, check out this book's cover to see the registered trademark, *For Dummies,* for this brand. Trademarks can last forever, as long as a business continues to use the trademark and file the proper paperwork periodically.

In order to show in financial statements that their values are being used up, all fixed assets are depreciated or amortised. Tangible assets are depreciated; see Chapter 12 for details on how to depreciate. Intangible assets such as patents and copyrights are amortised (amortisation is very similar to depreciation). Each intangible asset has a lifespan based on the number of years for which the rights are granted. After setting an initial value for the intangible asset, a business then divides that value by the number of years it has protection, and the resulting amount is then written off each year as an Amortisation Expense, which is shown on the profit and loss statement. You can find the total amortisation or depreciation expenses that have been written off during the life of the asset on the balance sheet in a line item called Accumulated Depreciation or Accumulated Amortisation, whichever is appropriate for the type of asset.

Acknowledging your debts

The Liabilities section of the balance sheet comes after the Assets section and shows all the money that your business owes to others, including banks, suppliers, contractors, financial institutions and individuals. Like assets, you divide your liabilities into two categories on the balance sheet:

- ✓ **Current liabilities:** All bills and debts that you plan to pay within the next 12 months. Accounts appearing in this section include Trade Creditors (bills due to suppliers, contractors and others), Credit Cards Payable and the current portion of a long-term debt (for example, if you have a mortgage on your premises, the payments due in the next 12 months appear in the Current Liabilities section).

- ✓ **Long-term liabilities:** All debts you owe to lenders that are to be paid over a period longer than 12 months. Mortgages Payable and Loans Payable are common accounts in the long-term liabilities section of the balance sheet.

Most businesses try to minimise their current liabilities because the interest rates on short-term loans, such as credit cards, are usually much higher than those on loans with longer terms. As you manage your business's liabilities, always look for ways to minimise your interest payments by seeking longer-term loans with lower interest rates than you can get on a credit card or short-term loan.

The fictional business used for the example balance sheets in this chapter has only one account in each liabilities section:

Current liabilities:

Trade Creditors   £2,200

Long-term liabilities:

Loans Payable   £29,150

Naming your investments

Every business has investors. Even a small family business requires money upfront to get the business on its feet. Investments are reflected on the balance sheet as *capital*. The line items that appear in a balance sheet's Capital section vary depending upon whether or not the business is incorporated. (Businesses incorporate primarily to minimise their personal legal liabilities; I talk more about incorporation in Chapter 22.)

If you're preparing the books for a business that isn't incorporated, the Capital section of your balance sheet contains these accounts:

- ✔ **Capital:** All money invested by the owners to start up the business as well as any additional contributions made after the start-up phase. If the business has more than one owner, the balance sheet usually has a Capital account for each owner so that individual stakes in the business can be recorded.

- ✔ **Drawings:** All money taken out of the business by the business's owners. Balance sheets usually have a Drawing account for each owner in order to record individual withdrawal amounts.

- ✔ **Retained Earnings:** All profits left in the business.

For an incorporated business, the Capital section of the balance sheet contains the following accounts:

- ✔ **Shares:** Portions of ownership in the business, purchased as investments by business owners.

- ✔ **Retained Earnings:** All profits that have been reinvested in the business.

Because the fictional business isn't incorporated, the accounts appearing in the Capital section of its balance sheet are:

Capital   £5,000

Retained Earnings   £4,500

Sorting out share investments

You're probably most familiar with the sale of shares on the open market through the various stock market exchanges, such as the London Stock Exchange (LSE) and the Alternative Investment Market (AIM). However, not all companies sell their shares through public exchanges; in fact, most companies aren't public companies but rather remain private operations.

Whether public or private, ownership in a business is obtained by buying shares. If the business isn't publicly traded, shares are bought and sold privately. In most small businesses, these exchanges are made among family members, close friends and occasionally outside investors who have been approached individually as a means to raise additional money to build the business.

The value of each share is set at the time the share is sold. Many businesses set the initial share value at £1 to £10.

Pulling Together the Final Balance Sheet

After you group together all your accounts (see the preceding section 'Gathering Balance Sheet Ingredients'), you're ready to produce a balance sheet. Businesses in the United Kingdom usually choose between two common formats for their balance sheets: the Horizontal format or the Vertical format, with the Vertical format preferred. The actual line items appearing in both formats are the same; the only difference is the way in which you lay out the information on the page.

Horizontal format

The Horizontal format is a two-column layout with assets on one side and liabilities and capital on the other side.

Figure 19-1 shows the elements of a sample balance sheet in the Horizontal format.

Balance Sheet
As of 31 May 2010

Fixed Assets			Capital	
Equipment	£ 5,050		Opening balance	£ 5,000
Furniture	£ 5,600		Net Profit for year	£ 14,500
Vehicles	£ 25,000			£ 19,500
		£ 35,650	Less Drawings	£ 10,000
				£ 9,500
			Long-term Liabilities	
			Loans Payable	£ 29,150
Current Assets			**Current Liabilities**	
Stock	£ 1,200		Trade Creditors	£ 2,200
Trade Debtors	£ 1,000			
Cash	£ 3,000			
		£ 5,200		
		£ 40,850		£ 40,850

Figure 19-1:
A sample balance sheet using the Horizontal format.

Vertical format

The Vertical format is a one-column layout showing assets first, followed by liabilities and then capital.

Using the Vertical Format, Figure 19-2 shows the balance sheet for a fictional business.

Whether you prepare your balance sheet as per Figure 19-1 or Figure 19-2, remember that Assets = Liabilities + Capital, so both sides of the balance sheet must balance to reflect this.

The Vertical format includes:

✔ **Net current assets:** Calculated by subtracting current assets from current liabilities – a quick test to see whether or not a business has the money on hand to pay bills. Net current assets is sometimes referred to as *working capital*.

✔ **Total assets less current liabilities:** What's left over for a business's owners after all liabilities have been subtracted from total assets. Total assets less current liabilities is sometimes referred to as *net assets*.

Balance Sheet
As of 31 May 2010

Fixed Assets

Equipment	£ 5,050	
Furniture	£ 5,600	
Vehicles	£ 25,000	
		£ 35,650

Current Assets

Stock	£ 1,200	
Trade Debtors	£ 1,000	
Cash	£ 3,000	
	£ 5,200	

Less: Current Liabilities

Trade Creditors	£ 2,200	
Net Current Assets		£ 3,000
Total Assets Less Current Liabilities		£ 38,650
Long-term Liabilities		
Loans Payable		£ 29,150
		£ 9,500

Capital

Opening Balance		£ 5,000
Net Profit for Year		£ 14,500
		£ 19,500
Less Drawings		£ 10,000
		£ 9,500

Figure 19-2: A sample balance sheet using the Vertical format.

Putting Your Balance Sheet to Work

With a complete balance sheet in your hands, you can analyse the numbers through a series of ratio tests to check your cash status and monitor your debt. These tests are the type of tests that financial institutions and potential investors use to determine whether or not to lend money to or invest in your business. Therefore, a good idea is to run these tests yourself before seeking loans or investors. Ultimately, the ratio tests in this section can help you determine whether or not your business is in a strong cash position.

Testing your cash

When you approach a bank or other financial institution for a loan, you can expect the lender to use one of two ratios to test your cash flow: the *current ratio* and the *acid test ratio* (also known as the *quick ratio*).

Current ratio

This ratio compares your current assets to your current liabilities and provides a quick glimpse of your business's ability to pay its bills in the short term.

The formula for calculating the current ratio is:

Current assets ÷ Current liabilities = Current ratio

The following is an example of a current ratio calculation:

£5,200 ÷ £2,200 = 2.36 (current ratio)

Lenders usually look for current ratios of 1.2 to 2, so any financial institution considers a current ratio of 2.36 a good sign. A current ratio under 1 is considered a danger sign because it indicates the business doesn't have enough cash to pay its current bills. This rule is only a rough guide and some business sectors may require a higher or lower current ratio figure. Get some advice to see what the norm is for your business sector.

A current ratio over 2.0 may indicate that your business isn't investing its assets well and may be able to make better use of its current assets. For example, if your business is holding a lot of cash, you may want to invest that money in some long-term assets, such as additional equipment, that you can use to help grow the business.

Acid test (quick) ratio

The acid test ratio uses only the financial figures in your business's Cash account, Trade Debtors and Marketable Securities – otherwise known as *liquid assets*. Although similar to the current ratio in that it examines current assets and liabilities, the acid test ratio is a stricter test of a business's ability to pay bills. The assets part of this calculation doesn't take stock into account because it can't always be converted to cash as quickly as other current assets and because, in a slow market, selling your stock may take a while.

Many lenders prefer the acid test ratio when determining whether or not to give a business a loan because of its strictness.

Calculating the acid test ratio is a two-step process:

1. **Determine your quick assets.**

   Cash + Trade Debtors + Marketable securities = Quick assets

2. **Calculate your quick ratio.**

   Quick assets ÷ Current liabilities = Quick ratio

The following is an example of an acid test ratio calculation:

£2,000 + £1,000 + £1,000 = £4,000 (quick assets)

£4,000 ÷ £2,200 = 1.8 (acid test ratio)

Lenders consider that a business with an acid test ratio around 1 is in good condition. An acid test ratio less than 1 indicates that the business may have to sell some of its marketable securities or take on additional debt until it can sell more of its stock.

Assessing your debt

Before you even consider whether or not to take on additional debt, always check out your debt condition. One common ratio that you can use to assess your business's debt position is the *gearing ratio*. This ratio compares what your business owes – *external borrowing* – to what your business owners have invested in the business – *internal funds*.

Calculating your debt to capital ratio is a two-step process:

1. **Calculate your total debt.**

   Current liabilities + Long-term liabilities = Total debt

2. **Calculate your gearing ratio.**

   Total debt ÷ Capital = Gearing ratio

The following is an example of a debt to capital ratio calculation:

£2,200 + £29,150 = £31,350 (total debt)

£31,350 ÷ £9,500 = 3.3 (gearing ratio)

Lenders like to see a gearing ratio close to 1 because it indicates that the amount of debt is equal to the amount of capital. Most banks probably wouldn't lend any more money to a business with a debt to capital ratio of

3.3 until its debt levels were lowered or the owners put more money into the business. The reason for this lack of confidence may be one of two:

- ✔ They don't want to have more money invested in the business than the owner.
- ✔ They are concerned about the business's ability to service the debt.

Generating Balance Sheets Electronically

If you use a computerised accounting system, you can take advantage of its report function to generate your balance sheets automatically. These balance sheets give you quick snapshots of the business's financial position but may require adjustments before you prepare your financial reports for external use.

One key adjustment you're likely to make involves the value of your stock. Most computerised accounting systems use the averaging method to value stock. This method totals all the stock purchased and then calculates an average price for the stock (see Chapter 9 for more information on stock valuation). However, your accountant may recommend a different valuation method that works better for your business. I discuss the options in Chapter 9. Therefore, if you use a method other than the default averaging method to value your stock, you need to adjust the stock value that appears on the balance sheet generated from your computerised accounting system.

Chapter 20

Reporting for Not-For-Profit Organisations

*U*nderstanding what motivates a business owner is easy – profit and business growth. Consequently these owners need a bookkeeping system that enables them to manage that process. But what if your organisation isn't motivated by profit, but drawn together by a common interest? What if you aren't driven by growing sales and forcing up margins? Up and down the United Kingdom thousands of clubs, associations and other not-for-profit organisations exist, for which trading and making a profit isn't the main purpose. The reality is that these organisations don't need to focus on sales, margins and profit. They really need to focus on good stewardship of the organisation's funds and reporting back to the members in a simple format that those members can understand. Therefore, preparing a conventional profit and loss account is overkill for their needs.

In this chapter, I cover the key types of financial statements that a not-for-profit organisation may need. The bookkeeping principles are exactly the same as covered in other chapters, but the financial statements are far more basic.

Keeping Only Receipts and Payments Accounts

The simplest not-for-profit organisations require only a simple annual summary of the Cash book. If a group operates entirely on a cash basis – that is, doesn't take credit for anything it buys and receives cash for any club subscriptions and other fund-raising activities – simple receipts and payment accounts meet their needs. This type of organisation can operate just with the Cash book, using that for both receipts and payments.

The only asset that this type of organisation has is a cash or bank balance. The books for this type of organisation are kept on a cash-basis, which is covered in Chapter 2.

Figure 20-1 shows what a typical Receipts and Payments account looks like for an imaginary club.

The Cirencester Running Club
Receipts and Payments account for the year ended 30 June 2010

Receipts		*Payments*	
Bank balance as at 1.7.09	£ 236	Printing and stationery	£ 150
Subscriptions received during the year	£ 650	Coach to London Marathon	£ 300
Annual fundraising event	£ 116	Village Hall rent	£ 500
Ban interest received	£ 11	Bank balance as at 30.6.10	£ 63
	£ 1,013		£ 1,013

Figure 20-1: A simple Receipts and Payments account.

The low volume of transactions doesn't warrant being computerised. No trading activity exists to report on. The only sources of income are the members' subs and an annual fund-raising event. Because these two income sources account for less than £1,000 in the year, no further analysis is really required.

The bookkeeping skills required to run this organisation and prepare this type of financial statement are minimal. The only ongoing monitoring is of the bank balance.

Tallying Income and Expenditure Accounts

Some types of not-for-profit organisations own assets and have liabilities. A sports club, for example, may own the grounds on which it plays and the clubhouse in which it socialises, or at least is responsible for paying to keep the grounds in good condition. An organisation may boost cash reserves with ongoing or frequent fund-generating activity. For example, it may have a club bar, which involves buying in and selling drink, snacks and maybe food.

Realising that you need more accounts

Even very simple business activity is likely to have accounting issues such as stock, purchases of supplies on credit and unpaid wages. If your organisation has any assets or liabilities, the Receipts and Payments account isn't a good way of preparing final accounts because it shows only the cash balances and not the other assets and liabilities. Instead, you need the following:

✔ A balance sheet (explained in Chapter 19)

✔ An Income and Expenditure account that shows changes in the organisation's capital

Instead of a Capital account, which is an element in a balance sheet for a sole trader or partnership, the balance sheet for a not-for-profit organisation has an Accumulated Fund.

A sole trader or partnership uses the formula:

Capital + Liabilities = Assets

In a not-for-profit organisation, you substitute:

Accumulated Fund + Liabilities = Assets

As far as accounting rules are concerned, an Income and Expenditure account follows the same principles as the profit and loss statement (covered in Chapter 18), which means that these books are kept on an accrual accounting basis. The only real difference is in the terminology used, which is highlighted in Table 20-1.

Table 20-1	Accounts Terminology Translation
Profit-making business	*Not-for-profit organisation*
Profit and loss statement	Income and Expenditure account
Net profit	Surplus of income over expenditure
Net loss	Excess of expenditure over income
Capital account	Accumulated Fund

This type of organisation has many characteristics similar to those of a business enterprise – the use of assets, trading activity and liabilities. The only real difference is the scale of operations and the motive for being in business. Any trading or fund-raising activities are on a much smaller scale and the motivation is to swell the organisation's funds so that it can prosper as a group.

A not-for-profit organisation may have reason to prepare a profit and loss statement: for example, where the organisation ran an event, say a disco, with the purpose of making a profit to provide funds for the repair of the clubhouse. For this type of activity, a profit and loss statement needs to be prepared and any profit made transferred into the main Income and Expenditure account.

Preparing Income and Expenditure accounts

Preparing an Income and Expenditure account is similar to preparing a profit and loss statement – just with different terminology, depth of information and format. The only new concept is that a not-for-profit organisation doesn't have shareholders or a proprietor. The organisation is owned by the members, and they usually pay annual subscriptions to enjoy the facilities of the club.

It follows therefore that in preparing Income and Expenditure accounts for a not-for-profit organisation, you need to maintain the full range of journals and ledgers that you do for a profit-based business. The information in Chapter 18 can guide you in preparing financial reports.

In this example, the treasurer of the Ashcroft Gardens Football Club prepared an Income and Expenditure account and a balance sheet for the club, as well as a separate profit and loss statement for the bar run to make a profit for the club.

The first step in preparing Income and Expenditure accounts is readying a Receipts and Payments account (see the preceding 'Keeping Only Receipts and Payments Accounts' section). A sample account is shown in Figure 20-2.

The Ashcroft Gardens Football Club
Receipts and Payments account for the year ended 31 December 2010

Receipts		*Payments*	
Bank balance as at 1.1.09	£ 500	Payment for bar supplies	£ 4,000
Subscriptions received		Wages:	
during the year:		Ground keeper	£ 1,000
2004 (arrears)	£ 70	Barman	£ 500
2005	£ 1,500	Bar expenses	£ 300
2006 (in advance)	£ 50	Club house repairs	£ 150
Bar sales	£ 6,000	Pitch maintenance	£ 200
Donations received	£ 150	Treasurer's expenses	£ 150
		Club travel	£ 300
		Bank balance as at 31.12.10	£ 1,670
	£ 8,270		£ 8,270

Figure 20-2: A sample Income and Expenditure account.

The members who saw this statement agreed that it was inadequate because it didn't give a clear picture of how well the bar had performed. Also, it treated overdue and prepaid subscriptions as part of the current year's receipts, which was clearly wrong. And to add insult to injury, no provision was made for depreciation of the clubhouse (£200 per annum), the club equipment (£110 per annum) and bar stocks of £600 (last year this figure had been £500). Also, unknown to the members, the club had several creditors, a schedule of which is shown in Table 20-2.

Table 20-2	Ashcroft Gardens Football Club Creditors	
Creditor	*31.12.09*	*31.12.10*
Bar supply creditor	£300	£340
Bar expenses owing	£30	£36
Club travel costs owing	£0	£65

Based on this information, the treasurer, with a little help from the accountant, prepared the following accounts:

- ✔ A Statement of Affairs, which is a type of cash-based balance sheet, as at 31 December 2009, shown in Figure 20-3. A *Statement of Affairs* is a simplified balance sheet for any organisation that does not have a formal bookkeeping system and few transactions within the accounting year. Quite often the accountant who prepares these statements does so from inadequate records – often referred to as *incomplete records*.

- ✔ A profit and loss statement for the bar for the year ending 31 December 2010, shown in Figure 20-4. This is prepared, as for a profit organisation, when you need to show the results for activity run to make a profit.

- ✔ The final accounts – Income and Expenditure for the year ended 31 December 2010 and balance sheet as at 31 December 2010, shown in Figures 20-6 and 20-8.

These accounts clearly show that the bar made a profit of £1,254, which was transferred into the Income and Expenditure account, as well as the healthy state of the club's balance sheet with net assets of £16,649.

Figure 20-5 shows how the purchases and bar expenses figures are calculated for the profit and loss statement in Figure 20-4.

The workings in Figure 20-6 show how the numbers for the transport costs and subscriptions received were calculated for the Income and Expenditure account shown in Figure 20-7.

In the example in Figure 20-7, the treasurer treats subscriptions owing as an asset. However, most subscriptions that have been overdue for a long time are never paid. Many clubs don't bring in unpaid subscriptions as an asset in the balance sheet. This obviously prudent approach ensures that the balance sheet assets aren't overstated. Good practice when preparing club accounts, or any other organisation that relies on subscription income, needs to exclude all outstanding subscriptions from the final accounts.

Donations must be treated as income during the year in which they are received. Also, new members at some clubs (such as golf clubs) have to pay an entrance fee when they join in addition to their annual membership fee. Entrance fees are usually included as income in the year of receipt.

The Ashcroft Gardens Football Club
Statement of Affairs as at 31 December 2009

	£	£	£
Fixed Assets			
Land			10,000
Clubhouse			4,000
Club equipment			1,100
			15,100
Current Assets			
Bar stock		500	
Subscription debtors		70	
Cash at bank		500	
		1,070	
Less Current Liabilities			
Creditors	300		
Bar expenses owing	30	330	
Net current assets			740
			15,840
Financed by:			
Accumulated fund (difference)			15,840

Figure 20-3: Statement of Affairs as at 31 December 2009.

The Ashcroft Gardens Football Club
Bar profit and loss statement for the year ended 31 December 2010

	£	£
Sales		6,000
Less Cost of Goods sold:		
Opening stock	500	
Add Purchases	4,040	
	4,540	
Less closing stock	600	3,940
Gross Profit		2,060
Less bar expenses	306	
Bar wages	500	806
Net profit (transferred to Income and Expenditure account)		1,254

Figure 20-4: Bar profit and loss statement for the year ended 31 December 2010.

Purchases Account			£
Cash	£ 4,000	Balance brought forward	£ 300
Balance carried down	£ 340	Profit & Loss	£ 4,040
	£ 4,340		£ 4,340

Bar Expenses			
Cash	£ 300	Balance brought forward	£ 30
Balance carried down	£ 36	Profit & Loss	£ 306
	£ 336		£ 336

Figure 20-5: Purchase and Expense accounts for the bar.

The Ashcroft Gardens Football Club

Income and Expenditure account for the year ended 31 December 2010

	£	£	£
Income			
Subscriptions for 2010			£ 1,580
Profit from the bar			£ 1,254
Donations received			£ 150
			£ 2,984
Less expenditure			
Wages — ground keeper		£ 1,000	
Repairs		£ 150	
Pitch maintenance		£ 200	
Treasurer's expenses		£ 150	
Club travel		£ 365	
Depreciation			
Clubhouse	£ 200		
Club equipment	£ 110	£ 310	£ 2,175
Surplus of income over expenditure			£ 809

Figure 20-6: Working for Transport Costs and Subscription Income.

Transport Costs			
Cash	£300	Balance brought forward	0
Balance carried down	£65	Profit or Loss	£365
	£365		£365

Subscription Income			
Balance brought forward	0	Cash	£1500
Profit or Loss	£1580	Balance carried down	£80
	£1580		£1580

Figure 20-7: Income and Expenditure Account

The Ashcroft Gardens Football Club
Balance sheet as at 31 December 2010

	£	£	£
Fixed Assets			
Land			£ 10,000
Clubhouse		£ 4,000	
Less depreciation		£ 200	£ 3,800
Club equipment		£ 1,100	
Less depreciation		£ 110	£ 990
			£ 14,790
Current Assets			
Bar stocks		£ 600	
Debtors (subscriptions)		£ 80	
Cash at bank		£ 1,670	
		£ 2,350	
Current Liabilities			
Creditors — bar supplies	£ 340		
Bar expenses owing	£ 36		
Travel costs owing	£ 65		
Prepaid subscriptions	£ 50	£ 491	
Net current assets			£ 1,859
			£ 16,649

Figure 20-8:
Balance
sheet for
the football
club.

Financed by:

		£
Accumulated fund		
Balance as at 1.1.10		£ 15,840
Add surplus of income over expenditure		£ 809
		£ 16,649

Chapter 21

Completing Year-End Payroll and Reports

. . . .

In This Chapter

▶ Mastering employee reporting

▶ Preparing forms for employees

▶ Taking care of annual statutory returns

. . . .

*E*ven when you keep diligently up to date with everything concerning your employee payroll and benefits, you still have some paperwork to complete at the end of the year. You need to submit forms for each of your employees as well as some summary reports.

Yes, you guessed it. End-of-the-year HM Revenue & Customs paperwork takes some time. To help make the process as painless as possible, this chapter reviews the forms you need to complete, the information you need for each form and the process for filing your business's payroll information with HM Revenue & Customs. I deal with some of the payroll basics in Chapter 11.

Reporting on Employees

You may think that you've done a lot of paperwork relating to your payroll throughout the year, but the job isn't yet complete. Although you keep individual records for deduction of PAYE tax and National Insurance for each employee, and make payments to HM Revenue & Customs throughout the year, at the end of the tax year on 5 April, HM Revenue & Customs wants more information, to be sure that you haven't missed out on any PAYE tax and National Insurance Contributions (NICs).

I cover the forms you need to submit in some detail in the following sections in the order in which they need to be submitted – so you know when to panic!

HM Revenue & Customs publishes an *Employer Helpbook E10* each year that covers finishing the tax year. You can obtain this from their website, www. hmrc.gov.uk.

Form P14

As far as forms go, the P14, shown in Figure 21-1, is pretty straightforward. In essence the P14 is a summary of each employee's P11 that you have been working with all tax year, and you don't need any more information than what you already have on the employee's P11. I cover the P11 in Chapter 11. Please remember that if you do not send a P14 to HM Revenue & Customs for every employee each tax year, they will not have a record of that person's PAYE, NICs and other deductions record. Also, if you have more than one employee please ensure that you send these to HM Revenue & Customs in alphabetical order. Table 21-1 tells you what to put in each section.

The P14 is due mid-May; check with HM Revenue & Customs for the exact date for the current year.

With this form, and all the end-of-the-year employee-related forms, the key word is accuracy – take care and complete the form slowly. Make sure that you pick up the correct tax year details.

HM Revenue & Customs ask that you submit your P14 forms in alphabetical order.

The last part of form P14 is the P60, but the form is blue (instead of orange). You don't send this to HM Revenue & Customs. Instead, you give each employee his or her own copy, which summarises pay, tax, NICs deductions and so on made during the year.

Don't give a P60 to employees who were no longer with the business at the end of the tax year.

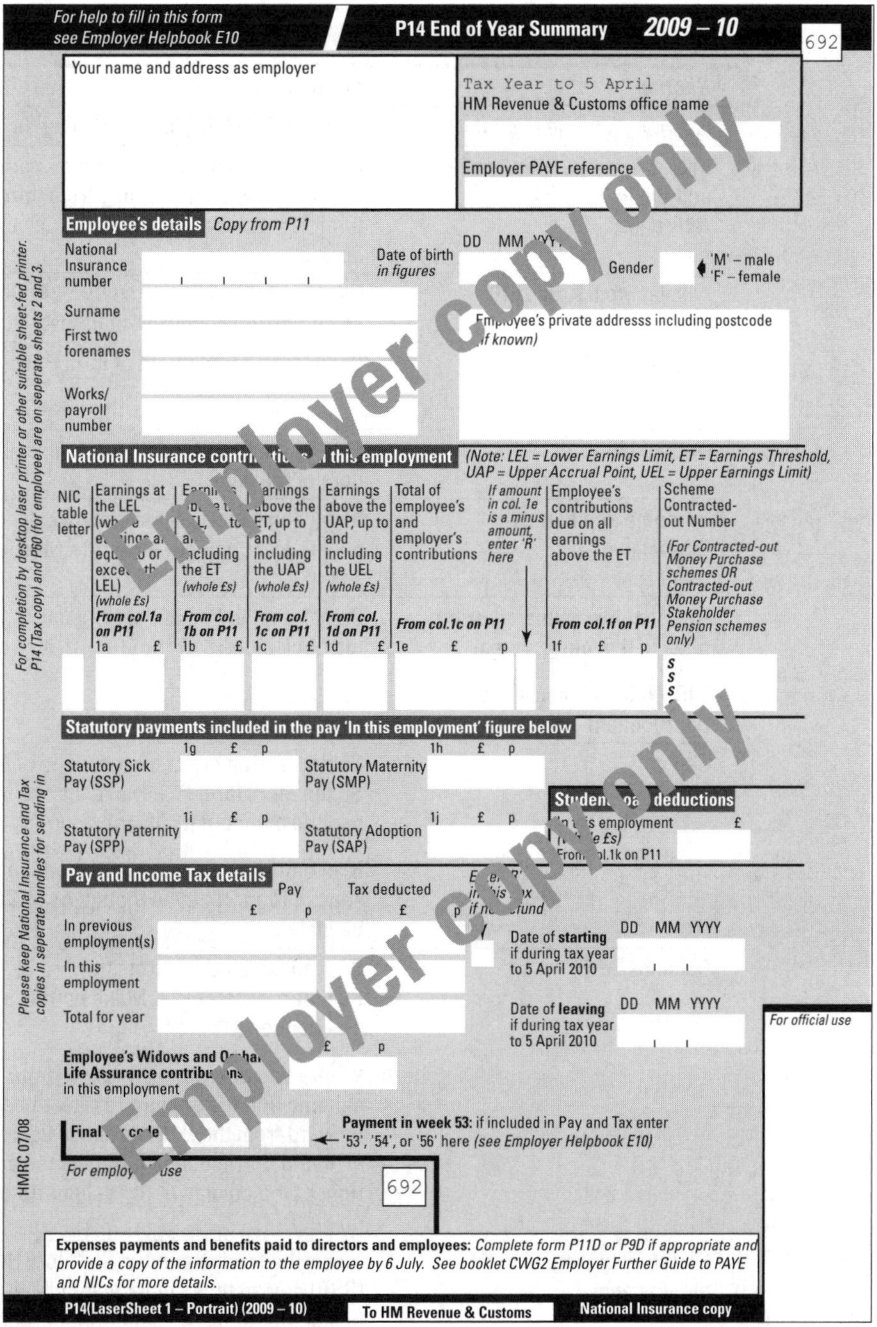

Figure 21-1: Sample P14 End of Year Summary for 2009/10.

© Crown Copyright.

Table 21-1	Sections of Form P14
Section	**What to Do**
Employer's name and address	Show your full address, including the postcode.
Inland Revenue office name and Employer's PAYE reference	Enter your Inland Revenue office name and Employer's PAYE reference from the front of form P35. You can also find this on your payslip booklet.
Tax year to 5 April 2010	Usually pre-printed on the form. Take care to submit the correct year's figures!
Employee's details National Insurance number	Copy this from the front of form P11.
Date of birth	Enter the day and month as well as all four numbers of the year.
Surname and first two forenames	If you don't know all the employee's forenames, put initials. Don't put titles (Mr, Mrs, Miss and so on).
National Insurance contributions in this employment NIC (National Insurance Contribution)Table letter	Copy from the End of Year Summary section on the back of form P11.
Columns 1a to 1c	Copy these amounts from the End of Year Summary of form P11. Make entries in whole pounds and right justify the figures. If an entry exists in column 1a, you must still send in form P14 even though no NICs may be payable.
Columns 1d to 1f	Copy these amounts from the End of Year Summary of form P11. Make entries in pounds and pence. Where you operate a contracted-out pension scheme and the column 1d total to be carried forward from the P11 is a minus figure, enter 'R' in the corresponding box immediately to the right of the column of the column 1d total boxes on the P14.
Statutory payments in this employment Box 1g	Insert the total amount of Statutory Sick Pay (SSP) paid in those months for which an amount has been recovered under the Percentage Threshold Scheme.
Boxes 1h to 1j	Copy these amounts from the corresponding columns on form P11.

Section	What to Do
Scheme Contracted-Out number	Complete this only if the employee is a member of a Contracted-Out Money Purchase (COMP) scheme, COMP Stakeholder Pension (COMPSHP) scheme, or the COMP part of the Contracted-Out Mixed Benefit (COMB) scheme you operate.
	Members of these schemes only receive their Age Related Rebate (ARR) if this part is entered correctly.
Student loan deductions	Copy this amount from the totals box at the bottom of column 1k on form P11.
	Enter whole pounds only.
Date of starting and date of leaving	Make entries if an employee starts and/or leaves your employment during the tax year (2009/10 in this example).
	Enter date as figures: 09 05 2010, for example.
Pay and income tax details In previous employment(s)	Copy these amounts from the End of Year Summary of form P11.
In this employment	Copy these amounts from the End of Year Summary of form P11.
Total for year	Copy these amounts from the End of Year Summary of form P11.
	Fill in these boxes only if the employee was still working for you at 5 April.
Employee's Widows and Orphans/Life Assurance con-tributions in this employment	Applies where an employee is legally obliged to pay contributions that qualify for tax relief but are not authorised under 'net pay arrangements' for tax relief. See *CWG2 Employers Further Guide to PAYE and NICs* for more information.
Final tax code	Fill in boxes from the left-hand side.
	Always show the last tax code you were using at the 5 April date.
Payment in week 53	Use only if Week 53 is included in the Pay and Tax totals, and then put one of the following in this box:
	'53' if 53 weekly pay days were in the year
	'54' if 27 fortnightly pay days were in the year
	'56' if 14 four-weekly pay days were in the year.

Detailing benefits on forms P9D, P11D and P11D (b)

Fortunately, you don't need these forms for the majority of your employees in the typical small business. Basically, these forms are used to report back to HM Revenue & Customs the various benefits in kind that employees received during the year.

The forms and the circumstances they address are as follows:

- ✔ Use the fairly simple form P9D if the employee in question earned at the rate of £8,500 per annum or less. Earnings includes all bonuses, tips and benefits.

- ✔ Use the significantly more complicated form P11D for employees who earned at the rate of £8,500 or more and for all directors, regardless of earnings.

- ✔ Use form P11D(b) to:

    - Confirm that by 6 July all forms P11D have been completed and sent to your HM Revenue & Customs office.

    - Declare the total amount of Class 1A NICs you are due to pay. *Class 1A* contributions are the extra NICs that may be due on taxable benefits that you provide to your employees.

HM Revenue & Customs produces a series of guides to help you get this area of reporting right. Look for the publication for the current tax year:

- ✔ *480 Expenses and Benefits – A Tax Guide:* This guide runs to some 100 pages and is the definitive guide.

- ✔ *CWG2 Employers' Further Guide to PAYE and NICs.*

- ✔ *CWG5 Class 1A NICs on benefits in kind.*

- ✔ *P11D Guide*: This guide is a four-page overview, which makes reference to the *480* guide for more detail.

Within the confines of this book, I can't possibly hope to do justice to the whole detail of benefit-in-kind reporting. However, the following list gives you a brief outline of the kind of things that are deemed to be benefits in kind and need to be included on the P9D or P11D:

- ✔ Assets transferred (cars, property, goods or other assets)

- ✔ Payments made on behalf of the employee

- ✔ Vouchers and credit cards

✔ Living accommodation

✔ Mileage allowance payments/passenger miles

✔ Cars, vans and car fuel

✔ Interest-free, low interest and notional loans

✔ Private medical treatment or insurance

✔ Qualifying relocation expenses payments and benefits

✔ Services supplied

✔ Assets placed at employees' disposal

✔ Computer equipment

✔ Other items – subscriptions, educational assistance, non-qualifying relocation benefits and expenses payments, incidental overnight expenses

✔ Employer-provided childcare

✔ Expenses payments made to, or on behalf of, the director or employee – general expenses for business travel, travel and subsistence, entertainment, home telephone, other non-qualifying relocation expenses

The list seems to go on and on.

Reporting PAYE-free earnings on forms P38, P38A and P38 (S)

Forms P38 and P38A ask you to report payments made to employees from whom you haven't deducted PAYE – such as part-time casual staff. Form P38 (S) applies to students. The following subsections show the type of payments that you need to include or omit on forms P38 or P38A.

Section A

In this section, you:

✔ Include payments above the PAYE threshold.

✔ Include payments to employees who have not produced a P45 and were engaged for more than one week, if both of the following conditions are met:

• The rate of pay was above £95 per week or £412 per month.

• The employee failed to complete certificate A or B on form P46.

✔ Exclude payments included on form P14.

Section B

In this section, you:

  ✔ Include payments that total over £100 made to any employee including casuals during this tax year.

  ✔ Exclude those included on forms P14, those in section A (above), those payments to employees with completed P46 certificates A and B, and payments returned on forms P38(S).

P38 (S)

P38(S) is the appropriate return for students who work for you solely during a holiday. You don't need to deduct tax from a student as long as:

  ✔ They fill in the student's declaration, *and*

  ✔ The student's pay in your employment doesn't exceed £6,475 during the tax year.

  If a student's pay in your employment exceeds this figure, you must deduct tax using code 'OT week 1/month 1' in accordance with paragraphs 110 and 111 of the booklet *CWG2 Employers' Further Guide to PAYE and NICs.*

Submitting Summary Information on Form P35

Form P35 is part of the Employers' Annual Return In essence it lists every employee, including directors (who must be shown first with an asterisk by their name), NIC amounts and income tax you deducted from their pay. If you have more than ten employees, you need one or more continuation sheets (form P35CS).

Also, as per the P14, you need to list employees in alphabetical order.

  ✔ Page 1 tells you what your obligations are and where to get further help: nothing to complete here.

  ✔ Pages 2 and 3 require you to list the details of your employees and summarise your payments of NICs, PAYE tax, SSP, SMP and SAP for the year.

  ✔ Page 4 contains several tick-box questions for you to complete before signing and dating the form.

Figure 21-2 shows an example of completed pages 2 and 3 of form P35.

Part 1 Summary of employees and directors

- If you are sending your form P35 and **all** of your forms P14 on paper you must:
  a. list **each employee or director** for whom you have completed a form P11 *Deductions Working Sheet* (or equivalent record). If you have more than ten entries, please prepare P35(CS) *Continuation Sheets*
  b. ensure that all forms P14 are enclosed with this return.
- If some or all of your forms P14 are not enclosed with this return because they are being sent by Internet, Electronic Data Interchange (EDI) or magnetic media, there is no need to complete the 'Part 1 Summary of employees and directors' section of this return. Instead you must begin by completing boxes 3 and 6 of the 'Part 2 Summary of payments for the year' section below.

Guidance notes –
Some useful hints are given below. For step-by-step guidance refer to the 'Help' section on page 1.

If any of the boxes do not apply to you, please leave them blank.

Employee name Put an asterisk (*) by the name if the person is a director.	National Insurance contributions (NICs) Enter the total NICs from column 1e on form P11. Write 'R' beside any minus amounts.	Income Tax deducted or refunded in this employment. Write 'R' if an amount to show a net refund.
ELLIOT CP	£ 3298.88	£ 3531.?
BARKER AL	£ 2713.36	£ 2787.7
DOE JM	£ 2864.01	£ 2?80.01
FRASER FM	£ 2612.68	£ ??.75
MILLS V	£ 2814.24	£ 24?.75
WILLIAMS TP	£ 1207.96	£ ?031.75
	£	£
	£	£
	£	£
	£	£

you... mistake and ...d th... ong entry:
... ... a li... ...hrough the entry so that it can still be read, **and**
... record the correct figure alongside.

	1256	30
10		850
?1		-2016 30 2106.30

NICs
Total NICs shown above *after deducting amounts marked 'R'* **1** £ 155?0.? 1

Income Tax
...tal tax shown above *after deducting amounts marked 'R'* **4** £ 15358 76

Totals from P35(CS) *Continuation Sheets* **2** £

Totals from P35(CS) *Continuation Sheets* **5** £

Part 2 Summary of payments for the year

Total ...C... 1 + 2 **3** £ 15510 99

Total tax 4 + 5 **6** £ 15358 76
see Note 2

Advance received from HM Revenue & Customs to refund tax **7** £

Total tax 6 + 7 **8** £ 15358 76

Combined amounts

Total NICs and tax 3 + 8 **9** £ 30869 75

Total Student Loan deductions *see Note 3* **10** £

9 + 10 **11** £ 30869 75

Statutory payments recovered *see Note 4*

Statutory Sick Pay (SSP) **recovered** **12** £ 225 31

Statutory Maternity Pay (SMP) **recovered** **13** £

NIC compensation on SMP **14** £

Statutory Paternity Pay (SPP) **recovered** **15** £

NIC compensation on SPP **16** £

Statutory Adoption Pay (SAP) **recovered** **17** £

NIC compensation on SAP **18** £

Total of boxes 12 to 18 **19** £ 225 31

Funding received from HM Revenue & Customs to pay SSP/SMP/SPP/SAP **20** £

19 ...us 20 **21** £ 225 31

11 minus 21 **22** £ 30869 75 *see Note 5*

Deductions made from subcontractors *see Note 6* **23** £

Amount payable for the year 22 + 23 **24** £ 30644 44

NICs and tax paid already **25** £ 30644 44

Tax-free Incentive payment received during the year *see Note 7* **26** £

NOW PAYABLE 24 minus 25 and 26 **27** £ NIL

Do not include a payment with this return. If a payment is due, please make it immediately. See page 1 for notes on how to pay.

Fill in boxes 28 and 29 only if you are a **limited company** that has had CIS deductions made from payments received for work in the construction industry.

CIS deductions suffered *Total of column E on form CIS132* **28** £

Revised amount now payable 27 minus 28 **29** £

Please now fill in page 4

Note 1
Boxes **1** to **6** Enter 'R' beside any minus amounts.

Note 2
Boxes **3** and **6** If you are not required to complete the 'Part 1 Summary of employees and directors' section you should begin by entering the respect... NICs and Income Tax totals for ...ll employees for whom ...ou... completed a form P11 ...equ... ... record).

Not... 3
Box **10** Whole pounds only. Do not enter pence in shaded area.

Note 4
Boxes **12** to **18** **Do not enter the totals paid.**
Only enter the amounts you are entitled to recover. You will find this in your P30BC *Payslip Booklet* or your own equivalent payment record.

Note 5
Box **22** If box **21** is a minus figure then add box **21** to box **11**

Note 6
Box **23** Add up boxes 4.6 on all your CIS300 monthly returns and enter the total amount in box 23 of the P35.

Note 7
Box **26** If a tax-free payment was credited to your PAYE payment record for this year, for having sent any previous year's return online, enter the amount. If the tax-free payment was repaid directly to you or your adviser by cheque, leave this box blank.

Page 2 / Page 3

© Crown Copyright.

Figure 21-2:
Sample P35 End of Year Summary for 2009/10.

Boxing out Parts 1 and 2

You can get much of the information you need to complete Parts 1 and 2 of form P35 from the P11 forms you have for each person to whom you pay money:

✔ The total of each employee's and the employer's NICs are in column 1e of the P14 End of Year Summary.

✔ The total tax deducted or refunded is in the 'In this employment' box in the Pay and Income Tax section towards the bottom of the page.

Completing Parts 1 and 2 makes you check that your payments to the accounts office are correct. If this form shows that you should have paid over more to HM Revenue & Customs during the year, you need to make an additional payment.

Okay, I can't put it off any longer; Table 21-2 ploughs through the 29 boxes of form P35.

Table 21-2	Boxes of Form P35
Box Number	**What to Do**
1	Add up all the entries from the NICs columns on the form.
2	If you have any continuation sheets (P35CS), add these up and put the total for all continuation sheets in this box.
3	Add boxes 1 and 2 together. If the figure is a refund, mark 'R'.
4	Add up the entries from the income tax column on the form.
5	If you have any continuation sheets (P35CS), add these up and put the total for all continuation sheets in this box.
6	Add boxes 4 and 5 together. If the figure is a refund, mark 'R'.
7	Use this box only if the business has asked your accounts office for an advance; if so, enter that amount here.
8	Add boxes 6 and 7 together and enter the total here.
9	Add NIC and Tax together (boxes 3 and 8) and enter the total here.
10	Fill in this box only if you made student loan deductions this year. Pick up the total of all the boxes at the bottom of column 1k on each of the form P11s and enter the total here (whole pounds only).
11	Add box 9 to box 10 and enter the total here.

Box Number	What to Do
12	If you have paid any Statutory Sick Pay (SSP) to employees, enter the amount you are entitled to recover under the Percentage Threshold Scheme (PTS) in this box. Include any payments you received directly from your accounts office to cover recovery of SSP, which you show in box 20. For further details see the *Employer Helpbook E14, What to do if your employee is sick.*
13	If you paid any SMP (Statutory Maternity Pay) to employees, enter in this box the amount you are entitled to. Include any payments you received directly from your accounts office to cover recovery of SMP, which you show in box 20. For further details see the *Employer Helpbook E15, Pay and time off work for parents.*
14	Enter here any compensation you are entitled to claim in addition to the SMP recovered. For further details see the *Employer Helpbook E15, Pay and time off work for parents.*
15	Enter here any SPP (Statutory Paternity Pay) you have paid to employees and are entitled to recover. For further details see the *Employer Helpbook E15, Pay and time off work for parents.*
16	Enter here any compensation you are entitled to claim in addition to the SPP recovered. For further details see the *Employer Helpbook E15, Pay and time off work for parents.*
17	Enter here any SAP (Statutory Adoption Pay) paid to employees that you are entitled to recover. Include any payments received directly from your accounts office to cover the recovery of SAP, also shown in box 20. For further details see the *Employer Helpbook E16, Pay and time off work for adoptive parents.*
18	Enter here any compensation you are entitled to claim in addition to the SAP recovered. For further details see the *Employer Helpbook E16, Pay and time off work for adoptive parents.*

(continued)

Table 21-2 *(continued)*

Box Number	What to Do
19	Add all boxes from 12 to 18 and enter the total in box 19.
20	Use this box only if you received funding from your accounts office to pay SSP/SMP/SPP/SAP. Enter here the amount you received in funding.
21	Calculate box 19 minus box 20 and enter the total here.
22	Calculate box 11 minus box 21 and enter the total here.
23	Use this box for deductions made from sub-contractors. Add up boxes 4.6 on your CIS300 monthly returns and enter the total amount here.
24	Calculate box 22 plus box 23 and enter the total here.
25	Enter here the total of NICs and tax paid over so far for the tax year.
26	Enter here any amount credited to the business's PAYE payment record for tax-free incentives for sending in its return electronically the previous year.
27	Calculate box 24 minus boxes 25 and 26.
The following boxes are only for limited companies that deducted CIS (Construction Industry Scheme) deductions from payments	
28	CIS deductions suffered. Refer to form CIS132 (which summarises all employees), column E, for the total deductions suffered and copy this amount here.
29	Calculate box 27 minus box 28.

Ticking off the Part 3 checklist

Page 4 of the form has three sections – Parts 3, 4, and 5. Part 3 has no numbers, just a checklist of questions to answer:

✔ **Question 1:** If you had any employees for whom you didn't complete a form P14 or P38(S), tick 'No'.

These employees are likely to be part-time or casual staff. If you tick 'No' you must complete a *P38A, Employer's Supplementary Return*.

✔ **Question 2:** Did you make any 'free-of-tax' payments to an employee? A free-of-tax payment is one where the employer bears any tax due.

✔ **Question 3:** Has anyone other than the employer paid expenses or provided benefits to any of your employees during the year as part of their employment with you?

✔ **Question 4:** This question is in two parts. If the answer to the first part is 'Yes', you have to complete a form P14 for each employee concerned.

✔ **Question 5:** This question asks if you have paid any part of an employee's pay direct to anyone else, for example, paying school fees direct to a school. If you did, you need to report whether the payment was included in the employee's pay for tax and NICs purposes and in the pay shown on form P14.

This question doesn't include attachment of earnings orders or payments to the Child Support Agency.

✔ **Question 6:** This question covers IR35 under which HM Revenue & Customs has restricted workers' ability to form services companies or partnerships through which they sell their services. Your best bet is to find out more about IR35 at www.hmrc.gov.uk/ir35, to make sure that you comply. If, for example, you don't deduct tax and NICs when you need to, you may become liable for any non-payment of tax and NICs by the person employed.

If you included PAYE and NICs from workers who you deemed to be employees, tick the second box 'Yes'. If you tick the second box 'Yes' but the amount of the deemed payment is provisional, confirm on a separate sheet and send it with the form P35.

Pensioning out Part 4

If you have a company pension scheme that was contracted-out of the State Second pension, enter your employer's contracted-out number here (you can find this on your contracting-out certificate).

Certifying your employer status in Part 5

This part is the check-up part, where you make sure that you've included all the necessary forms and then sign on the dotted line.

Computerised systems

If you use a computerised payroll system, you can save a lot of grief because most of the year-end reports (certainly P14, P35 and P60) are done automatically.

Also, if you use the HM Revenue & Customs payroll CD-ROM that comes with the New Employer Pack, you can enjoy the same benefits of a computerised payroll system and all the online HM Revenue & Customs guides.

Tick to confirm that you enclose all forms P14, P38A, P11D and P11D(b).

Also, confirm that P38A (see question 1 in the checklist of Part 3) is enclosed or not due.

Sign and print the name and capacity of the person signing and the date.

Phew! Everything's done at last!

Chapter 22

Satisfying the Tax Inspector

. . . .

In This Chapter

▶ Sorting out business legal structures

▶ Reporting on self-employment and partnership tax

▶ Filing taxes for limited companies

. . . .

*P*aying taxes and reporting income for your business are very important jobs, and the way in which you complete these tasks properly depends on your business's legal structure. From sole traders (self-employment) to limited companies and everything in between, this chapter briefly reviews business types and explains how taxes are handled for each type.

Finding the Right Business Type

Business type and tax preparation and reporting go hand in hand. If you work as a bookkeeper for a small business, you need to know the business's legal structure before you can proceed with reporting and paying tax on the business income. Not all businesses have the same legal structure, so they don't all pay tax on the profits they make in the same way.

But before you get into the subject of tax procedures, you need to understand the various business structures you may encounter as a bookkeeper. This section outlines each type of business. You can find out how these structures pay taxes in the separate sections that follow.

Sole trader

The simplest legal structure for a business is the *sole trader,* a business owned by one individual. Most new businesses with only one owner start out as sole traders, and some never change this status. Others, however, grow by adding partners and become *partnerships*. Some businesses add lots of staff and want to protect themselves from lawsuits, so they become *Limited Liability Partnerships (LLPs)*. Those seeking the greatest protection from individual lawsuits, whether they have employees or are simply single-owner companies without employees, become limited companies. I cover these other structures later in this chapter.

Partnership

HM Revenue & Customs considers any unincorporated business owned by more than one person to be a *partnership*. The partnership is the most flexible type of business structure involving more than one owner. Each partner in the business is equally liable for the activities of the business. This structure is slightly more complicated than a sole trader (see the preceding 'Sole trader' section), and partners need to work out certain key issues before the business opens its doors. These issues include:

- ✔ How are the partners going to divide the profits?
- ✔ How does each partner sell his or her share of the business, if he or she so chooses?
- ✔ What happens to each partner's share if a partner becomes sick or dies?
- ✔ How is the partnership going to be dissolved if one of the partners wants out?

Partners in a partnership don't always have to share equal risks. A partnership may have two different types of partners: general and limited. The general partner runs the day-to-day business and is held personally responsible for all activities of the business, no matter how much he or she has personally invested. Limited partners, on the other hand, are passive owners of the business and not involved in day-to-day operations. If a claim is filed against the business, the limited partners can be held personally liable only for the amount of money they individually invested in the business.

Limited Liability Partnerships (LLPs)

The *Limited Liability Partnership*, or LLP, is a structure that provides the owners of partnerships with some protection from being held personally liable for their businesses' activities. This business structure is somewhere between a partnership and a limited company: The business ownership and tax rules are similar to those of a partnership, but like a limited company, if the business is sued, the owners aren't held personally liable.

Rather like forming a limited company, an LLP is formed by filing the appropriate forms with Companies House. On receipt of these forms, the Registrar of Companies issues a Certificate of Incorporation.

Growth of the LLP

Limited Liability Partnerships are the latest business vehicle and were introduced on 6 April 2001 after the Limited Liability Partnerships Act 2000 received royal assent on 20 July 2000. Many law firms and accounting firms are set up as LLPs. More and more small-business owners are choosing this structure rather than a limited company because the LLP is easier and cheaper to maintain (it involves a lot less paperwork, plus fewer legal and accounting fees), and yet still provides personal protection from legal entanglements.

Both for business and practical reasons, I recommend drawing up an agreement to establish the rights, responsibilities and duties of the partners to each other, and to outline how the business is going to be run, because few provisions are contained within the act governing these relationships.

Limited companies

If your business faces a great risk of being sued, the safest business structure for you is the *limited company.* Courts in the UK have clearly determined that a limited company is a separate legal entity (Saloman v Saloman 1897) and that its owners' personal assets are protected from claims against the company. Essentially, an owner or shareholder in a company can't be sued or face collections because of actions taken by the company. This veil of protection is the reason many small-business owners choose to incorporate even though it involves a lot of expense (to pay for both lawyers and accountants) and paperwork.

In a limited company, each share represents a portion of ownership, and profits must be split based on share ownership. You don't have to sell shares on the public stock markets in order to be a limited company, though. In fact, most limited companies are private entities that sell their shares privately among friends and investors.

If you're a small-business owner who wants to incorporate, first you must form a *board of directors* (see the sidebar 'Roles and responsibilities of the limited company board'). Boards can be made up of owners of the company as well as non-owners. You can even have your spouse and children on the board – I bet those board meetings are interesting.

Roles and responsibilities of the limited company board

Limited companies provide a veil of protection for company owners, but in order to maintain that protection, the owners must comply with many rules unique to corporations. The *board of directors* takes on the key role of complying with these rules, and it must maintain a record of meeting minutes that prove the board is following key operating procedures, such as:

✔ Establishment of records of banking associations and any changes to those arrangements

✔ Tracking of loans from shareholders or third parties

✔ Selling or redeeming shares

✔ Payment of dividends

✔ Authorisation of salaries or bonuses for officers and key executives

✔ Undertaking of any purchases, sales or leases of corporate assets

✔ Buying another company

✔ Merging with another company

✔ Making changes to the Articles of Incorporation

✔ Election of corporate officers and directors

Corporate board minutes are considered official and must be available for review by HM Revenue & Customs and the courts. If a company's owners want to invoke the veil of protection that corporate status provides, they must prove that the board has met its obligations and that the company operated as a limited company. In other words, you can't form a board and have no proof that it ever met and managed these key functions.

Tax Reporting for Sole Traders

HM Revenue & Customs doesn't consider sole traders and partnerships to be individual legal entities, so they're not taxed as such. Instead, sole proprietors report any business earnings on their annual tax returns – that's the only financial reporting they must do. In effect, sole traders and partnerships pay income tax on their business profits. To be technical, they pay their income tax on their business profit under what is called *trading income*. A sole trader may well have another job as well, on which he or she pays tax under the normal PAYE system. All these (and other sources of income) are pulled together on his or her tax return to assess the overall income tax liability.

The basic tax return covers everything that a person in paid employment needs to tell HM Revenue & Customs to get his or her tax assessed correctly. The numerous pages of questions cover every aspect of tax related to normal tax life – working, receiving dividends, earning interest, paying and receiving pensions, making small capital gains – as I said, everything.

As the bookkeeper for a sole trader, you're probably responsible for pulling together the sales, Cost of Goods Sold and expense information needed for the forms. In most cases, you then hand off this information to the business's accountant to fill out all the required forms.

Ultimately, because sole traders pay income tax on all their earnings, you need to note the current rates of tax for sole traders (and other unincorporated bodies) based on their taxable profits. Table 22-1 gives this information.

Table 22-1	2010/11 Tax Rates
Tax Rate	*2010/11 Taxable Profits*
Basic rate: 20%	£0– £37,400
Higher rate: 40%	£37,401–£150,000
Additional rate: 50%	Over £150,000

Fortunately most people have simple tax affairs. Because employment is usually taxed under the PAYE system (the employer acts as the unpaid tax collector) and most other sources of income have basic rate of tax deducted at source, you don't need to complete a tax return each year. The tax return is needed to pull all the earnings together only where an individual may have a liability to higher rate tax, for example other earnings that have not had tax deducted at source that pushes their taxable earnings above the basic tax rate.

Expanding to the supplementary pages

To deal with liability at a higher tax rate or areas too complex for the standard annual tax return, you need supplementary pages. The supplementary pages cover:

- ✔ **Employment:** To cover more complicated employment situations, for example, an employee who has more than one job.

- ✔ **Share schemes:** To cover an employee who receives shares under an employee share ownership scheme.

- ✔ **Self-employment:** These pages cover business profits for the sole trader. I look at this more closely in the next section.

- ✔ **Partnerships:** To declare your share of any partnership profits.

- ✔ **Land and property**: For example, where any rental income is received from any property.

✔ **Foreign:** To cover any overseas sources of income.

✔ **Trusts:** To cover any income received by means of a distribution from any trust set up for you.

✔ **Capital gains:** To cover any gains made from the disposal of assets rather than trading income.

✔ **Non-residence:** To cover any income received by non-residents in the UK and thus liable to UK tax.

HM Revenue & Customs sends supplementary pages only if you ask for them or have received them before. As a taxpayer, you are responsible for asking for a tax return and completing one every year.

Filling out the self-employment supplementary pages

This section concentrates on the supplementary pages that relate to running a business. If you want to know more about filling in the rest of your tax return and saving tax, you may find *Paying Less Tax For Dummies* useful – if only such a title existed.

Depending on your turnover, you use one of two different self-employment supplementary pages. If your turnover is less than £68,000, you can complete the shortened version, which is only two pages long. (See Figures 22-1 and 22-2.) Double-check that you are eligible to use the shortened form by referring to the guide to completing the self-employment supplementary pages. You can find it on the HMRC website, www.hmrc.gov.uk.

On the first page, SES1, shown in Figure 22-1, you put down details of the business name and address and when it began or ceased trading. You also use this page to enter your business income and allowable business expenses. (Refer to Chapter 18 for a refresher.) You put your total business expenses in box 19 if your turnover is less than £68,000. On the second page, SES 2 (shown in Figure 22-2), you summarise the capital allowances that the business is claiming for any of its assets (capital allowances are covered in Chapter 12). You then calculate your taxable profits and read page SESN9 of the notes to see if you need to make any adjustments.

Losses, Class 4 NICs and CIS deductions are entered in the final section. (Make sure you read page SESN10 of the notes to help you complete this section correctly.)

HM Revenue & Customs

Self-employment (short)

Tax year 6 April 2009 to 5 April 2010

Your name

Your unique taxpayer reference (UTR)

Read page SESN 1 of the *notes* to check if you should use this page or the *Self-employment (full)* page.

Business details

1 Description of business

2 Postcode of your business address

3 If your business name, description, address or postcode have changed in the last 12 months, put 'X' in the box and give details in the 'Any other information' box of your tax return

4 If you are a foster carer or adult placement carer, put 'X' in the box – *read page SESN 2 of the notes*

5 If your business started after 5 April 2009, enter the start date *DD MM YYYY*

6 If your business ceased before 6 April 2010, enter the final date of trading

7 Date your books or accounts are made up to – *read page SESN 2 of the notes*

Business income – if your annual business turnover was below £68,000

8 Your turnover – *the takings, fees, sales or money earned by your business*

£ • 0 0

9 Any other business income not included in box 8 – *excluding Business Start-up Allowance*

£ • 0 0

Allowable business expenses

If your annual turnover was below £68,000 you may just put your total expenses in box 19, rather than filling in the whole section.

10 Costs of goods bought for resale or goods used

£ • 0 0

11 Car, van and travel expenses – *after private use proportion*

£ • 0 0

12 Wages, salaries and other staff costs

£ • 0 0

13 Rent, rates, power and insurance costs

£ • 0 0

14 Repairs and renewals of property and equipment

£ • 0 0

15 Accountancy, legal and other professional fees

£ • 0 0

16 Interest and bank and credit card etc. financial charges

£ • 0 0

17 Phone, fax, stationery and other office costs

£ • 0 0

18 Other allowable business expenses – *client entertaining costs are not an allowable expense*

£ • 0 0

19 Total allowable expenses – *total of boxes 10 to 18*

£ • 0 0

SA103S 2010 | Tax return: Self-employment (short): Page SES 1 | HMRC 12/09 net

Figure 22-1: Page SES1 of the self-employment supplementary pages shows business details, capital allowances and income and expenditure for annual turnover below £68,000.

Net profit or loss

20 Net profit – *if your business income is more than your expenses (if box 8 + box 9 minus box 19 is positive)*

£ [   ] • [0] [0]

21 Or, net loss –*if your expenses exceed your business income (if box 19 minus (box 8 + box 9) is positive)*

£ [   ] • [0] [0]

Tax allowances for vehicles and equipment (capital allowances)

There are 'capital' tax allowances for vehicles and equipment used in your business (you should not have included the cost of these in your business expenses). Read pages SESN 4 to SESN 8 of the *notes* and use the example and Working Sheets to work out your capital allowances.

22 Annual Investment Allowance

£ [   ] • [0] [0]

24 Other capital allowances

£ [   ] • [0] [0]

23 Allowance for small balance of unrelieved expenditure

£ [   ] • [0] [0]

25 Total balancing charges – where you have disposed of items for more than their value

£ [   ] • [0] [0]

Calculating your taxable profits

Your taxable profit may not be the same as your net profit. Read page SESN 9 of the *notes* to see if you need to make any adjustments and fill in the boxes which apply to arrive at your taxable profit for the year.

26 Goods or services for your own use – *read page SESN 9 of the notes*

£ [   ] • [0] [0]

28 Loss brought forward from earlier years set off against this year's profits – *up to the amount in box 27*

£ [   ] • [0] [0]

27 Net business profit for tax purposes (*if box 20 + box 25 + box 26 minus (boxes 21 to 24) is positive*)

£ [   ] • [0] [0]

29 Any other business income not included in boxes 8 or 9 – *for example, Business Start-up Allowance*

£ [   ] • [0] [0]

Total taxable profits or net business loss

30 Total taxable profits from this business (*if box 27 + box 29 minus box 28 is positive*)

£ [   ] • [0] [0]

31 Net business loss for tax purposes (*if boxes 21 to 24 minus (box 20 + box 25 + box 26) is positive*)

£ [   ] • [0] [0]

Losses, Class 4 NICs and CIS deductions

If you have made a loss for tax purposes (box 31), read page SESN 10 of the *notes* and fill in boxes 32 to 34 as appropriate

32 Loss from this tax year set off against other income for 2009–10

£ [   ] • [0] [0]

35 If you are exempt from paying Class 4 NICs, put 'X' in the box – *read page SESN 10 of the notes*

[   ]

33 Loss to be carried back to previous year(s) and set off against income (or capital gains)

£ [   ] • [0] [0]

36 If you have been given a 2009–10 Class 4 NICs deferment certificate, put 'X' in the box – *read page SESN 10 of the notes*

[   ]

34 Total loss to carry forward after all other set-offs – *including unused losses brought forward*

£ [   ] • [0] [0]

37 Deductions on payment and deduction statements from contractors – *construction industry subcontractors only*

£ [   ] • [0] [0]

SA103S 2010   Tax return: Self-employment (short): Page SES 2

Figure 22-2: Page SES2 of the self-employment supplementary pages shows details of capital allowances, taxable profits, losses and Class 4 NICs.

Filing Tax Forms for Partnerships

If your business is structured as a partnership (meaning it has more than one owner) and is not a limited liability company, your business doesn't pay taxes. Instead, all money earned by the business is split up among the partners and they pay the tax due between them very much as if they were sole traders. However, a partnership is required to complete a partnership tax return to aid the assessment of the members of the partnership. Essentially, the partnership tax return is sent out to the nominated partner and he or she completes the partnership tax return in a manner similar to the sole trader tax return explained in the preceding sections. That partner states what profit share is attributable to each partner, and each partner is responsible for showing this profit figure in his or her own personal tax return.

Don't be tempted to forget to include partnership profits (or any other source of income for that matter), because HM Revenue & Customs knows from the partnership tax return what you earned in that tax year.

Paying Taxes for Limited Companies

Limited companies are more complex than sole traders and partnerships. Although many aspects of their accounting and taxation are similar, their accounts are open to public scrutiny because each year a limited company must file its accounts at Companies House, the UK government organisation responsible for tracking information about all UK limited companies. This means that although only HM Revenue & Customs knows the full details of a sole trader or partnership, the whole world has access (for a fee) to a limited company's accounts.

Companies make a separate tax return, known as a CT600, to HM Revenue & Customs, in which they detail their financial affairs. As a result, the limited company pays corporation tax on its earnings (profit) as well as tax on any dividends paid out to its shareholders. This means that its shareholders receive dividends net of basic rate of income tax because the company has already paid it for them.

Two forms of CT600 exist: a short version, only four pages, is sufficient for companies with straightforward tax affairs, but more complicated companies, as designated by HM Revenue & Customs, must complete the eight-page return. The following (among others) must file the eight-page return:

✔ Any company that owns 25 per cent of another non-UK company

✔ Any insurance company (or friendly society) having business treated as overseas life assurance business

✔ Any company liable to pay its corporation tax in instalments (profit in excess of £1.5m)

For full details, please refer to the *CT600 Guide (2010)*, which can be obtained from the HMRC website at www.hmrc.gov.uk.

Corporation tax rates vary according to how much taxable profit the company makes. Although starting rates are low for a limited company, they soon escalate to the higher (main) rate. Current corporation tax rates on profits are shown in Table 22-2.

Table 22-2	Corporation Tax Rates	
Tax Rate	*2010/11 Taxable Profits*	*2011/12 Taxable Profits*
Small profits rate:	21%	20%
Small profits rate can be claimed by qualifying companies with profits not exceeding:	£300,000	N/A
Marginal relief: lower limit	£300, 000	N/A
Marginal relief: upper limit	£1,500,000	N/A
Main rate:	28%	27%

Check with your accountant to determine whether incorporating your business makes sense for you. A strong argument exists in favour of some smaller businesses incorporating, because they pay less corporation tax than income tax at some levels. But tax savings isn't the only issue you have to think about; operating a limited company also increases administrative, legal and accounting costs. Make sure that you understand all the costs before incorporating.

Chapter 23

Adding the Cost of
Value Added Tax (VAT)

. . . .

. . . .

A lot of mystery and tales of horror surround the subject of VAT (Value Added Tax). Now that HM Revenue & Customs administers both tax and VAT, the average business person is facing an even more powerful organisation with a right to know even more about your business.

The rules governing which goods and services are subject to VAT and which items of VAT are reclaimable can be quite complex. This chapter can only scratch the surface and give a broad understanding. Contact both HM Revenue & Customs and your accountant/auditor at an early stage to find out whether all your sales are subject to VAT and how you can ensure that you are only reclaiming allowable VAT. Remember the following – get it right from the beginning.

Looking into VAT

VAT (Value Added Tax) is a tax charged on most business transactions made in the UK or the Isle of Man. VAT is also charged on goods and some services imported from certain places outside the European Union and on some goods and services coming into the UK from other EU countries. VAT applies to all businesses – sole traders, partnerships, limited companies, charities and so on. In simple terms, all VAT-registered businesses act as unpaid collectors of VAT for HM Revenue & Customs.

Examples of taxable transactions are:

- ✔ Selling new and used goods, including hire purchase
- ✔ Renting and hiring out goods
- ✔ Using business stock for private purposes
- ✔ Providing a service, for example plumbing or manicure
- ✔ Charging admission to enter buildings

As you can see, this list covers most business activities.

Certain services are exempt from VAT, including money lending, some property transactions, insurance and certain types of education and training. Supplies exempt from VAT don't form part of your turnover for VAT purposes.

As the name suggests, Value Added Tax is a tax on the difference between what you buy (inputs) and what you sell (outputs), as long as these items fall within the definition of taxable transactions (see the next sections). At the end of a VAT reporting period, you pay over to HM Revenue & Customs the difference between all your output tax and input tax.

- ✔ **Input tax** is the VAT you pay out to your suppliers for goods and services you purchase for your business. You can reclaim the VAT on these goods or services coming *in* to your business. (See 'Getting VAT back', later in this chapter.) It is in effect a tax added to all your purchases.
- ✔ **Output tax** is the VAT that you must charge on your goods and services when you make each sale. You collect output tax from your customers on each sale you make of items or services going *out* of your business. It is in effect a tax added to all your sales.

Notice 700: The VAT Guide needs to be your bible in determining how much you need to pay and what you can reclaim.

Knowing what to charge

In addition to the obvious trading activities, you need to charge VAT on a whole range of other activities, including the following:

- ✔ **Business assets:** If you sell off any unneeded business assets, such as office equipment, commercial vehicles and so on, you must charge VAT.
- ✔ **Sales to staff:** Sales to staff are treated no differently than sales to other customers. Therefore you must charge VAT on sales such as canteen meals, goods at reduced prices, vending machines and so on.

✔ **Hire or loans:** If you make a charge for the use of a business asset, this amount must incur VAT.

✔ **Gifts:** If you give away goods that cost more than $50, you must add VAT. Treat gifts as if they are a sale for your VAT records.

✔ **Goods for own use:** Anything you or your family take out of the business must go on the VAT return. HM Revenue & Customs doesn't let you reclaim the VAT on goods or services that aren't used for the complete benefit of the business.

HM Revenue & Customs is really hot on using business stock for your own use, which is very common in restaurants, for example. HM Revenue & Customs knows you do it and has statistics to show how much on average businesses 'take out' this way. If you don't declare this item when you've used business stock, be prepared to have HM Revenue & Customs jump on you from a great height.

✔ **Commission earned:** If you sell someone else's goods or services and get paid by means of a commission, you must include VAT on this income.

✔ **Bartered goods:** If you swap your goods or services for someone else's goods or services, you must account for VAT on the full value of your goods or services that are part of this arrangement.

✔ **Advance payments:** If a customer gives you any sum of money, you must account for VAT on this amount and the balance when he or she collects the goods. If, for example, you accept payment by instalments, you collect VAT on each instalment.

✔ **Credit notes:** These items are treated exactly like negative sales invoices, so make sure that you include VAT so you can effectively reclaim the VAT on the output that you're going to, or may have already, paid.

In general you don't have to charge VAT on goods you sell to a VAT-registered business in another European Community (EC) member state. However, you must charge UK VAT if you sell goods to private individuals.

Knowing how much to charge

The rate of VAT applicable to any transaction is determined by the nature of that transaction. The 20 per cent rate applies to most transactions. The type of business (size or sector) generally has no bearing on the VAT rates. Three rates of VAT currently exist in the UK:

✔ A standard rate is 20 per cent from 1st Januray 2011. This is the rate at which most businesses should add VAT to products and services that they sell.

✔ A reduced rate, currently 5 per cent. Some products and services have a lower rate of VAT, including domestic fuel, energy-saving installations and the renovation of dwellings.

✔ A zero per cent rate. Many products and services are given a zero rating, including some foods, books and children's clothing. A zero rating for a product or service is not the same as a total exemption.

You can view a list of business areas where sales are reduced-rated or zero-rated in *Notice 700,* which you can download from www.hmrc.gov.uk. You can call the National Advice Service on 0845-0109000 if you have queries about the list.

Registering for VAT

The starting point is registering for VAT so that you can charge VAT on your sales and reclaim VAT on your purchases.

The current VAT registration threshold is £70,000 (this changes each year, so check with HM Revenue & Customs for the current threshold). So, if your annual turnover (sales, not profit) is less than this figure, you don't have to register for VAT.

You may find it advantageous to register for VAT even though your sales fall below the VAT registration threshold (and may never exceed it). Registering for VAT gives your business increased credibility – if your customers are large businesses, they expect their suppliers to be VAT registered. Also, you can't reclaim VAT if you're not registered. If your business makes zero-rated supplies but buys in goods and services on which you pay VAT, you want to be able to reclaim this VAT.

As your business grows, it may be difficult to know whether you have broken through the VAT registration threshold. HM Revenue & Customs states that you must register for VAT if:

✔ At the end of any month the total value of the sales you made in the past 12 months (or less) is more than the current threshold.

✔ At any time you have reasonable grounds to expect your sales to be more than the threshold in the next 30 days.

After you register for VAT, you're on the VAT treadmill and have to account for output tax on all your sales, keep proper VAT records and accounts and send in VAT returns regularly.

Paying in and Reclaiming VAT

HM Revenue & Customs adopts a very simple process, laying down and policing the rules in two ways:

- ✔ Businesses must file periodic returns to the VAT Central Unit (see 'Completing Your VAT Return', later in this chapter, for when to file VAT payments).
- ✔ Businesses receive periodic enquiries and visits from HM Revenue & Customs to verify that these returns are correct.

VAT returns must be posted to arrive at the VAT Central Unit by the due date, which is shown on the form, and is usually one month after the period covered by the return. Yes, this schedule means that you have one month to complete your VAT return. Any payment due to HM Revenue & Customs must be sent with the VAT return.

As long as you complete your VAT return on time and don't arouse the suspicions of HM Revenue & Customs, you may not meet the staff for many years.

You face a financial penalty if your return is late and/or seriously inaccurate. HM Revenue & Customs can and does impose hefty fines on businesses that transgress. Also, offenders who previously had the luxury of quarterly VAT returns often find themselves having to complete monthly VAT returns. Don't mess around with HM Revenue & Customs!

HM Revenue & Customs targets some business sectors. In general, businesses structured in a complex manner (such as offshore companies) that involve a lot of cash are likely to come in for extra scrutiny. Experience tells HM Revenue & Customs that looking closely at certain types of businesses often yields extra revenues. Also, businesses that submit VAT returns late on a regular basis attract fines and may be forced to submit monthly VAT returns together with payments on account.

Choosing paper or ether

HM Revenue & Customs is phasing out paper VAT returns, and from April 2010 you may need to file your VAT return online and pay your VAT electronically. The advantage of paying online is that you qualify for seven additional calendar days after the date shown on your return to pay. Visit the HM Revenue & Customs website at www.hmrc.gov.uk and click VAT Online Services to find out about doing your VAT return online.

If you are still eligible to submit paper VAT returns, you must pay the VAT one month after the end of the VAT period. For example, if the VAT period ends 30 September 2010, you need to pay your VAT by 31 October 2010. However, if you file your return online, you don't need to pay until 7 November 2010, giving you an obvious cash-flow advantage.

What to look out for on your paper VAT return

Fill in boxes 1 to 9, but complete boxes 8 and 9 only if you trade in goods with other EC member states. Write one amount in each box or put 'NONE' if appropriate.

- ✔ Correct any mistakes by crossing out, writing in the correct figure and initialling the amendment.
- ✔ Enclose negative figures in brackets.
- ✔ Write your VAT registration number on the back of all cheques.
- ✔ Inform your local HM Revenue & Customs office if any of the details printed on the return are incorrect. Don't make any alterations on the return, but write a separate letter to your local VAT Business Advice Centre.
- ✔ Leave blank boxes or areas labelled 'For Official Use'.
- ✔ Send *only* cheques or crossed postal orders with your return.
- ✔ Do *not* send post-dated cheques.

What to look out for on your electronic VAT return

Fill in the appropriate boxes, using 0.00 for nil amounts.

- ✔ Make any payment due by electronic methods (BACS, CHAPS or bank giro).
- ✔ Wait for the acknowledgement that your electronic return was received.
- ✔ Keep a copy of the electronic acknowledgement page for your records.

Meeting deadlines for small businesses

Most businesses pay VAT quarterly, regardless of size. Return forms are sent out in advance by post. Generally, you get your next VAT return about a month in advance of when you need to send it in. If your next VAT return doesn't arrive within this time scale, call your local HM Revenue & Customs office and ask for another. Remember that you're responsible for completing a VAT return even if you don't receive a form!

HM Revenue & Customs has introduced some arrangements to make VAT accounting easier for small businesses. The accounting method that your business uses determines when you pay VAT:

- ✔ **Annual Accounting:** If you use the Annual Accounting scheme, you make interim payments, either three or nine, spread across the year, towards an estimated annual VAT bill. This arrangement evens out VAT payments and helps to smooth cash flow. At the end of the year, you submit a single annual return and settle up for any balance due (or maybe receive a cheque back from HM Revenue & Customs). In effect, you complete one annual VAT return at the end of the year but make periodic payments on account (you agree with HM Revenue & Customs which you want).

  This arrangement may suit the disorganised business that struggles to complete the more traditional four quarterly VAT returns.

  You can use this scheme if your annual sales (excluding VAT) aren't expected to exceed £1,350,000 and continue up to annual sales of £1,600,000.

  The range is based on estimates of your total sales. If your sales have a boost and exceed £1,350,000, you can stay on this scheme just as long as sales don't go beyond £1,600,000. If sales exceed £1,600,000, you must come off this scheme.

- ✔ **Cash Accounting:** If you use the Cash Accounting scheme, your business accounts for income and expenses when they're actually incurred. Therefore, you don't pay HM Revenue & Customs VAT until your customers pay you. This arrangement may suit a business that has regular slow-paying customers. You can use this scheme if your estimated VAT taxable turnover is not more than £1,350,000.

- ✔ **Flat Rate Scheme:** This arrangement makes VAT much simpler by allowing you to calculate your VAT payment as a flat percentage of your turnover. The percentage is determined according to the trade sector in which your business operates.

  Under this scheme you can't reclaim any VAT on your actual purchases, which may mean you lose out if your business is significantly different to the business model HM Revenue & Customs applies to you. Also, if your business undertakes a large capital spend, which has a lot of VAT on it, you are unlikely to get the entire amount back under this scheme.

  You can use this scheme if your annual sales (excluding VAT) aren't expected to exceed £150,000.

- ✔ **Retail Schemes:** If you make lots of quite small sales to the public, you may find it difficult to issue a VAT invoice for each sale. Several available retail schemes may help. For example, you can use a simpler receipt that a till can print out.

To find out more about the numerous retail schemes, visit the HM Revenue & Customs website www.hmrc.gov.uk and click the link to VAT, under Businesses and Corporations. You must then follow the next steps:

Click on Getting Started with VAT, followed by Accounting schemes to simplify VAT accounting or save money, and then scroll down the screen and select VAT retail scheme.

Getting VAT back

When you are completing your VAT return, you want to reclaim the VAT on every legitimate business purchase. However, you must make sure that you only reclaim legitimate business purchases. The following is the guidance that HM Revenue & Customs gives:

- ✔ **Business purchases:** You can reclaim the VAT on all business purchases and expenses, not just on the raw materials and goods you buy for resale. These purchases include things like business equipment, telephone and utility bills, and payments for other services such as accountants and solicitors' fees.

  You can't deduct your input tax for certain purchases, including cars, business entertainment and second-hand goods that you bought under one of the VAT second-hand schemes.

- ✔ **Business/private use:** If you use services for both business and private purposes, such as your telephone, you can reclaim VAT only on the business use. No hard and fast rules exist on how you split the bill – your local HM Revenue & Customs office is likely to consider any reasonable method.

- ✔ **Pro-forma invoice:** If a supplier issues a pro-forma invoice, which includes VAT that you have to pay before you are supplied with the goods or service, you can't deduct this amount from your VAT bill on your next return. You can only deduct VAT when you get the proper invoice.

- ✔ **Private motoring:** If you use a business car for both business and private use, you can reclaim all the VAT as input tax, but you have to account for tax on any private motoring using a scale charge (see 'Using fuel for private motoring', later in this chapter).

✔ **Lost invoices:** You can't reclaim any VAT on non-existent invoices. If you do and you get a VAT visit, you're in for the high jump!

✔ **Bad debt relief:** Occasionally customers don't pay you, and if you have already paid over to HM Revenue & Customs the output VAT on this sale, you're going to be doubly annoyed. Fortunately HM Revenue & Customs isn't totally heartless – you can reclaim this VAT on a later VAT return.

Completing Your VAT Return

As mentioned earlier, HM Revenue & Customs are phasing out paper returns and you are required to submit your returns online. Letting your accounting software complete your VAT return is the easiest method. Sage 50 Accounts does VAT returns as a matter of routine, picking up all the necessary information automatically. You just need to tell the program when to start and when to stop picking up the invoice information. Sage 50 Accounts even prints out the VAT return in a format very similar to HM Revenue & Customs' own VAT return form. Figure 23-1 shows Sage 50 Accounts VAT return.

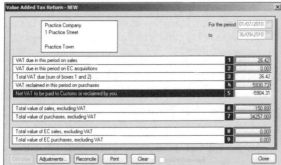

Figure 23-1:
The Sage 50
Accounts
VAT return.

Filling in the boxes

At last I come to the nitty-gritty of what figures go into each of the nine boxes on the VAT return. Table 23-1 helps keep the process simple.

Table 23-1	VAT Return Boxes
Box	*Information Required*
1	VAT due on sales and other outputs in the period. Notice 700: The VAT Guide gives further help.
2	VAT due from you on acquisitions of goods from other EC Member States. Notice 725 VAT: The Single Market gives further help.
3	For paper returns, enter the sum of boxes 1 and 2. The electronic form handles all the maths needed in completing the form.
4	The input tax you are entitled to claim for the period.
5	The difference between the figures from boxes 3 and 4. Deduct the smaller from the larger. If the figure in box 3 is more than the figure in box 4, you owe this amount to HM Revenue & Customs.
	If the figure in box 3 is less than the figure in box 4, HM Revenue & Customs owes you this amount.
6	Your total sales/outputs excluding any VAT.
7	Your total purchases/inputs excluding any VAT.
8	Complete this box only if you supplied goods to another EC member state. Put in this box the total value of all supplies of goods (sales) to other member states.
	Note: If you include anything in box 8, make sure that you include the amount in the box 6 total.
9	Complete this box only if you acquired goods from another EC member state. Put in this box the total value of all goods acquired (purchases) from other member states.
	Note: If you include anything in box 9 make sure that you include the amount in the box 7 total.

I deliberately keep this process simple, but remember that behind every box is a multitude of traps set to ensnare you. The HM Revenue & Customs website, www.hmrc.gov.uk has detailed notes to help you complete your VAT return.

Glancing at some problem areas

Not all businesses are entirely straightforward for VAT purposes. Some business activities have their own unique rules and regulations. The list below outlines the exceptions to the rule:

- **Building developer:** See *VAT Notice 708: Buildings and construction* about non-deductible input tax on fixtures and fittings. Also *Notice 742 Land and Property*, regarding land and new-build property sales.

- **Tour operator:** See *VAT Notice 709/5: Tour operators' margin scheme* about VAT you can't reclaim on margin scheme supplies.

- **Second-hand dealer:** See *VAT Notice 718: margin schemes for second-hand goods, works of art, antiques, and collectors' items* about VAT you can't reclaim on second-hand dealing.

Using fuel for private motoring

If your business pays for non-business fuel for company car users, you must reduce the amount of VAT you reclaim on fuel by means of the scale charge.

Notice 700/64: Motoring expenses gives full details. If you use the scale charge, you can recover all the VAT charged on road fuel without having to split your mileage between business and private use. A *scale charge* is a method of accounting for output VAT on road fuel bought by a business that is then used for private mileage. Until 2007, the scale charge was calculated on the engine size, but since the budget of 2007 it has been based on the CO_2 emissions of each vehicle.

You can obtain your CO_2 emissions from your vehicle registration certificate (for cars registered after 2001). The HMRC website offers full details of all CO_2 emissions and the associated fuel scale charge. See www.hmrc.gov.uk for further details.

Leasing a motor car

You may find that you are able to claim only 50 per cent of the input tax on contract hire rentals in certain situations. If you lease a car for business purposes, you normally can't recover 50 per cent of the VAT charged. The 50 per cent block is to cover the private use of the car. You can reclaim the remaining 50 per cent of the VAT charged. If you lease a qualifying car that is used exclusively for business purposes and not available for private use, you can recover the input tax in full.

Filing under special circumstances

If you're filing your first VAT return, your final return or a return with no payment, bear a few things in mind:

- **First return:** On your first return, you may want to reclaim VAT on money you spent prior to the period covered by your first VAT return. In general, you can recover VAT on capital and pre-start up costs and expenses incurred before you registered for VAT as long as they are VAT qualifying. For further help on this, refer to *Notice 700: The VAT Guide,* available from HM Revenue & Customs.

  If you're completing a VAT return for the first time, go onto the HM Revenue & Customs website for help (www.hmrc.gov.uk) and/or speak with your accountant. You may be missing a trick in not reclaiming VAT on something you bought but didn't reclaim the VAT on. More importantly, you may be reclaiming VAT on something that you aren't permitted to reclaim.

- **Final return:** For help with your final return, read *Notice 700/11: Cancelling your registration.* If you have any business assets, such as equipment, vehicles or stock on which you previously reclaimed VAT, you must include these items in your final VAT return. In effect HM Revenue & Customs wants to recover this VAT (unless the amount is less than £1,000) in your last return. Note that even if you previously completed electronic returns, you must complete a paper-based return for this final return.

  As soon as your business circumstances change, you must inform HM Revenue & Customs, which has specified time limits, depending on the circumstances. If you ignore these time limits, you may incur penalties. If in doubt, contact the National Advice Service on 0845-0109000.

- **Nil return:** You can file a Nil return if you:

  - Have not traded in the period covered by the VAT return *and*

  - No VAT exists on purchases (inputs) to recover *or*

  - No VAT exists on sales (outputs) to declare.

  Complete all boxes on the return as 'None' on your paper-based return or '0.00' on your electronic return.

Correcting mistakes

HM Revenue & Customs accepts the fact that people make mistakes (after all, we are only human!) and they don't expect perfection. However, they do have strict rules concerning mistakes. If you find a mistake on a previous return, you may be able to adjust your VAT account and include the value of that adjustment on your current VAT return. You can only do this if the mistake is found to be genuine and not deliberate, and is also below the error-correcting threshold (currently £10,000). If the amount is payable to HM Revenue & Customs, include it in the total for box 1 or box 2 (acquisitions). If the amount is repayable to you, include it in the total for box 4.

If you make a bigger mistake (the net value of the mistake is more than £10,000), *do not* include the amount on your current return. Inform your local VAT Business Advice Centre by letter or on form *VAT 652: Voluntary disclosure of errors on VAT returns*. A Notice of Voluntary Disclosure is then issued showing only the corrections to the period in question, and you become liable to the under-declared VAT and interest. Under these circumstances, no mis-declaration penalty is applied. Form *Notice 700/45: How to correct VAT errors and make adjustments or claims* helps you.

If you discover that a deliberate error has been made, you must disclose it to HM Revenue & Customs immediately. You cannot adjust these errors in a later VAT return.

Pursuing Payments and Repayments

Your completed VAT return results in one of two outcomes: you owe HM Revenue & Customs money or it owes you money – unless of course you complete a Nil return, in which case you and HM Revenue & Customs are quits.

If you owe VAT but can't afford to pay by the due date, still send in your completed VAT return, and then contact the Business Payment Support Line on 0845-3021435. This service was set up on 24 November 2008 to meet the needs of businesses and individuals affected by the current economic downturn. You can discuss temporary options with them, such as extending the period of payment.

If you are owed money, you should receive a repayment about two weeks after you submit your VAT return. If after three weeks you haven't received your repayment, contact the Customs and Excise National Advice Service on 0845-0109000.

If your business is due a repayment of VAT on a regular basis and you are on quarterly VAT returns, switch to monthly VAT returns at the earliest opportunity. Under a monthly system you wait only two weeks for your VAT repayment rather than an additional two months.

If for any reason you receive a 'Notice of assessment and/or over-declaration' as a result of a mistake found by a visiting officer, don't wait until your next VAT return to rectify the issue. If you owe VAT, send your payment and the remittance advice in the envelope provided. If you are owed, suppress a large smile and pay in the cheque, or check your bank account if you normally pay electronically.

Chapter 24

Preparing the Books for a New Accounting Cycle

*I*n bookkeeping, an accounting period, or cycle, can be a month, a quarter or a year (or any other division of time that makes business sense). All these occur within the accounting year. At the end of every accounting year, known as the *year-end,* certain accounts need to be closed while others remain open.

Just as the best method is to add accounts to your bookkeeping system at the beginning of an accounting year (so you don't have to move information from one account to another), you also need to wait until the end of the accounting year to delete any accounts that you no longer require. With this approach, you start each year fresh with only the accounts you need to best manage your business's financial activities.

In this chapter, I explain the accounts that must be closed and start with a zero balance in the next accounting cycle (see Chapter 2 for more detail about the accounting cycle). I also review the accounts that continue from one accounting cycle to the next, such as Assets and Liabilities. In addition, I discuss the process of closing the books at year-end and how to begin a new accounting cycle for the next year.

Finalising the Nominal Ledger

After you complete your accounting work for the accounting cycle in which your business operates, you need to re-examine your Nominal Ledger. Some accounts in the Nominal Ledger need to be zeroed out so that they start the new accounting cycle with no detail from the previous cycle, whereas other accounts continue to accumulate detail from one cycle to the next. When you break down the Nominal Ledger, the balance sheet accounts carry forward into the next accounting cycle, and the profit and loss statement accounts start with a zero balance.

Zeroing out profit and loss statement accounts

When you're sure that you've made all necessary corrections and adjustments to your accounts and you have your year-end numbers, you can zero out all Nominal Ledger accounts listed on the profit and loss statement – that's revenues, Cost of Goods Sold and Expense accounts. Because the profit and loss statement reflects the activities of an accounting period, these accounts always start with a zero balance at the beginning of an accounting cycle.

If you use a computerised accounting system, you may not actually have to zero out the profit and loss statement accounts. For example, Sage 50 Accounts zeroes out your income and expenses accounts at year-end (by transferring them to retained earnings), so you start with a zero net profit, but the program also maintains the data in an archive so you're always able to access it. Sage 50 Accounts makes the year-end process reasonably straightforward. Click the Company tab, select Manage Year End from the Tasks list, and you're presented with the Sage Year End Procedure screen shown in Figure 24-1.

The main purpose of this screen is to remind you of all the tasks you need to do prior to the year-end. Click through buttons 1 to 5 in sequence and Sage guides you through the year-end process. When you click to run your year-end process, the screen shown in Figure 24-2 appears. This screen confirms that the program now transfers all the profit and loss figures to retained earnings and carries forward the remaining balance sheet figures. Click OK and complete the year-end process.

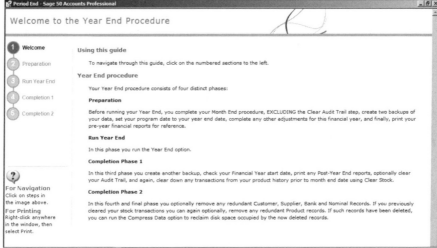

Figure 24-1:
Starting the
year-end
process
in Sage 50
Accounts.

Figure 24-2:
Zeroing out
the profit
and loss
figures at
year-end
in Sage 50
Accounts.

Carrying over balance sheet accounts

Unlike profit and loss statement accounts, you never zero out the accounts
listed on a balance sheet – that's assets, liabilities and capital. Instead, you
note your ending balances for each of these accounts so you can prepare
a balance sheet (see Chapter 19), and you carry forward the data in the
accounts into the next accounting period. The balance sheet just gives you

a snapshot of the financial state of your business at a particular date in time. From one accounting cycle to the next, your assets and (unfortunately) liabilities remain. You also need to maintain information about how much capital your investors have put into the business.

Conducting Special Year-End Bookkeeping Tasks

Before you start the process of closing the books for the year, print a summary of your account information from your computerised accounting system. If you make an error while closing the books, you can always use this printout to backtrack and fix any problems. (There's no manual equivalent of this process.)

Sage 50 Accounts provides a Year End Guide Checklist as you go through the Year End Procedure screens to help you keep track of all the necessary year-end activities. In Sage 50 Accounts, follow these steps to complete the year-end processing:

1. **Before running the year-end, make sure you take two back-ups of your data, in case things go wrong or you discover you weren't quite ready for the year-end.**

2. **Set your program date to your year-end date.**

3. **Print any pre-year-end reports, such as audit trails and nominal activity reports.**

4. **After running the Year-End option, check that your starting date for the new financial year is correct.**

5. **Clear your audit trail and clear down any product history using Clear Stock, if required.**

6. **Finally, you can clear any redundant bank accounts, supplier accounts, customer accounts or product records.**

Checking customer accounts

As you prepare your books for the end of an accounting year, review your customer accounts (Trade Debtors). Unless it's the end of the year, don't close the Trade Debtors accounts you don't need any more. When you start a new accounting year, you certainly want to carry over any balance still due from customers.

Before closing your books at the end of the accounting cycle, review the customer accounts for possible bad debt expenses. (I talk about bad debt in greater detail in Chapter 10.) Now is the time to be more critical of past-due accounts. You can use any bad debt to reduce your tax bill, so if you believe that a customer isn't likely to make good on a past-due account, write off the loss.

Assessing supplier accounts

The end of an accounting period is the perfect time to review your supplier accounts to make sure that they're all paid in full and ready for the new cycle. Also, ensure that you enter any bills into your supplier accounts that reflect business activity for the period being closed; otherwise, expenses from the period may not show up in the appropriate year-end financial statements.

Review any outstanding purchase orders to make sure that your supplier accounts aren't missing orders that have been completed but not yet billed by the supplier. For example, if you receive stock on 23 December but the supplier isn't going to bill for that stock until January, accrue for the bill in December to reflect the receipt of that stock during that accounting year (accruals are covered in Chapter 2).

Deleting accounts

The closing process at the end of an accounting year is a good time to assess all your open accounts and verify that you still need them. If an account contains no transactions, you're free to delete it at any time. However, wait until the end of the year to delete any accounts you don't think you're going to need in the next year. If you're assessing accounts at the end of an accounting period that isn't also the end of the year, just make a list of the accounts to be deleted and wait for the year-end.

Sage doesn't allow you to delete an account with transactions on that account. An account can only be deleted if it has no transactions and the balance is zero.

Starting the Cycle Anew

You certainly don't want to close the doors of your business while preparing all your year-end reports, such as the financial statements and HM Revenue & Customs reports – after all, that process can take two to three months. So you need to continue making entries for the new year as you close the books for the previous year.

If you do the books manually, you probably need easy access to two sets of books: the current year and the previous year. In a manual bookkeeping system, you just start new journal pages for each of the active accounts. If you have some accounts that aren't very active, rather than start a new page, you can leave some space for adjustments or corrections, draw a line and start the transactions for the new year on the same page.

If you keep your books using a computerised accounting system such as Sage 50 Accounts, you can continue posting transactions past the year-end date, while you wait for all the final invoices and bank statements to come through. The year-end can be run at a later date.

Part of closing your books is starting new files for each of your accounts. Most businesses keep two years of data – the current year and the previous year – in the on-site office files and put older files into storage. As you start a new year, box up your two-year-old files for storage and use the newly empty drawers for the new year's new files. For example, suppose that you're creating files for 2011. Keep the 2010 files easily accessible in filing cabinet drawers in your office, but box up the 2009 files for storage. Then keep your 2011 files in the drawers where the 2009 files were.

No hard and fast rule exists about file storage. You may find that you need to access some files regularly and therefore don't want to put them in storage. No problem. Pull out any files related to ongoing activity and keep them in the office so you don't have to run to the storage area every time you need the files. For example, if you have an ongoing legal case, keep any files related to that matter out of storage and easily accessible. Also remember that you have a legal obligation to keep your account records for six tax years.

Part VI
The Part of Tens

'You say my bookkeeping predecessor
was incompetent. What happened to him?'

In this part . . .

We join the *For Dummies* series tradition by providing you with some lists of tens. In this case, the lists contain key factors to maintaining your books and using the information collected. We highlight the top ten accounts that all bookkeepers must know in order to manage the books and give you the ten best ways to use your books to manage your business's cash.

Chapter 25

Top Ten Ways to Manage Your Business Cash with Your Books

In This Chapter

▶ Keeping a handle on internal bookkeeping tools

▶ Monitoring profits and expenses

▶ Dealing smartly with suppliers, contractors and customers

*M*any business owners think of bookkeeping as a necessary evil, but in reality, if you make effective use of the data you collect, bookkeeping can be your best ally when it comes to managing your cash. The key to taking advantage of what bookkeeping offers is to understand the value of basic bookkeeping principles and how to use the information collected efficiently and effectively. This chapter reviews the top ten ways to use your books to help you manage your business cash.

Charting the Way

You may not think that a list of accounts, called the Chart of Accounts, is worth much attention, but this chart dictates how you collect your financial data and where in the books you put your business's transactions. In order for you to be able to use the information effectively, your Chart of Accounts must define each account precisely and determine exactly what types of transactions go where. (I talk about the Chart of Accounts and how to set one up in Chapter 3.)

Balancing Your Entries

Balanced books are the only way to know how your business is doing. Without them, you can never know whether your profit numbers are accurate. In bookkeeping, you use a process called *double-entry bookkeeping* to keep the books balanced. I talk more about this basic principle and how to keep the books balanced in Chapter 2.

Posting Your Transactions

In order to be able to use the information you collect regarding your business transactions, the transactions must be posted accurately to your accounts. If you forget to post a transaction to your books, your reports don't reflect that financial activity, and you have a serious problem. Or, if you post an incorrect transaction to your books, any reports that draw on that information are going to be wrong – again, a problem. I talk more about the posting process in Chapters 4 and 5.

Keeping on Top of Credit Control

If your business sells to customers on credit, you certainly want to make sure that your customers pay for their purchases in the future. (Customer account information is gathered in the Trade Debtors account as well as in individual records for each customer.) Review the reports based on customer payment history, called *Aged Debtor reports,* on a monthly basis to make sure that customers pay on time. Remember that you set the rules for credit, so you may want to cut off customers from future purchases if their accounts are overdue for 90 days or more. I talk more about how to manage customer accounts in Chapter 10.

Paying Bills Accurately and on Time

If you want to continue getting supplies, products and services from your suppliers and contractors, you must pay them accurately and on time. Managing your payments through the Trade Creditors account ensures accuracy and timeliness, and also saves you from mistakenly paying bills twice. To be safe, you need to review Aged Creditor reports on your payment history, to ensure that you make timely and accurate payments. I talk more about managing your payments in Chapter 9.

Planning Profits

Nothing is more important to a business owner than the profits he or she may ultimately make. Yet many business owners don't take time to plan their profit expectations at the beginning of each year, so they have no way to measure how well their businesses are doing throughout the year. Avoid this problem by taking time before the year starts to develop profit expectations and a budget that can help you meet those expectations. Then develop a series of internal financial reports from the numbers in your bookkeeping system to help determine whether or not you're meeting your sales targets and maintaining control over your product costs and operating expenses. I talk more about sales tracking in Chapter 10, costs and expense tracking in Chapter 9 and how to determine your net profit in Chapter 18.

Comparing Budget to Actual Expenses

Keeping a careful watch on how well your budget planning reflects what's actually happening in your business can help you meet your profit goals. As with profits (see the preceding section), take time to develop a budget that sets your expectations for the year and then develop internal reports that give you the ability to track how closely your actual expenses match that budget. If you see any major problems, correct them as soon as possible to make sure that you meet your target profit at the end of the year. I talk more about internal financial reporting in Chapter 18.

Comparing Sales Goals to Actual Sales

In addition to watching your expenses, you need to monitor your actual sales so that they match the sales goals you set at the beginning of the year. Designing an internal report that tracks sales goals versus actual sales allows you to monitor how well your business is doing. If you find your actual sales are below expectations, take steps to correct the problem as early in the year as possible in order to improve your chances of meeting those year-end goals. To find out how to use internal financial reports to track your sales activity, check out Chapters 10 and 18.

Monitoring Cost Trends

Awareness of the costs involved in purchasing the products you sell or the raw materials you use to manufacture your products is very important because these costs can have a major impact on whether or not your business earns the net income you expect. If you find that the costs are going up, you may need to adjust the prices of the products you sell in order to meet your profit goals. I talk more about tracking cost trends in Chapters 9 and 18.

Making Pricing Decisions

Properly pricing your product can be a critical factor in determining whether or not your product sells. If the price is too high, you may not find any customers willing to buy the product; if the price is too low, you lose money.

When determining what price to charge your customers, you must consider a number of different factors, including how much you pay to buy or manufacture the products you sell, the market research about what customers are willing to pay for a product, what you pay your employees and the advertising and administrative expenses you incur in order to set a price. All these items are factors in what you're going to spend to sell that product. I talk more about tracking costs and expenses in Chapters 9 and 18.

Chapter 26

Top Ten Most Important Accounts for Any Bookkeeper

*E*ach and every account has its purpose in bookkeeping, but all accounts certainly aren't created equal. For most businesses, some accounts are more essential than others, so in case you're having trouble knowing where to start your account set-up and what's necessary, this chapter looks at the top must-have accounts for bookkeepers.

Cash

All your business transactions pass through the Cash account, which is so important that you actually need two books, Cash Receipts and Cash Payments, to track the activity. (I discuss these books at length in Chapter 5.) As the bookkeeper, your responsibility is to make sure that all cash – coming into the business or being sent out – is handled and recorded properly in the Cash account.

Trade Debtors (Accounts Receivable)

If your business sells its products or services to customers on credit, you definitely need a Trade Debtors account, where you monitor all money due from customers. As the bookkeeper, keeping Trade Debtors up to date is critical, so make sure that you send timely and accurate bills to customers. I talk more about Trade Debtor processes in Chapter 10.

Stock

Every business must have products to sell. Those money-making products must be carefully accounted for and monitored, because this process is the only way a business knows what it has on hand to sell. As the bookkeeper, you contribute to this process by keeping accurate stock records in a Stock account. The numbers you have in your books are periodically verified by doing physical counts of the stock on hand. I talk more about how to manage stock and Stock accounts in Chapter 9.

Trade Creditors (Accounts Payable)

No one likes to send money out of the business, but you can ease the pain and strain by monitoring and paying bills in your Trade Creditors (or Accrual) account. You certainly don't want to pay anyone twice, but you also want to make sure that you pay bills on time or else your business may no longer get the supplies, stock or other things needed to operate. Suppliers often penalise late-paying businesses by cutting them off or putting them on cash-with-order status. On the flipside, if you pay your bills early, you may be able to get discounts and save money with suppliers, so the early bird definitely gets the worm. For more on the Trade Creditors account, check out Chapter 9.

Loans Payable

A time is bound to come when your business needs to purchase major items such as equipment, vehicles and furniture. Unfortunately, you may find that you don't have the money to pay for such purchases. The solution is to take on long-term loans to be paid over more than a 12-month period. The Loans Payable account allows you to monitor the activity on these loans, in order to get and keep the best rates, and make all loan payments on time and accurately. I talk more about the Loans Payable account in Chapter 13.

Sales

No business can operate without taking in cash, mostly through sales of the business's products or services. The Sales account is where you record all incoming revenue collected from these sales. Recording sales in a timely and accurate manner is a critical job of the bookkeeper, because otherwise you can't know how much revenue your business has collected every day. To find out more about sales and the Sales account, see Chapter 10.

Purchases

Purchases are unavoidable. In order to have a tangible product to sell, your business has to manufacture the product, in which case you have to purchase raw materials, or purchase a finished product from a supplier. In the Purchases account, you track the purchases of any raw materials or finished goods. The Purchases account is a key component in calculating Cost of Goods Sold, which you subtract from Sales to find your business's gross profit. I talk more about the Purchases account in Chapter 9.

Payroll Expenses

You need to pay employees to get them to stay around. No matter how much you beg, few people want to work for nothing! To keep up to date with the biggest expense of many businesses, you record all money paid to employees in the Payroll Expenses account. Accurate maintenance of this account is essential because it ensures that all reports are filed and payroll taxes are paid. And if you don't take care of these responsibilities to HM Revenue & Customs, you can find yourself in some serious hot water. I talk more about payroll obligations and the Payroll Expenses account in Chapters 11 and 21.

Office Expenses

Key expenses that can drain a business's profits are office expenses. From paper, pens and paperclips to expenses related to office machinery, these expenses tend to creep up if not carefully monitored in the Office Expenses account. I talk more about the Office Expenses account, as well as internal controls that you can put into place to keep costs down, in Chapter 9.

Retained Earnings

The Retained Earnings account tracks any profits made by the business that are reinvested for growing the business and not paid out to business owners. This account is *cumulative,* which means it shows a running total of earnings retained since the business opened its doors. Although managing this account doesn't take you a lot of time, the ongoing accuracy of the Retained Earnings account is important to investors and lenders who want to track how well the business is doing. I talk more about Retained Earnings in Chapter 19.

Glossary

accrual accounting: An accounting method in which transactions are recorded when they actually occur, even if cash hasn't changed hands. Income is recorded when earned (not when the business is actually paid for the products or services), and expenses are counted when goods or services are received, even if the business hasn't yet been paid for the goods or services. Most businesses use this accounting method. See also *cash-based accounting*.

accumulated fund: A form of capital account or retained earnings for a not-for-profit organisation. It shows all the surpluses the organisation has ever made.

amortisation: An accounting method used to show the using-up of an intangible asset by writing off a portion of the asset's value each year.

assets: Everything the business owns, such as cash, buildings, vehicles, furniture, and any other item used to run the business and help it generate money in the future.

averaging: An accounting method used to value stock by calculating an average cost per unit sold.

bad debts expense: A categorisation used to write off customer accounts with outstanding payments that the business determines can never be collected.

balance sheet: A snapshot of a business's financial picture at a point in time (usually the year-end) that shows all assets and liabilities. It also shows who has invested in the business and how the investments were used.

capital: A term used to describe the owner's equity. In the case of a limited company, it is the nominal value of the shares issued. In the case of a sole trader, it records the owner's investment in the business.

capital accounts: Used to track the value of assets owned by the business owners or shareholders after accounting for liabilities.

cash-based accounting: An accounting method based on actual cash flow. Expenses are recorded only when the business actually pays out cash for the goods or services, and income is recorded only when the business collects cash from the customer. See also *accrual accounting*.

chart of accounts: A list of all the Nominal accounts used by a business to analyse its income, expenses, assets, and liabilities.

corporation tax: A tax paid by limited companies on their earnings.

cost of goods sold: The full cost of those goods and services sold in any period. This usually includes stock, direct labour, and any other direct costs.

credits: Accounting entries that increase Liability or Income accounts and decrease Asset or Expense accounts. Credits always appear on the right-hand side of an accounting entry.

current assets: All items the business owns that are expected to be used in the next 12 months, including items, like cash, that can be easily liquidated. Other examples include cash equivalents, Trade debtors, stock, marketable securities, and prepaid expenses.

current liabilities: All financial obligations the business owes that are due in less than 12 months, such as Trade Creditors (money due to suppliers, contractors, and consultants) and Credit Cards Payable (payments due on credit cards).

debits: Accounting entries that increase Asset or Expense accounts and decrease Liability and Income accounts. Debits always appear on the left-hand side of an accounting entry.

depreciation: An accounting method used to account for the reduction of the value of an asset over time. Depreciation is taken over a set number of years to show that an asset is being used up and its value is diminishing.

expenses: All costs of operating a business.

First-In, First Out (FIFO): An accounting method used to value stock that assumes the first items put on the shelf are the first items sold.

fixed asset: An asset with an expected life greater than 12 months, which will in general be in permanent use by the business. Land and buildings, motor vehicles, and plant and equipment are all examples of fixed assets.

gross profit: The difference between sales and cost of goods sold. Often described as the key measure of business performance, it measures the margin made on each sale.

income: Money earned by a business from its trading activities; synonyms are sales and revenue.

income and expenditure account: A version of the profit and loss statement for not-for-profit organisations used to find the amount of surplus or deficit during a period.

income tax: A tax paid by individuals and partnerships on all their earnings, including earnings from direct employment and self-employment.

intangible asset: Anything the business owns that has value but can't be touched, such as licences, patents, trademarks, and brand names.

interest: Income earned from money invested in money markets, such as bank deposits.

Last In, First Out (LIFO): An accounting method used to value stock that assumes the last items put on the shelf are the first items sold.

liabilities: All debts the business owes, such as Trade Creditors, and Mortgages Payable.

long-term assets: All things a business owns that are expected to be due in more than 12 months, such as buildings, factories, vehicles, and furniture.

long-term liabilities: All debts a business owes that it expects to repay in more than 12 months. Examples are mortgages and long-term loans.

Lower of Cost or Market Valuation (LCM): An accounting method used to value stock based on whichever is lower: the actual cost of the stock or its current market value.

net profit: The bottom line after all costs, expenses, interest, taxes, depreciation, and amortisation are accounted for. Net profit reflects how much money the business makes.

Nominal Journal entries: Any entries made to correct or adjust balances in the Nominal Ledger accounts.

Nominal Ledger: A summary of all historical transactions that occurred since the business first opened its doors. This ledger is the summary of a business's financial information.

operating cash flow: The cash that a business's operations generate to produce and sell its products.

operating expenses: Expenses that a business incurs in order to continue its operations, such as advertising, equipment rental, premises rental, insurance, legal and accounting fees, entertainment, salaries, office expenses, repairs and maintenance, travel, utilities, vehicles, and just about anything else that goes into operating a business and isn't directly involved in selling a business's products.

operating profit: A measure of a business's earning power from its ongoing operations.

periodic stock method: Tracking stock that a business has on hand by doing a physical count of stock on a periodic basis, whether daily, monthly, yearly, or any other time period that meets a business's needs.

perpetual stock method: Tracking stock that a business has on hand by adjusting the stock counts after each transaction. A computerised stock control system is needed to manage stock using this method.

petty cash: All cash kept on hand at business locations for incidental expenses.

point of sale: The location where customers pay for products or services they want to buy, such as a register or service counter.

profit: All the earnings of a business after all business expenses.

profit and loss statement: A statement for-profit organisations use to find the amount of profit or loss during a period. It shows such key measures as Sales, Gross Profit and Net Profit.

receipts and payments account: A summary of the cash book/journals of a not-for-profit organisation.

retained earnings account: An account used to show net profits left in the business from accounting period to accounting period and reinvested in the business for future growth.

short-term liabilities: Those assets not kept permanently within the business and expected to change within 12 months. Examples are stock, debtors, and prepayments.

specific identification: An accounting method used to value stock based on the actual items sold and their individual costs.

tangible assets: Any items the business owns that can be held in one's hand or touched, such as cash, stock, or vehicles.

Trade creditors: An account used to record money due to suppliers, contractors, and consultants for products or services purchased by the business. Sometimes known as accounts payable.

Trade debtors: An account used to record income not yet received on products sold or services provided to customers that is to be collected at a later date. Sometimes known as accounts receivable.

Value Added Tax (VAT): A tax charged on most business transactions made in the UK and the Isle of Man. VAT is also charged on goods and some services imported from certain places outside the European Community (EC), as well as on some goods and services coming into the UK from other EC countries. VAT applies to all business types – sole traders, partnerships, limited companies, charities, and so on.

Index

FOR DUMMIES®

Making Everything Easier! ™

UK editions

BUSINESS

978-0-470-74490-1

978-0-470-74381-2

978-0-470-71119-4

Asperger's Syndrome For Dummies
978-0-470-66087-4

Boosting Self-Esteem For Dummies
978-0-470-74193-1

British Sign Language
For Dummies
978-0-470-69477-0

Business NLP For Dummies
978-0-470-69757-3

Cricket For Dummies
978-0-470-03454-5

Diabetes For Dummies, 3rd Edition
978-0-470-97711-8

English Grammar For Dummies
978-0-470-05752-0

Flirting For Dummies
978-0-470-74259-4

Football For Dummies
978-0-470-68837-3

IBS For Dummies
978-0-470-51737-6

Improving Your Relationship For
Dummies
978-0-470-68472-6

Lean Six Sigma For Dummies
978-0-470-75626-3

Life Coaching For Dummies,
2nd Edition
978-0-470-66554-1

Nutrition For Dummies, 2nd Edition
978-0-470-97276-2

REFERENCE

978-0-470-68637-9

978-0-470-97450-6

978-0-470-74535-9

HOBBIES

978-0-470-69960-7

978-0-470-68641-6

978-0-470-68178-7

24940 (p1)

FOR DUMMIES®

A world of resources to help you grow

UK editions

SELF-HELP

Cognitive Behavioural Therapy FOR DUMMIES
Rhena Branch
Rob Willson
978-0-470-66541-1

Neuro-linguistic Programming FOR DUMMIES
Kate Burton
Romilla Ready
978-0-470-66543-5

Mindfulness FOR DUMMIES
Shamash Alidina
978-0-470-66086-7

STUDENTS

Philosophy FOR DUMMIES
Martin Cohen
978-0-470-68820-5

Student Cookbook FOR DUMMIES
Oliver Harrison
978-0-470-74711-7

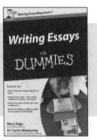

Writing Essays FOR DUMMIES
Mary Page
Dr Carrie Winstanley
978-0-470-74290-7

HISTORY

The Tudors FOR DUMMIES
David Loades
Mei Trow
978-0-470-68792-5

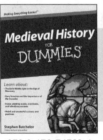

Medieval History FOR DUMMIES
Stephen Batchelor
978-0-470-74783-4

British History FOR DUMMIES
Dr. Seán Lang
978-0-470-97819-1

Origami Kit For Dummies
978-0-470-75857-1

Overcoming Depression For Dummies
978-0-470-69430-5

Positive Psychology For Dummies
978-0-470-72136-0

PRINCE2 For Dummies, 2009 Edition
978-0-470-71025-8

Psychometric Tests For Dummies
978-0-470-75366-8

Raising Happy Children
For Dummies
978-0-470-05978-4

Reading the Financial Pages
For Dummies
978-0-470-71432-4

Sage 50 Accounts For Dummies
978-0-470-71558-1

Self-Hypnosis For Dummies
978-0-470-66073-7

Starting a Business For Dummies,
2nd Edition
978-0-470-51806-9

Study Skills For Dummies
978-0-470-74047-7

Teaching English as a Foreign Language
For Dummies
978-0-470-74576-2

Teaching Skills For Dummies
978-0-470-74084-2

Time Management For Dummies
978-0-470-77765-7

Training Your Brain For Dummies
978-0-470-97449-0

Work-Life Balance For Dummies
978-0-470-71380-8

Available wherever books are sold. For more information or to order direct go to www.wiley.com or call +44 (0) 1243 843291

24940 (p2)